What people are s

Dr. Goff succeeds in developing a "common sense approach to religion." Between the covers of this book, one finds inspirational guidance and constant companionship.

Ronald W. Roskens
President-Emeritus
University of Nebraska

This book is a remarkable demonstration of what can happen when a serious preacher takes responsibility for refining the theological dimension of his work. Goff works with process modes of thought, and has developed a comprehensive and incisive discussion of the themes that have informed his preaching throughout his career.

Benjamin A. Reist, Stuart Professor
of Systematic Theology, Emeritus
San Francisco Theological Seminary

No religion satisfied my examination until I looked at Christianity through Vernon's eyes. Simple, straightforward, logical — this book can help anyone struggling with their spirituality.

Process religion, as Dr. Goff teaches, is a logical, believable explanation for anyone struggling with their spirituality.

Ron Parks
President, Millard Manufacturing company

Built on the basic concepts of respect for a loving God and love for one another, this book presents an approach to religion that is compatible with the way we understand the world in which we live, rather than being tied to beliefs or rituals developed at a time when the knowledge concerning our world was considerably different than it is today. Just as we have continued to learn and grow in other areas of our lives, such as science, health and communication, this approach encourages us to search and to grow in our understanding of God, as we work with him, using the resources he has provided to make this a better world.

Dale Salzman
Omaha, Nebraska

Dr. Goff has produced a book which is stimulating, inspirational, challenging, non-traditional, hopeful, thoughtful, and trusting of recognizable data when tested by other minds.

This book is designed to encourage a constant questioning of assumptions and conclusions, yet recognizing that one's basic assumption strongly influences one's conclusion.

Dr. Goff has produced a clear testimony to the conviction that our clear thinking and committed actions are more dependable and constructive than intuition and feeling.

Dr. Goff looks upon all honest inquiry as a tool for understanding how God works and human progress is realized. He provides a credible witness to the process by which knowledge and skill may replace magic and miracles.

Alva H. Clark, ThM. ThD.
Retired Minister, United Methodist Church

Should Christian theology promote a rhetoric of evasions and euphemisms? Should faith depend on learning to have the correct emotional response to troubling doctrines? Dr. Goff argues that reason and experience are worthy tools for evaluating scripture and theology. He gives guidance in the search for pearls, and justification for learning when to say "no." Making God Talk Make Sense *is written in a straight-forward style, with clarity and integrity.*

Elaine S. Rich, Rph.
Omaha, NE

Dr. Goff not only gives us permission to THINK for ourselves, he challenges us to do so.

Karen Dageforde
Omaha, NE

Bringing ancient (2000 year old) theology into the 21st Century — logical interpretation of biblical events makes the Christian message more believable and acceptable.

Wes Rieke
Omaha, NE

Goff addresses the important theological matters in a frank and forthright manner. He credits the religious contributions of 4,000 to 2,000 years ago, with being a valuable start in religious thinking, but shows that we have learned so much since then which requires new and continuing additions and revisions of that early thinking.

Goff discards those parts of the Bible which made good sense to people thousands of years ago, but are dysfunctional for modern people. And, he offers his own penetrating contributions to the great issues of God, of Jesus, of life and death, and how God works with us, today. Four Stars!!

Goff shows that we can find God and understand how He (or She) works with us, today. He honors the past, but he shows that we need not swallow everything in the Bible in order to find God and work with God for our own benefit and to advance God's goals for the World. Four Stars!!

F. Ivan Nye, PhD.
Ret. Prof. of Sociology
Washington State University

Its approach to contemporizing a 2000-year-old faith is remarkable. It is an on-the-edge view of the world and of God. Dr. Goff challenges our faith talk and expressions we use today.

Ronald C. Croom
District Superintendent
United Methodist Church

Making God Talk Make Sense

A Common Sense Approach to Religion

VERNON G. GOFF

Dageforde Publishing, Inc.

ISBN 1-886225-67-2
Cover design by Angie Johnson
Photography by Lee Vernon Studio

CIP information forthcoming

Dageforde Publishing, Inc.
122 South 29th Street
Lincoln, Nebraska 68510
Ph: (402) 475-1123 FAX: (402) 475-1176
email: info@dageforde.com

Visit our website: www.dageforde.com

Printed in the United States of America
10   9   8   7   6   5   4   3   2   1

To Alice
My wife and best friend
who has critically read and reread
the manuscript for this book many
times, and loves me still.

Ted, Vern, Kandy, Debbie
(In Order of Arrival)
My children who have
often admonished
but never rejected me.

Theodore
My Father
who taught me the values
of honesty and hard work.

The Memory of Mattie
My Mother
who, along with her love,
provided an example of
balanced mind and heart.

Dale, Bobbie and Sharon
My siblings who tolerate my views even
if they think I have lost both my
religious "way" and my senses.

The Parents and Grandparents of Alice
Whose hearts were always "in the
right place," whose love was never
doubted, who demonstrated the kind
of grandmotherly sweetness that makes
poetry and in whose "Mission" which
she started and sustained in Detroit
I received my first ordination.

The Memory of Doris
The only sister of Alice who
had a keen mind but was fearful
of using it in religious thought
lest she "lose the faith."

David
Alice's brother who introduced
us to each other at Taylor University
and who will read this book with
proud interest and then lay it
to one side.

Contents

Acknowledgments

Without the encouragement of the St. Luke congregation, the patience of Alice, my wife and companion in all my endeavors for over fifty years, the curiosity of my children, Deb, Kandy, Ted, and Vern, and the incessant and helpful consultations of Dr. Ivan Nye, this book would never have come into existence.

St. Luke tolerated, and occasionally demonstrated great appreciation for my theological curiosity and candid honesty for thirty-five years. Alice cooperated with "working vacations" which focused on "the book" for over ten years. My children, sometimes bored by theology, but always curious and supportive have listened politely to most of what I have to say for as long as they can remember. Vern, a professional photographer, videotaped sermons for fifteen years, provided the photography for the book cover, and has also been an integral part of the support group which has made it impossible for me not to write.

Dr. Ivan Nye, retired Professor of Sociology, was a member of my congregation for many years and has encouraged me at every point to record my religious thinking in a book, so that it could be of benefit to persons beyond St. Luke. Dr. Nye taught at several major universities including Ohio State, Florida State and Washington State. He has authored many articles and several books and is a recipient of the Burgess Award for Continuing Distinguished Contributions to Research and Theory. His impressive research, considerable contributions to social theory, and extensive writing have made him a person with whom I found it helpful to converse on many of the topics that I explore in this volume.

To the many who have served as readers, and especially to all those who demonstrated confidence by ordering books before the manuscript went to print, I say a sincere "thanks."

To all my colleagues in ministry who, though they may have watched the direction of my ministry from the corner of their eye, have never openly opposed my honest expressions of thought, I am grateful.

Many professionals along the way have contributed, sometimes quite intentionally, and other times unwittingly. Early grade school teachers, notably Thelma Deland Ewers and Thelma Miller, helped make religion important to me. The late M.F. Gordon, converted from Judaism to a Nazarene evangelist and who served as my first pastor in an interdenominational rural church, caused me to feel that if I did not become a minister I would surely go to hell. (I became a minister for all the wrong reasons and remained in ministry for the right reasons.) The late Dr. Milo Rediger at Taylor University (a fundamentalist college in Upland, Indiana) without knowing it provided my first insight into the possibility of a thinking, rather than primarily an emotional, religious experience. The late Dr. Wm. Bernhardt, in classes and in his "Critical Analysis of Religion," helped me intellectually and emotionally reach the conclusion that it was indeed OK to think beyond the literal words of the Bible in my effort to rationally relate religious beliefs with a contemporary view of the world. Dr. Harvey Pothoff nurtured my sense of balance between the intellectual and the emotional. (Dr. Bernhardt and Dr. Pothoff were at Iliff School of Theology in Denver, CO.) I have great appreciation for, and give special thanks to Dr. Benjamin Reist, now retired from the San Francisco School of Theology, who guided and encouraged me through the challenges of my Doctoral Dissertation and told me that he enjoyed reading my "stuff."

It was Dr. Alva Clark (now retired after 28 years as Senior Pastor of St. Paul UMC, Omaha, NE) who, by his invitation to join the St. Paul clergy staff in 1960, was most responsible for my coming to Omaha. Omaha and St. Paul opened doors for learning and service that might not otherwise have been opened. Dr. Clark is a skilled "on the job trainer" and demonstrated patience and support for most of my excursions of curiosity and commitment. It was he who, through example, taught me the value of writing sermons in full manuscript before sharing them from the pulpit. (However, I always left the manuscript in the office while preaching.) It was he who, more than anyone else, dreamed the dream and opened the way for my appointment as founding pastor and thus the eventual thirty-five-year ministry at St. Luke.

To all those mentioned and hundreds of others, I express deep gratitude.

Vernon G. Goff, ThM, D Min

Foreword

The importance of religion is evident in a number of ways. History testifies to its importance in human life both individually and in the variety of its developing societies at any given point in human history.

The impact of religion, past and present, on architecture, government, education, literature, values, and mores, is evident to all who examine the broad spectrum of human development.

Even if one confines an examination of religious influence on human society to contemporary America, the magnitude of cost and number of edifices dedicated to some aspect of religion is impressive. The vast number of church buildings in America symbolizes the importance placed on religion in our society. A similar thing can be said of many societies in the world, past and present.

Among other things, religion has to do with *God Talk*. *God Talk* is a primary tool used by religion to communicate whatever it is that a given "brand" of religion believes is important. Some *God Talk* is easily understood and makes sense. Much of it is neither easily understood nor does it make sense to a majority of persons with whom it seeks to communicate.

The purpose of this book is to interpret *God Talk* from a Christian perspective in a way that is understandable and meaningful in the world of our day. I hope it will serve as a guide to many who seek the values which healthy religion provides but who find much *God Talk* to be empty and sometimes offensive. Healthy religion contributes to a more harmonious and sacred experience of life.

The purpose of this book is also to stimulate thought and encourage faith for those who value the contributions of the Judeo-Christian tradition, but who find much of the belief system in this tradition out of harmony with the knowledge and technological explosion of the past several decades. It is a book for those who enjoy and are comfortable with the challenge of religious thought and who insist on honesty of expression. It is not for those who already "know" that their belief system is "right," "adequate," and not at all in need of growth, or who are satisfied to live in one world of religious beliefs and another world of beliefs which guide their life.

Persons who are in the church but whose intellect is insulted by much that the church preaches and teaches may find this book helpful. It may be equally helpful to those who value the functional goals of the tradition but who, for the same reasons as those just mentioned, elect not to be aligned with institutional religion. It may also be helpful for those who think progressively and are searching for a bridge of theological communication with their fundamentalist peers. Clergy who know more than they teach or preach may also find it helpful.

The theme of the book is built on several basic assumptions.

- What persons believe makes a difference in their attitude toward and expression of life.

- Measurable and exciting progress has been made in most areas of importance to the human family. Included in these areas but not limited to them are: education; health care; transportation; communication; technology; government; race relations; gender equality; international relations; longevity; quality of life for those specially challenged; economics; and national infrastructures.

- Religion is notably lacking in experiencing exciting progress and is often part of the problem it seeks to solve rather than part of the solution.

- The same general principles of methodology should be followed in the search for religious progress as have been effective in other areas.
- The Bible is of great value as a resource but is insufficient to meet the challenges of this present age, and, in some instances, provides outdated instruction.
- Revelation and intervention by God in the traditional sense are not dependable, therefore should not be relied on for either truth or change.
- God communicates in a variety of ways, including but not limited to Scripture.
- God does not force human beings to express their lives in ways that are harmonious with His, but is forever nudging them in the general direction of goodness. At the heart of goodness is love, reverence, respect, and personal responsibility.

This book assumes that much meaningful progress in the world has been, and continues to be, made by persons of basic goodness. It is supposed that these persons would welcome a theology that enhances the meaning of the specific kind of progress with which they are involved. It is also supposed that these persons would be delighted to know that their insights and contributions make a worthwhile contribution to a functional theology.

Part I indicates a specific theological approach, typically identified as "Process Theology." Part II is an application of Process thought to traditional beliefs.

Appendix I deals with Process thought in greater depth than the typical reader might have interest, but shares information from several writers for those inclined toward critical study. Appendix II provides Scripture references for the chapters of Part II, for those who like to relate scriptural thought to the subject matter of the book.

This is not intended to be a book for those seeking resources for in-depth critical study of various theories, Process or otherwise. It is a "digestion" of much study from a wide variety of sources over a period of many years.

References to God are consistent with biblical references in speaking of God as male. This is done only for the sake of convenience and should not be interpreted as a sexist approach to theology. From the author's perspective God can as well be referenced as female, male/female, of without personification. It should also be noted that sexual preference is a non-issue in this book. All persons are assumed to be "just that" regardless of sexual persuasion.

Finally, the purpose of this book is not to "spoon feed" anyone. Instead, the goal is to stimulate thought that will result in the continual creation of a *belief system* that works well for the individual doing the reading. Surely God must respect honesty, harmonious relational thinking, and a curiosity about theology that at least equals that of any other discipline.

It is the author's belief that the general principles that guide the thinking presented in this book represent a common sense approach to theology which makes *God Talk* make sense. These principles are timeless in their application.

Part I

Bringing Religion Up to Date
(A Formidable Challenge)

Chapter 1

Change, a Constant in Religion and Life

Our world is characterized by change. Evolution as a process of creativity is characterized by change. Life in our world is characterized by change. Regardless of whether or not we like change, it is part of things as they are and there is no reason to believe that will not always be true. It is reasonable to assume, given our present level of knowledge, that the only thing that does not and will not change is the fact of change itself. We can count on change!

My nephew, who manages a tire store, recently repaired a slow leaking tire for me. When I approached him at the cashier's desk to pay for the service, he refused payment. Not desiring special treatment, I insisted that I would like very much to pay the going rate. His response was simple, but the principle of his response has many applications: "I know you would like to pay, but not today—get over it!"

That is the way it is with change in life. Change will eventually come, regardless of how much we resist it. We may as well accept that fact and "get over it."

This is not to suggest that there are not situations where change should be resisted, nor is it to suggest that change should always be resisted. It is true, however, that when change is resisted it is sometimes postponed and sometimes a more desirable kind of change occurs than would otherwise have been true. It is also true that, if not overwhelmed, resistance tends to increase the strength of that which opposes it.

Resistance Is the Norm to Change in Religious Belief

There is no area of human experience where change comes with greater resistance than in the belief system which is perceived to be fundamental to any specific religion. The intent of this book is to discuss the application of this assumption to our Judeo-Christian tradition, especially as it relates to Christianity.

Religion has to do with self-perception and worth. It has to do with the relationship of past, present, and future. It has to do with human relationships. Religion has to do with perceived God/human relationships. It has to do with perception in relation to many facets of life. Religion has to do with values. It has to do with ethics and morality. It has to do with purpose. It has to do with hope. It has to do with mortality and immortality.

Healthy religion has to do with much more than can be described in one paragraph, but suffice it to say that there is no aspect or facet of life which should not be touched in a positive manner by a healthy system of religious belief.

Healthy Religion Accommodates Positive Change

Healthy religion is one which promotes and accommodates change, even within its own belief system. Such religious change by its very nature must be slow. If the religion is to be healthy, however, change must occur in a manner which keeps its belief system harmonious with a defensible view of the world at any given point in time.

Religious change in the life of an individual can be both challenging and painful. There is that about religion which both binds people together and separates them from one another. Judaism, with its concept of "the chosen people," has perpetuated a kind of religious arrogance. Christianity by its very nature has historically nurtured a kind of arrogance among its adherents and continues to do so. Any discipline which is embraced and taught as having all truth is, by its very nature, arrogant. Those who are bound together by it will be inseparable. They may feel strongly about keeping themselves untainted by the "wrongness" of others, and thus maintain a rigid attitude of separation. They may view their mission in life to be that of persuading others of their rightness. Those who reject their pressures for conversion may be alienated, persecuted, and either destroyed or threatened with destruction. After all, if "truth" is rejected when offered so "lovingly," do those who reject it really deserve to live? Isn't it only reasonable that they should be branded as "the evil ones" and "damned to eternal hell" either now, or in the future! So goes the thinking of many who seek to protect and promote the fundamentals of the past.

Proposed ideas about change in theological thought can be understood best in the context of the developmental background and experience of the one proposing the ideas. Some knowledge of my own religious journey to this point in the time sequence of my life may therefore be helpful.

A Personal Perspective

As suggested in a previous chapter, my cultural background is rural, i.e., agricultural with a combination of farming and animal husbandry.

My family background includes parents with a strong work ethic and an unbendable, elevated standard of ethics and morality.

Educationally, my background includes a one-room school through the eighth grade, a high school class of twenty-nine seniors, an undergraduate degree with majors in science and Bible, a Masters degree in Theology, and a Doctorate in Ministry with a dissertation in Theology.

I have a vocational history which includes farm/ranch, car service, factory work, door-to-door sales, and fifty years in the general professional ministry with its own broad application of experience and responsibilities. Under the umbrella of professional ministry falls the experience of starting and managing a Child Development Center for thirty-five years and a Senior Life Enhancement Center for five years.

My religious journey has its roots in a family which, for the first twelve years of my life, professed no religious faith and only occasionally attended religious services, but functioned on level of high moral and ethical values with roots in Christian teaching and tradition. We were not members of any denominational church.

The first religious thoughts were spawned by a rare visit to a rural Sunday School at the early age of three or four. They had to do with concern as to whether or not my parents would go to heaven or hell when they died. My earliest introduction to meaningful personal religion was from rural school teachers who started a religious youth group in the school and offered religious pictures and plaques as rewards for the memorization of Scripture. There was no general community resistance to this religious emphasis which utilized the school building at times other than usual school hours.

My family was "converted" to a fundamentalist, but not radical, brand of Christianity through the evangelistic ministry of a Jew converted from Orthodox Judaism to the Nazarene brand of Christianity. In response to his religious change, his family considered him dead and erected a tombstone for him in a cemetery to emphasize their point. He was the one who contributed most to my "beginnings in the faith."

This evangelist-converted-from-Judaism became my first pastor. He instilled a legalistic brand of Christian thought in my mind which included both threat and promise of reward, and scared me into the experience of being a "born again Christian." He insisted that I must become a minister or go to hell. When I was in college, he asked me to marry his daughter, suggesting that, after all, marriage is "just a shot in the dark." It was three years of teen-age training in his ministry that nudged my early religious journey in the direction of unbending, biblically based fundamentalism.

I came to acquire a certainty that I had all necessary "truth." This certainty of truth was a great motivator! After college I elected to "skip" seminary and, along with my new wife, Alice, began pastoring churches in South Central Iowa, having already served a "student charge" at the tender age of eighteen in Indiana. At the end of three years, Alice and I decided to leave the local pastorate in favor of being an evangelistic team. She provided the music. I provided the "spoken word." For five years we traveled the Midwest, "spreading the gospel" in music and sermon.

As an evangelist, and during my early years as a pastor, I cajoled people to a born-again experience. I witnessed altars lined with repenting persons of all ages in response to sermons that were both threatening and promising. That psychological leverage is essential to successful evangelism, whether the evangelist is Billy Sunday, Billy Graham, any TV evangelist, or a younger "yours truly." I once preached on the street in front of the courthouse in Marion, Indiana, while Alice supported the service with music from a folding pump organ. The organ had been transformed into an electric instrument by attaching a tank vacuum cleaner which provided the air to create sounds through the pipes. I recall preaching in the salvation army on skid row in Detroit as drunks were being thrown out the back door. Alice and I have experienced the trauma of being awakened by a drunk man who was welcomed into our trailer house living room by our four year old son. We were holding revival services on the Pine Ridge Reservation in South Dakota at the time.

As the world was thrust into the new experience of space exploration, I began to sense inadequacy in my biblically centered theology. I also developed a sense that, in some ways, it was out of harmony with defensible scientific knowledge which was beginning to "explode." In the Fall of 1957, while conducting revival meetings in the Methodist Church in Arapahoe, Nebraska, the first Sputnik was sent up by Russia. This "out of world" reality convinced me that change had to occur in the basics of my biblically centered system of theological belief.

Ingredients Essential to Healthful Change

The growing uneasiness with my belief system led to the completion of a Masters degree and later a Doctor of Ministry which targeted the need for a "course correction" in traditional Christian theology. Learning, experience, and sincerity nudged me in a process of gradual change in my belief system. This was a change which I resisted but could not avoid. This change was challenging and painful and, in the beginning, came with considerable fear and great difficulty.

There was a sense in which I felt I was betraying a "past" which had been very meaningful to me. My confidence in the Bible as the framework for all my theological beliefs had been shaken by a combination of learning about its developmental background and the rapid changes in contemporary knowledge. My entire being resisted respecting common sense as an important theological element. The most difficult time was a transitional period of two years during which I examined most aspects of my entire theological belief system. During this transitional period, I was a miserable and insecure specimen of humanity. Physical manifestations of inner turmoil became pronounced. I developed a spastic colon and heart palpitations. Doctors repeatedly asked why I was stressed. I was succeeding in my profession and had a beautiful and supportive wife. My family was healthy and en route to becoming what I had always dreamed of, two boys and two girls. Having a sense that medical professionals could not understand my need to "break new theological ground," I just took the medicine they prescribed and continued to think. A background which nurtured common sense enabled me to survive, and finally to thrive.

I had a growing sense that God would not be in contradiction to himself. His creation would not contradict the Bible if the Bible was, in fact, his infallible and complete "Word." I began to perceive less of God's intervention in the world and noticed more of God's work through human beings and the natural order of things. That was part of the obvious that I had been refusing to see. Little wonder! The Bible and many who interpret it emphasize the greatness and holiness of God and the smallness and evil of "man."

I came to learn that the secret of a healthy and productive religious life includes all aspects of life and is found in a sense of humble but confident partnership with God. Taking a cue from my understanding of Jesus, I embraced the idea of God as a loving and supportive parent. On the basis of growing human knowledge as to how and why things are as they are, I further embraced the idea that God is non-intervening in the sense that the Judeo-Christian tradition has taught and in the manner which we would often like to believe.

God and Change

Experience and study to date have brought me to a point of intellectual clarity concerning the ways of God being evident through change. I perceive that God works through a process which involves change—some call it evolutionary change which, in relation to human behavior and choices, occurs as a result of God's nudging, but never as a result of direct divine intervention.

Scientific evolutionary beliefs and biblical beliefs about creation contradict one another in detail but not in fundamental truth. Both credit God as Creator but assume a different methodology of creation. A common sense approach that is harmonious with what we have come to learn about our environment is that God creates through change, i.e., through an evolutionary process in which any given change builds on those before it. An evolutionary method in process is not inherently anti-religious. It is a description of what we are currently learning about how God works in an amazing expression of creativity. This is about as religious as it gets!

A Partnership of Science and Religion

Scientific inquiry and theological thought should not, therefore, be viewed as being at odds with one another. Science could better be viewed as our human effort to understand the creative ways of God and how to better utilize that knowledge in a manner that improves the human situation. Science thus becomes another means of our learning about how God works and how we can best work with God, i.e., another way of acquiring religious truth. Healthy religion is one which nurtures the process of a developing belief system which instructs and empowers human beings. The desired result is an expression of human life in ways that are harmonious with the ways of God.

Security in Change

Human beings should not therefore seek to find their greatest security in a changeless God. Our greatest security should be found in living harmoniously with the creative activity of a dynamic God who is always in the process of creating, i.e., bringing about change. A healthy religion invites us to be in creative partnership with whatever it is that God is about. As we journey through this life and experience the universe which God has provided for us, we can do so with a belief that we are partners with God and with no need to know about everything that lies around the next corner. The lack of need "to know" is "faith." The dynamic of moving forward hopefully is "faith in action."

Why bother to pursue a "Common Sense Approach to Religion?" Why bother, especially in view of the inevitable? This resistance typically comes from those who think religiously in relation to a world view thousands of years old. It is ironic that many of these same people live functionally in relation to a contemporary view of the world. In reality, such persons live life on two levels. One is the unreal world of religion. The other is the real world of "making life work." Such persons are often convinced that their purpose in life should be that of protecting beliefs in a static and unchanging God whose ultimate goal is to destroy a creation which has become evil and replace it with a "new heaven and a new earth." The method of fulfilling their sense of mission is typically self-centered and sometimes brutal. We can take heart in the fact that crucifixion and burning to death are now both outlawed in civilized society. Most damage is done today with psychological beating, i.e., ruining the reputation of another. In politics it has come to be called "the politics of personal destruction."

Why bother in the face of a Christian church that is both lethargic and threatening. Much of the church seeks to accommodate outdated beliefs that have proven to be popular. In politics this is called governing by polls. The church is very experienced in harboring and protecting those who seek to "defend the faith." Such protection is often provided by threat or other behavior which is in direct contradiction to the traditional tenets of love. Why bother when it is obvious that there will be more rejection than understanding, even among those who profess Christian discipleship?

The goal of this book is not to disturb the belief system of persons who express their lives in ways which recognize the common parentage of God to all human beings and who work hard at implementing the "golden rule." The world is in much greater need of loving behavior than it is in need of a common thread of intellectual assent. It is a good thing, however, when good behavior and relevant thinking are in harmonious support of one another. Intellectual assent is typically a forerunner to behavior. With that in mind, good thinking is a worthy goal. If one must choose, however, between good behavior and thinking that is not relevant or that is inconsistent with what is known, the choice for good behavior is easy.

The golden rule insists that we respond to others as we want them to respond to us. Much of religion is about "faith." It is "faith," rather than the object(s) of faith, which has spiritual power. In other words, the greatest need is not to disturb the serenity of those who live in harmony and support of the human family, and who are at peace with themselves in relation to their past, present, and future. Although their religious belief system may not now be harmonious with the world view on which the expression of their daily life is based, if they do good and not harm they are to be commended and supported.

The purpose of this book is to give permission and provide support for those who wish to bring their belief system into harmony with the expression of a life that is reverent, respectful, and harmonious with the wonderful environment in which we have been placed, as we now understand it.

The other side of the coin, however, has to do with what is happening to our world and within our human family. Power is now available to human beings which can either destroy or enhance the world. Change is occurring at a pace of rapidity never before experienced by human beings. The world of the human family is experientially shrinking in size so rapidly that even those yet in their youth are aware of this fact. The economics of

Europe or Asia, for example, affect the personal wealth of Americans from day to day. The most distant place on earth is only hours away by transportation and seconds away by communication. In contrast to an ancient world composed of "many worlds" with a variety of civilizations along the rivers and in the valleys of geography, we have functionally become a "global village." The power available to us in relation to this "village" is massive. It is important that religion enables us to save rather than destroy.

Not only are we experiencing change in ways never before experienced, but we are experiencing it with a rapidity not experienced ever before in history. Centuries ago, there was a luxury of time which is not available to us today. We can no longer afford to take the same amount of time to initiate change in religious thought, which was available when the world changed more slowly.

Many good and wonderful opportunities are available to human beings as a result of the rapidity with which change occurs. Only a brief reminder is needed to point out, however, that the powers of destruction are just as available to us as are the powers of construction. To use words attributed to Jesus, the ability to bring "God's kingdom on earth" is ours but we must use it now.

We need to "bother" with this matter of bringing theological beliefs in line with contemporary world views if we are to save our world and all the wonderful progress we have experienced as a human family.

Why Bother?

We need to "bother" because there are many wonderful people both in and out of organized religion who have "given up" on "professional religion" and thus choose to distance themselves from it. Such persons may be making a wonderful contribution to the world and may be experiencing life with great happiness, but they are being deprived of a depth of spirituality to which they have a right, and organized religion — and thus the human family — is being deprived of the wonderful contributions they could otherwise make to and through it. It is possible and desirable for persons to express their lives religiously in ways that contribute to intellectual integrity. Much contemporary religious belief is so out of harmony with current understanding of "how things are" that many who would otherwise add their values to organized religion do not, because to do so would diminish their sense of intellectual integrity.

We need to "bother" because of a need to universalize the spirit of our approach to religion and thus harmonize the spirit of the "global village." Neither is it necessary that we all use the same symbolic rhetoric nor is it necessary that we all observe the same "holy" days or symbolic rituals. It is necessary that we understand that our symbolic overtures, different though they may be, are all designed with the same purpose in mind. It is necessary that we respect the positive religious expressions of others, though we may not understand them, and thus nurture the spirit of love and acceptance which makes the human family a "family." Through the process of such respect we will come to understand better that which we do not now understand and which may therefore be threatening to us.

That which is "old" is not necessarily sacred because it is "old." Its value should be appreciated and preserved, not through servitude to it, but through building on it. Religion, perhaps more than any other major area of human concern, tends to be bound by a servitude to the past, rather than by a spirit which appreciates the past as a resource with which to build a better future.

God may be a dreamer, but God also wants things done and invites us to "do" in partnership with Him/Her. Dreams are fulfilled only through the reality of "doing." A common sense approach to religion requires harmony between the dreams that inspire us and the behavior which characterizes us. If one is to experience the best in life, the belief system which instructs us must be harmonious with the knowledge which empowers us to live meaningfully and hopefully in the world as we understand it to be! *God Talk* which is rooted in this perspective makes sense.

Chapter II

Toward a Functional Theology of Relevance

Theology has to do with, but is not limited to, beliefs related to God, human beings, and the relationship between the two. From theology should come a philosophy of life. From a philosophy of life should come an expression of life. The manner in which persons express their lives ultimately affects the world on every level.

Theology Makes a Difference

To the degree that the relationship between theology, a philosophy of life, and an expression of life exists on either the individual or corporate level, theology is important. We typically think of theology as a system of beliefs created in seminaries by professional "theologians," taught by Priests, Ministers, and Rabbis in local congregations, and embraced by laypersons. While this is generally true, it is not entirely accurate for many persons develop their own theology without benefit of theologian or clergy. Whatever the roots of a developing theology may be, theology ought to be harmonious with and supportive of the world view that provides a framework within which persons function. A reasonable world view typically comes from a combination of experience, knowledge, and religious values.

To the degree that the development of theology comes from professionals, a heavy responsibility is placed on theologians and clergy. This means that they are the ones who lay a foundation for the development of philosophies of life. Carried to the ultimate, this means that they bear much responsibility for the kind of life expressed by persons in the local church.

Sources of Theological Beliefs

While I do not wish to diminish the importance of the work of theologians, I think it is prudent for us to realize that they do not have the level of power in human life that this theory suggests. For this, we can be glad. Some professional theologians and clergy do not give evidence of being grounded firmly in the realities of life. Their theology thus becomes outdated as changes occur in a growing understanding of life and its environment. Theological irrelevance is also accentuated as human expressions of life change with the passing of time. Many theologians and clergy are beating the same "theological drum" that was beaten thousands of years ago. Many of "the flock" have long since started marching to the beat of a different drum. Some march to no theological drumbeat at all, believing that they can maintain greater intellectual integrity by professing to believe nothing, or by claiming to be agnostic. Some give evidence of "believing," for reasons of social respectability, family peace, or for purposes of gaining other values offered by institutional religion, when in reality they don't believe a given theology at all.

Herein lie two major concerns that deserve consideration. First, there should be a healthy mix of all aspects of life's major areas of experience and concern, in the development of theology. Second, it should be kept clearly in mind that there is, and should be, a tension between the theory of theological idealism proclaimed by theologians, and the understanding of life coming from the experience of laypersons. Put in another way, theology should be an outgrowth of what we learn about life and the existential medium in which life occurs. There is a need for theologians to correlate information that comes from the total spectrum of life and to articulate a theology consistent with that information. In other words, that which religion teaches should make sense in all areas and on all levels of life. To the degree that it does not, it falls short.

Of course this is not a new concept in the development of theology. This is the way theology, in our Judeo-Christian tradition, began. It was an outgrowth of human experience which was developed within the framework of the world as people understood it. When the words, "In the beginning God created the heavens and the earth" were first spoken and later written, science was not well developed as a discipline of learning. When it was said that God created everything that exists in six days and rested on the seventh, there was no knowledge of the slow evolving process that is at work in the development of the earth and various parts of it. Any concept of creativity continuing over a period of billions of years would have made no sense at all to people living then.

There are, however, two very important insights in these scriptural thoughts about creation which we need to assimilate. The first is the idea that we are created beings and there is that which is much greater than we are as individuals, which is responsible for the "whole." There is an implication that we do well to coordinate our lives with the intent and movement of that Creator, which we have come to call "God." The second is that life and its environment is characterized by movement from one kind of experience to another, and it is essential that we harmonize with this process of movement and change, if we are to experience healthy living. The story implies that God doesn't work all the time, but works and rests. The lesson is that we should follow that example. That which God created is filled with variety which we should enjoy and which teaches us something about the great power and creativity of God. The environment for our lives provides wonderful variety in such realities as: There is day and night; There is a sun during the day and a moon at night; There are clouds and stars; There are seasons and years; and there is the continual movement from sleep to being awake. The truth here is clear. This variety keeps life vital and exciting.

Theology from Knowledge or Knowledge from Theology?

As early theological concepts were developed, they were passed from generation to generation through the medium of stories around the campfire. Change and adjustment was easy to make, as it seemed necessary. With no effective means for learning and more than was readily evident about their environment, people found no great need to make changes in the stories. Basic understanding of the universe remained very much the same for thousands of years, and was closely related to the environmental conditions which existed wherever specific people lived on the earth. With the advent of writing, and later printing presses, it became much easier to record theological ideas and have them remain unchanged as written. With the sacred aura that came to enhance these unchanged ideas with age, it became much more difficult for changes to ever be made. Theology thus became difficult to adjust. Attitudes were solidified through such expressions as those found in the old Gospel song, "the old time religion, it was good for our parents, it was good for our grandparents, and it is good enough for me."

Our understanding of the world is much different than it was when the first creation stories of our religious tradition were told. It is much different than it was when Jesus walked the shores of the Sea of Galilee. We freely acknowledge that there is much about creation that we don't know, and we are still looking. We try to understand more by digging deep into the earth, and archeology has given us its share of secrets. We try to gain knowledge that will help us understand more by sending technical devices deep into space, and what we observe through cameras and telescopes in space, is beginning to bring new, and sometimes startling, information to us.

We now know the earth is not flat, but is in fact round. We now know that what we see above the earth consists of more than a lower heaven for the clouds, and a middle heaven for the stars and moon, and a third heaven where God dwells. We now know about space, and what we know causes us to marvel at what we don't know.

We now know that human beings have changed over the centuries through a long process of evolvement. We don't know all about what we have been like, and we don't know all about what we will become. We do have reason to believe, however, that change is a characteristic of our nature. That is the way God has made, or is making, us.

We also know that the process of evolvement which we can trace in human beings, occurs in other areas of nature. Certainly it is true in the animal world. It is even true with the geography of our earth with evidence of islands "being born" and the changing geographical face of continents.

It is now clear that creation has not stopped. It is not just past tense. It is also present and future tense. Creativity is still taking place within us and all about us. This seems to be true throughout the world of nature. Ideas are examples. As a result of the work of the human brain in the creation of ideas, much has changed in the way people communicate, travel, and do their work. The kind of work human beings do has also changed greatly over the centuries as a result of human creativity.

It may be that through space probes we can witness part of the process at work by which new planets, or even universes, are being created. The theoretical possibilities from this discovery exceed our ability to imagine. Are there other planets out there on which other intelligent beings live? If so, how many? What kind of beings inhabit them, and how intelligent are they? When interplanetary communication and transportation become reality, how will we get along with them and they with us? Will they have religion? What will their theology be like? Will they relate to the same Creator that we do? While I would not attempt to guess at the answers to some of the former questions, I would venture a guess that if their theology is up to date, and if ours is up to date, we will be able to relate to one another with the same religious values of love for God and love for one another, that should be nurturing our own theological development and expression of life.

Theological Adjustments Are Necessary

The concept that human beings had of God during the fifteen hundred year period of time in which the process of creating Judeo-Christian Scripture occurred, ought to be miniature compared to what ours should be today. The awe brought about by the senses of sight and hearing, which inspired the author of the 8th Psalm to say, "O Lord, Our Lord, how excellent is thy name in all the earth, who has set thy glory about the heavens. When I consider thy heavens, the work of thy fingers, the moon and stars that thou has ordained, what is man that thou art mindful of him, and the son of man that thou visiteth him..." The realization that inspired this kind of awe is small compared with what we should feel about the universe today.

A major difference in our understanding of our existential medium today as compared with our ancestors, has to do with distance as well as time. The Bible speaks of the eternal nature of God, but the secular and religious mind really thought about beginnings. It appears now that beginnings, and endings, only relate to certain aspects of our existential medium, and at different times. Perhaps there is no beginning and no end—just change. We have become familiar with the cycles that function in nature. Water is a good example. It appears to change in form, but it is still two parts of hydrogen to one part of oxygen, whether it is the liquid we drink, the ice with which we cool our tea, or the vapor which rises from the ocean and deposits itself on the mountains in Colorado as snow, or as water on the corn fields of Nebraska.

Another major difference is the understanding of what is static and what is always in movement. Our ancestors assumed that creation was done, and finished. We know now that it is still occurring. One of the wonderful gifts religion should give us is the realization that we are privileged to work with God in much important creativity. That is what happens when we create and bear children. That is what is happening when we give birth to ideas that nurture and enrich the values of human beings as persons, and of the human family.

We now understand, for example, that even the stick of wood that appears to be static, is, in reality, very dynamic. In it there is dynamic movement with atoms, molecules and electrons, none of which are ever at rest. There is in fact, reason to believe that there are macro worlds and micro worlds in which the same dynamic process of energy is at work on both levels, but in different ways and with components of different sizes.

There is a major difference in how we understand ourselves and our environment today, as compared to the period of time during which Scripture was being written. Our understanding of creation, both in terms of "how" and "essence," should impact our theology. Changes in theology should therefore be concurrent with changes in how we understand ourselves and our environment.

I am suggesting that because of our changing understanding of "how things are," we also need to make adjustments in our theology, which in turn will make adjustments in our philosophy of life, which in turn will make adjustments in the way we express our lives. Not only this, but to the degree that we are able to keep theology and world view harmonious, religion will become a much greater positive influence on our lives. It will not be in contradiction with what motivates us in our expression of life. Theology can and ought to be a source of security and hope, not a creator of confusion.

Theological Change Requires Time And Adjustments

Following World War I, The League of Nations did not live long but the idea of what could be accomplished by nations working together for common values survived. After World War II, the United Nations was born from a theory that to that time, had not proven workable. The United Nations has certainly fallen far short of accomplishing all of its goals. It has, however, accomplished some noteworthy things, in spite of its imperfections and shortcomings. One of the great things it has accomplished is the provision of a forum wherein nations can talk with one another instead of going to war with one another.

If they do go to war, they can still talk to one another during or after the war. The influence of other, less emotionally involved nations, can also thus make a positive contribution towards preventing or ending hostilities. With this experience, just think of the implications that exist as many nations move toward a broader platform of agreement on an ideology of government.

The important point here related to the United Nations is not political in any sense. The fact that lofty ideals often find a practical application, only after a process involving tedious and determined effort, deserves close attention.

Theological change presents challenges at least equal to those presented by political change among the nations of the world. Tedious and determined effort will be required to bring "worldly" and theological wisdom to a point of harmony.

In the world of today, events in one nation may have an immediate impact on other nations halfway around the world. World economics illustrates this fact of modern life. The importance of engaging the process of theological adjustment in a manner that is relevant to changing knowledge and experience in the world of today and tomorrow is critical. The distance in space and time which once separated nations from one another left room for fundamental theological differences. The proximity of cultures, nations and religions is now demanding theological adjustment.

Theology And The Future

What will happen if the human family wakes up one day to a proven realization that there are civilizations of intelligent beings, other than on the earth? We will probably assume that if we have the means of determining their existence, very soon we must reckon with them both in terms of communication and transportation. Communication means an exchange of ideas. Such an exchange may be positive or negative, hostile or conciliatory. Transportation means presence. Presence may be hostile or friendly. In the beginning, it will likely be at best, an experience that produces anxiety and fear. In the event of such an incontestable realization, the relational atmosphere of the nations on earth will immediately change greatly. We may become a union of "old friends" who forget all past differences, and form a bond designed to protect us against a common threat. On the other hand, we and they, may each clamor to get potential new "earth" friends "on our side," with the hope of making the whole world, "just like us." The former response, rather than the latter, is most likely to occur.

Whether or not we ever experience the need to respond to civilizations "out there," there is a need for closer bonding of the nations on earth. If the greatest need is not to save ourselves and our earth home from potential enemies "out there," it is to save us from ourselves. No one will survive if concern for self does not expand to concern for all of God's creation. The means of catastrophic destruction is no longer just in the hands of the rich and powerful. The possibility of such power being in the arsenal of rogue nations is very real. Rogue nations in the world of today tend to include a majority who are poor, traditionally weak, frustrated, and envious.

Even if the poor, and the weak, do not become so frustrated that they do something very foolish just to get even with the rich and the strong, it is possible that greed and self-centeredness can destroy us all. Much imagination is not required to understand that the rich, the poor, the weak and the strong, can all perish in a general nuclear war. The rich, the poor, the weak and the strong might all perish if the earth's environment becomes so contaminated through the waste of the rich and the powerful that the earth becomes uninhabitable by human beings. Self centeredness is no longer an option if the future of humanity is to be secure.

The only choice which assures a future for the human family is for its components to become "friendly" with one another. Nationalism must eventually "go." Racism must eventually "go." The rich and the poor must eventually be definitions that do not apply to the extremes which distinguish them today.

What must happen, can happen. A few years before the end of the twentieth century, only a few believed that the various economies of the world would become so interdependent so soon. There is a tendency to believe that animosity among the peoples of the world is a necessary evil which cannot be overcome. If that is true, then what is the future for the human family? If such negativism is perceived as truth, then the process of human development is slowed. Optimism, however, will hasten the process and accelerate the day of achievement.

Jesus was not so foolish as to waste his life promoting a way of life that could not "be sold." He was not foolish enough to "give his life" in defense of "a dead horse." As can be said for much of institutional religion, Christianity has done many wonderful things. As can also be said for much of institutional religion, it has also done some very foolish things. If those who profess to follow the letter of the law of Jesus, can reach deep inside, and work at following the spirit of Jesus, great progress will have been made. With such a spirit, Christianity can hope to become a unifying, rather than disruptive, force among the people of the world. The divisions within institutional Christianity do not contribute to the credibility of the church. The non-Christian population of the world is more impressed with loving behavior than with lofty rhetoric. The traditional arrogance of the church in insisting that the symbols of its expression are the only "true" symbols, does not nurture a spirit of understanding and love.

The basics which Jesus taught, of love for God and love for one another, have to do with expressions of life more than with the need for universal symbols. There is no need for all Christians to become Protestant or Catholic. There is no need for all Protestants to become Lutheran, United Methodist, United Presbyterian, or United Church of Christ. Whatever symbols are important to each group, may remain important. The reality of the meaning of the "love symbols" is what matters.

Healthy religion, whether under the umbrella of the Judeo-Christian tradition, or that of other great religions of the world, must use symbols with which to communicate. It must also recognize and also teach, that the symbol is only a tool of communication and is not an absolute value. The value must be seen as that which the symbol communicates. The symbol speaks to a frame of mind. The frame of mind comes from training and cultural background. Cultural backgrounds can be remembered and appreciated. Training should always be relevant to the world at any given point in the process of its evolvement.

All people of the world can have a similar experience of meaningful religion, though the symbols of their religion may differ greatly. Religion can thus become a unifying force rather than one that promotes divisions. Love for Creator and Creation can thus become a bond that unites us for the common good of one another. This is a dream worth dreaming.

Chapter III

Growth Plateaus In
The Judeo-Christian
Tradition

Making Good Come from Bad

That which, for a period of time, brought about the greatest sense of security in my life, was later responsible for giving birth to my greatest sense of uneasiness. A biblically based theology was great as long as it was adequate for the world as I understood it. When my biblically based theology "came up short," however, I was forced to find a better way, or give up religion. Because I believed that genuine religion must be totally integrated in life and vice versa, I wasn't able to give it up. Stress forced me to accept the alternative of finding a more realistic basis for religious understanding and expression.

One of the ironies of life is the fact that so many good things come from so many bad things. War, for example, brings out the ingenuity of a nation. The "miracle drugs" came as a result of need during World War II. Medical uses of the atom came about as a result of study related to using the atom in warfare. Originally, ventures into space were related to the need for protection from aggression as well as providing a new medium of aggression. A great variety of "good things" in the areas of medicine, food, and technology have come about as a result of research related to space exploration. The broad use of computers in so many different ways is a direct product of space technology. If one were to compile a list of all the good things that come from bad things, it would be an extremely long list.

It should be noted that "bad" is not essential in making "good" possible. Every good thing that has come as a result of "bad," could have been brought to reality had the same creativity been exercised without being forced by the "bad." Every example that I have given of good things coming from bad, could have happened just as well and just as quickly without the bad. There is need for humans to improve on their ability to nurture motivation to a point where we bring all necessary "good" to pass, without needing a nudge from the "bad."

The same principle of good coming from bad, has been at work in the development of our religious tradition. Most religion in our tradition has its greatest appeal to those who are "down and out," or who are made to believe they are "down and out." It is unusual to find an expression of religion that does not have its roots deep in a response to the negative. One of the great general emphases that needs to be made in religious expression is one which enables religion to make the "good" better, rather than simply making life tolerable by nurturing a psychological adjustment to the negative. We need the one, but we also need the other.

The First Plateau

Plateaus are geographical levels which are higher than the plains about them. In addition to altitude, the major difference in a plateau and the summit of a mountain is space area. When one climbs to the summit of a mountain, if he continues in the same direction he is soon going down the mountain to the base. When one is on a plateau, one can both see and travel great distances on approximately the same level. I have chosen to speak of the Old Testament unfolding of Judaism as the "First Plateau." This is an arbitrary analogy. We could talk about many plateaus. For the sake of simplicity I shall speak of only three.

For several years I have been licensed to pilot small planes. I shall never forget my first and only flight piloting a small plane with a single radio across the Rocky Mountains from Nebraska to California. I had driven through the mountains. I had flown high above the mountains in a jet. I had never before flown over the mountains at an altitude where every mountain range appeared to be the last, only to discover when I reached it that there was still another, and another, and another. I suspect this is the way it is with religion. When we attain one level where it appears there is space to stay a while and move about freely and happily, we soon discover there is another range, perhaps even higher, and thus a need and invitation to explore further.

Biblical stories which are history, fiction, or a combination of both, have been important to the development of Judaism and Christianity. The message and impact of the story is more important than whether it should be interpreted literally or otherwise.

The Abraham and "promised land" stories are basic to the larger Judeo-Christian story. He ventured out into unknown territory because he became dissatisfied at home with his family, religion, and culture. There were other stresses. He probably needed more pasture for his flocks or more room for his family and possessions. He became disenchanted with the idolatry practiced by his family. Tradition has it that his father was a maker of idols. One day as a child Abraham knocked over one of the idols breaking it. He could not understand why an idol which had godly powers attributed to it could not take care of itself.

Abraham's geographical journey also became a journey of faith. The stresses of the unfamiliar and dangers not before encountered demanded that he either "rise to the occasion" or shrink away in fear, returning to the safety and security of "home." He chose to continue on by faith, rising to the occasion, and thus became the Father of the great religion of Old Testament Judaism, which I am speaking of as "The First Plateau."

A Religion of Response to Stress

The experiences of Abraham were only the first of many stresses encountered on this Plateau. The prosperity first enjoyed by Abraham did not endure forever. There was famine. Abraham's descendants went to Egypt to buy food, expecting to be there only briefly. Instead, they settled there as guests of Joseph, one of Abraham's great grandsons who had become a high official in the Egyptian government. Joseph eventually died and generations gave way to one another. There arose a Pharaoh "who knew not Joseph" and the "welcome guest" status of the Hebrews was changed to slavery. They were compelled to make bricks for use in building some of the great cities of Egypt.

The outcry of the Hebrews was painful and loud. A young man by the name of Moses heard and felt it. Moses was a Hebrew by ancestry and an Egyptian by culture and training. He knew of the spiritual journey of his ancestors. He was also familiar with the Egyptian cultures, and others, having received his training in the court of the Pharaoh.

Moses determined to lead the Hebrews from the bondage of Egypt back to the Land of Promise. There were three great obstacles in his way. First, he must secure the unwavering loyalty of his people to his leadership. Second, he must overcome the resistance of the Egyptians. Third, he must overcome the obstacles that lay between Egypt and The Promised Land in the form of wilderness and unfriendly people.

Moses knew that if he would be successful in overcoming these obstacles, a religious commitment by his people involving the entirety of their being would be necessary. The Hebrews must view themselves as a people of destiny. They must understand themselves to be chosen by One God, as a special people to accomplish a special task on the face of the earth.

Moses therefore pulled on the knowledge he had acquired from his own cultural ancestry as a Hebrew. He drew from all the knowledge he had gained from the Hebrew and Babylonian cultures in which he had been trained in the Court of the Pharaoh. When he got the people away from the influence of the Egyptians, gathered about Mt. Sinai, he impressed on them that they were the followers of One God, Yahweh, and that this God could tell them how to live. We know the basics of the law by which they were instructed to live as "The Ten Commandments." Not only would Yahweh tell them how to live, but Yahweh would lead them across the wilderness by a cloud during daylight and a pillar of fire at night. The Ten Commandments became elaborated into a broad "law for living." A law of worship was also devised which included a movable Tabernacle symbolizing the constant presence of Yahweh in their midst.

As they journeyed toward the land of promise, there were regressions. Sometimes people complained. Sometimes they refused to go on. Sometimes they "broke the law" by which they were to live. In response, there was cultivated a philosophy which said, "Obey God and prosper; disobey God and reap retribution." This philosophy is evident in some belief systems today, especially those which have rootage in the Judeo-Christian tradition.

It was not easy moving into a land which was already inhabited. The Promised Land didn't meet all expectations. The people who already lived there had not been told by any God of authority that they should make room for newcomers. There were wars with defeats and victories. Even after the Hebrews felt they had secured themselves in destiny, they were victims of oppression from the Babylonians, the Persians, the Greeks, and prior to, during, and after the time of Jesus, the Romans.

Faith, a Foundation for Hope

The stories of the First Plateau teach an important lesson about an essential element in the religion of the ancient Hebrews. What carried them through these great times of challenge, stress, and defeat? It was their religious faith. It was a faith that not only told them how to live, but it told them they were a special people, needed by God for a special purpose. It told them that if they would "shape up" and be obedient to their religious law, God would hear their cry and relieve them from their oppression, just as he had done through Moses, with the Egyptians. They believed that there would be better days ahead, and that these "better days" would come through a special leader whom they anticipated as "The Messiah."

While the "First Plateau" was very nationalistic, it was also personalized. It was believed that the nation would become what the people were. It was a religion with a strong nationalistic hope, but one which had its roots firmly planted in an individual relationship with a God of love and justice who demanded strict obedience and held their destiny in his hands.

The Second Plateau

When I speak of the "Second Plateau," I speak of the of Jesus story, and the resulting ministry of the general church to this date. Whereas a primary emphasis of Old Testament Judaism was nationalistic, the primary emphasis of the ministry of Jesus was individualistic and universal. In his perception, the Old Testament law had gotten out of hand. Not only was there the Law of the Old Testament contained in the Torah, but the interpretations of these laws, which in turn became laws, numbering more than six hundred. People were told how far they could walk on the Sabbath before walking became work, and thus sin. They were told what they could eat and how it must be prepared. Some were told how often they could have sexual intercourse and under what circumstances. Jesus viewed this kind of religious law as a burden too heavy to be borne. He was openly critical of those who taught and enforced it. He taught that there was a better way.

The "better way" as Jesus viewed it, was not a flat rejection of everything that had come before, but was instead, an outgrowth of it, and complementary to it. He contended that all of the Old Testament Law (the First Plateau) could be summarized in a law of love. He said that if individuals would love the Lord their God, with all their heart, all their soul, and all their strength, and love their neighbor as **themselves,** the law would be fulfilled. He believed that the fulfillment of the law in this way would remove the burden of legalism because people would do good because they wanted to, not because they were afraid not to.

His interpretation of what religion ought to be and what it ought to do in a growth experience, was interpreted as a threat to the power of the religious authorities of his day. The record is candid and clear. The insecurity of those in religious power nudged them to pressure those in political/military power into putting Jesus to death on a cross. The cross was a common instrument by which criminals were put to death by the Romans. The death of Jesus gave rise to a whole new set of dynamics which resulted in the blossoming of the "Second Plateau."

"Good" Can Come from "Bad" But "Bad" Is Not a Requirement

The hardship and oppression suffered by Hebrews had brought forth a noble religion that related morality, personal obedience to God, government, and national hope. The "Second Plateau" rose from the ashes of the dashed hopes of the disciples and the life blood of their leader, Jesus. It is another case of "good" coming from "bad," not because it "must," but because it often does in the absence of other adequate motivation.

If one is to properly understand the impetus that gave rise to the "Second Plateau," it is essential to mentally compare the high hopes the disciples had in Jesus before his death, with the depths of despair they experienced following the crucifixion. Not only must one be able to relate to their despair, but do so with knowledge and objectivity.

The knowledge of which I speak is related to the strong place of sacrifice in the development of our religious tradition. When I speak of objectivity, I speak of the ability to emotionally separate oneself from the need to embrace beliefs because of the pressure religious teaching places upon us, rather than because it makes any kind of logical sense. In other words, we must accept the fact of animal and human sacrifice in the Judeo-Christian tradition, while understanding that apart from a primitive point of view, such sacrifice makes no practical sense at all.

The world of primitive people was small but often viewed as being controlled by one or more gods. Events, especially natural events, were often perceived as a response, good or bad, of a god who was either pleased or displeased with the behavior of human beings. A primary goal of religion was to appease the gods with the hope of experiencing good and avoiding that which threatened happiness, health, or life. Religion often taught that gods could be appeased by the offering of precious gifts called sacrifices. A sacrifice could be a precious possession, such as the best animal in the flock or herd. It could be a person one loved more than all others, such as the firstborn son or daughter.

The belief that the world is controlled by a god or gods was primary in circumstances where human beings felt out of control. A primary goal of religion was therefore to appease the god(s). A primary means by which religion sought to do this was by the offering of a sacrifice. The kind of sacrifice might be determined either by custom or by the nature of the need. Examples of this are found in the Old Testament laws of Moses concerning worship and sacrifice.

The story of Abraham and his need to demonstrate total devotion to Yahweh by offering his son, Isaac, as a sacrifice, is an example of this belief in the Judeo-Christian tradition. Human sacrifice is alluded to elsewhere in the Old Testament as well. It was a big step forward for Abraham to understand that the sacrifice of an animal could do just as well. The Judaism of which Moses was the architect, gave animal sacrifice a strong position of importance. It was important for the atonement of the people as a nation and for individuals as persons. It was believed that God often needed to be appeased. It is the ritual which gave the altar a place of prominence in Judeo-Christian symbolism. Many religious roots have their source in very primitive thinking! This is true for many religions, including Christianity and Judaism.

It is of more than passing interest that whereas Judaism had totally dispensed with human sacrifice by the time of Jesus, and that animal sacrifice played a role of decreasing importance, that the disciples of Jesus made it important once again. There is a reasonable and logical explanation. The explanation has to do with two important questions which confronted the disciples following the death of Jesus. What should they now do? How could they accept the reality of the death of Jesus in the face of what they had come to believe about him?

The disciples had grown to have total confidence in Jesus, both as a teacher and as a person. There was no doubt in their minds that he had a very special relationship with God, whom he called Heavenly Father. They had no doubt about the "rightness" of what he taught. They had come to believe that he was the Son of God in a way that his mortality was out of the question. When he died on the cross as other humans died with him, and had died before him, it shook the disciples to the core of their being. Not only did they fear for their own safety, but they felt totally alone and utterly insecure. He had not proven himself to be "in charge" as they had understood him to be.

The disciples were left with the formidable task of finding some way to make sense out of what had happened to Jesus. They must quickly make some very practical decisions concerning their own lives. Should they give up their experience with him as a bad dream and attempt to forget it? Should they go back to their fishing nets and other occupations and become the laughing stock of their countrymen? Should they try to make some kind of constructive sense out of what had happened?

They did what most human beings would do. They hid together in fear, seeking some small bit of security in their presence with one another. After a time, a leader emerged to whom they gave attention. It was Peter. His message was quite simple. How could they have been so foolish, Peter reasoned, as to have taken everything Jesus said literally. His message of love still stood. The message of his continued presence with them, must be given a symbolic and spiritual interpretation. Jesus was trying to tell them, Peter said, that even if he was killed, he would be with them in spirit to inspire and empower.

As this realization of inspiration and empowerment from the spirit of Jesus took root in their consciousness, they began to see themselves as the ones on whom Jesus had depended to carry on his work, after he was no longer with them. If his work was to be done, they must do it. The organized church was thus born! But what would be the source of the strength they would need? The cornerstone of a new religion was being laid in a belief concerning who Jesus was, what he had done, and the responsibilities of his followers. The "Second Plateau" was being formed!

Rationalization and World View Give Birth to Religious Beliefs

But what about this matter of his death? The ancient idea of sacrifice was resurrected. What about this old idea of sacrifice in relation to Jesus and his death? Jesus had not practiced sacrifice. There is no record that he encouraged his disciples to practice sacrifice. It must not have been important to his understanding of "good religion." The belief in the requirement for sacrifice was in the religious background of the disciples, however, and it was as though they utilized a mental and emotional relapse into primitive thought as a means of explaining the death of Jesus. The utilization of a primitive belief in rationalizing the death of Jesus gave temporary relief in response to the immediate and painful "why" question. Jesus was the sacrifice to end all need for sacrifice, and he was resurrected from the dead to prove it! Unfortunately it also provided rootage for a long term problem in that it was quite contrary to the spirit of Jesus and the primary emphasis of his teachings.

The early church reasoned that God must still require sacrifice as a means of atoning for sins. God, the disciples of Jesus reasoned, had permitted animal sacrifice as a temporary measure until his own Son, Jesus, would come into the world and willingly give himself as a sacrifice for the sins of the world. They thus came to understand the crucifixion as a good thing rather than as a bad thing. They came to see it as something God demanded, and that Jesus was willing to give, in order to accomplish the noble goal of providing salvation for the world. This is the reason the day of his crucifixion is celebrated in the church as Good Friday. This special day celebrates an event in which Jesus was gladly obedient to his "Heavenly Father" and thus met the requirements of a sternly judgmental, but lovingly just, God.

All of this fits neatly into a doctrine that would later be developed by the early church concerning the nature and being of God. In an effort to simplify an explanation of God in ways through which it was believed persons experienced God, there was created the doctrine of God as Trinity. This basic belief of the Christian Church has been a fundamentally basic companion to the idea of Jesus as sacrifice in traditional Christian theology.

In brief, the doctrine goes like this. God the Father was Creator who had created a perfect universe with a perfect human family. The human family had become imperfect through its own choices thus demanding its ultimate demise, or requiring some means of affecting its salvation. Jesus, the Son, came into the world and gave himself as a sacrifice for the sins of the world to satisfy the demands of God, the Father. God's presence is experienced in and among human beings through spirit, and is identified as The Holy Spirit.

The church thus offered a theology to the world that satisfied the needs of minds seeking appeasement from a blood thirsty God. It offered release from the shackles of the law of Judaism. It offered strength and inspiration through the presence of The Holy Spirit. It thus set the stage for the development of a Scripture that would one day become as authoritative to the church as the law had become to the Jews who rejected Jesus.

The individual hope offered by the church through the centuries has come in the form of personal salvation. This personal salvation has been made available through the sacrificial offering of Jesus. The church has generally held that the world is bad and will become increasingly so. One day it will become so bad that God will choose to destroy it. Jesus will return and claim his followers from the earth who will thus be saved forever. The earth will be cleansed and there will be a new heaven and a new earth on which those who have been faithful to Jesus Christ will dwell, forever, and forever. This is heaven. No more tears. No more pain. No more sorrow. No more death. Just happy living — forever!

This is the foundational belief of the "Second Plateau!"

Chapter IV

A Third Plateau— Now!

An attempt to cover all the material that is related to the title of this chapter would fill volumes. On the other hand, a brief paragraph might serve to remind us of a general truth which we already know. Without an effort to see the whole picture, it can be a chapter which nurtures depressing pessimism. The goal of this chapter, however, is to avoid denial and support reasonable optimism.

A World in Trouble

Because I know that you know this, that the world is in trouble, I will neither be dedicated to detail, nor will I simply make an affirmative statement of what you already know. Instead, I wish to suggest several general, but important things: First, some ways in which the world is in trouble; Second, some possible religiously related reasons why it is in as deep trouble as it is; and Third, some religious expressions which might light the way for reasonable hope.

When speaking of the world in trouble we need to make at least three applications. First, there is a need to consider the "macro-world." That is the entire world which involves all the international relationships and all the concerns related to environment, economics, health, warfare, peace, and exchange of ideas, which affect the total environment in which the human family must live. These are matters of concern for all nations. Second, there is a need to consider the "middle-world." That is the smaller world where groups of people are banded together in organized units under one kind of government. This "world" is represented by individual nations and their specific concerns, as well as the interdependent concerns of all the nations of the world. Third, there is the "micro-world." This is "your" world and "my" world. Concerns here include, but are not limited to, self-esteem, health, marriage, family, relationships, personal economics, education, vocation, security, religion, and personal happiness. This involves all of those things which are so important to our individual lives that they affect our perception of the other "worlds." For example, if we are happy, we can deal with the problems of the larger worlds much better than if we are in a state of depression. On the other hand, if we have a terminal disease and are in great physical pain and psychological depression, whatever good or bad things that may be happening in the other "worlds" have a lesser effect on our perception of life.

There is general consensus among persons informed about the nature and condition of land, sea, and air, that the world is in trouble environmentally. Land is being polluted with waste that will remain in its present condition for hundreds or thousands of years before the pollution "returns to the dust." In an effort to enrich soil for productivity and protect our crops from the ravages of insects and weeds, it has been loaded with fertilizer, pesticides, and herbicides which in turn have found their way into much of our water system. Waste from industrial nations has polluted rivers, streams, lakes and oceans. The atmosphere has been polluted to a degree that, in some locations, acid rain falls from the skies. Climates are believed to be changing as a result of the pollution that we have placed between ourselves and the sun. Space has been so polluted with trash that space vehicles are now in danger of damaging collisions.

The personal "worlds" of each of us are affected by many of the same concerns experienced on the national and international level. Certainly the personal "worlds" of millions are affected by each of those situations. We all deal with matters of self-esteem, and with personal concerns and disappointments. There are always the matters of health, economic security, and personal relationships. One out of every two marriages ends in divorce. An increasing number of persons find themselves coping with parenthood as single parents.

Support groups are proliferating in our society. They are designed for persons finding themselves in a variety of situations, ranging from struggling with an addiction to the need for support in the face of health concerns or loss of loved ones. The number of persons trained in the helping professions of social work, counseling, psychology, and psychiatry has expanded very significantly in the past twenty-five years.

There are more senior citizens in our society than has ever been true before, not just in actual numbers, but in ratio to the rest of the population. Many are retiring earlier. Medical science and a general concern for health has lengthened life expectancy. The challenge is for people who are no longer involved in careers to find a meaningful experience in their continuing life. The further challenge is to make it possible for persons to die with dignity, and as quickly and painlessly as possible when it is clear that "their time has come." We are not yet always sufficiently humane as to make death as easy as possible, when body, mind, and spirit indicate in every possible way that it is time for physical life to end.

A Healthy Religion Is Essential

What is the contribution of religion, or what should it be? A healthy religion is essential to the best health of human beings, collectively and individually. There are a number of ways in which religion needs to become more healthy and to grow in quality. Unfortunately, religion has been, and continues to often be part of the problem. Religion tends to change slowly if at all. It often contradicts in practice what it teaches in theory. Healthy religion should consistently be contributing to the solution of problems found on every level of human experience.

The institution of religion has done much good. It has made it possible for positive contributions to be made to human society through the teamwork of many persons with similar religious motivation. Western society can thank the religious institution and religious influence for historically nurturing much interest in education, social concerns, and government. This is evidenced by great educational and health care organizations started or given support by the church. It is evidenced by the strong commitment to humanitarian concerns made basic in the formation of the democratic government of our own society.

On the other hand, historically, the church has been responsible for keeping some of the poor in poverty. Great cathedrals in Europe were built with funds extracted from donors, many of whom were poor. Donors were often persuaded to give by being told that dead loved ones would spend less time in purgatory through the contribution of "indulgences." In the same way that Jesus believed the religious institution of his own people kept them in spiritual bondage, the church holds power over many in the world today. Examples of mind control and bondage to poverty can be found historically and in many places in the world today. Such abuses can also be observed in the work of some televangelists, and in certain churches.

Religion and Mind Control

There was a time when the church did not permit the Bible to be freely read and interpreted by its adherents. It was chained to the pulpit. The church maintained control by permitting biblical interpretation to be made only through church authority. The Pope became a primary figure in biblical interpretation and in the exercise of church power. It was technology with the advent of the printing press and religious social upheaval in the form of the Protestant Reformation, that made major changes in the accessibility which people had to the Bible. The church, however, through biblical interpretation and the promise of reward or the threat of punishment, has continued to exercise control over the minds of millions, even to this day.

Consider, for example, a general tactic which has been commonly used by the church in maintaining control of the human mind. While there is a bit of the "chicken and the egg" principle at work here, in terms of what comes first, a case can be made for church responsibility. Apart from genetic instincts, the infant human brain is similar to a computer disk in function. Apart from directing physical functions necessary for the survival and growth of the body, it comes clean and empty, ready to receive wonderful ideas and/or trash. As an empty "disk" it is of no value beyond potential, until the process of loading begins. Fortunately this process begins very early, either at or before birth.

The work of institutional religion with children typically begins very early through parental influence. At an early age, if religion is of significant value to the parents, the child is introduced to institutional religion, i.e., the church. If the religious experience of the parents is to be nurtured, the child should be brought to church in early infancy. At some point in infancy, the child will also begin to receive some social value through associating with persons outside the family and home, and in coming to know the church as a safe and loving place to be. By the time the child is toddling, there will be definite social value through interaction with other children. Typically, by age three, the opportunity for important social growth is provided and emotional and intellectual receptivity begins.

The benefits of church involvement for a child thus begin indirectly through the parents at or before birth. They begin coming directly to the child within the first two years. Religious benefits in terms of experiencing the value of love beyond the family, and extending the "warmth experience" further into the world, may accelerate from that point.

It is at the point when a child begins to assimilate intellectual ideas that religion can do damage and thus become part of the "world's problems" rather than part of the solution. Small children respond with total attentive involvement to a story that is well told, whether that story is fact or fiction. Typically, religious stories told on the level of small children are fiction, but told as though they were fact. Often the story comes from the Bible and the teacher may not know whether it is fact or fiction. Regardless of the story, it is probably told as fact because there is typically a belief on the part of the teller that all Bible stories are fact. It is often believed that not only are all Bible stories fact, but that since they are "Bible" stories, they should all be told. Thus, in the child's mind, there is often injected confusion through being told contradictory stories of God's great love on one occasion, and stories of God's anger and judgment on another. One day the child may hear about God's love shown through the baby Jesus, and on another day hear how wonderful it was that God worked through the boy, David, to kill the giant, Goliath. The message received is that God's love is neither universal nor dependable. The solid basis of religious security for the child thus erodes, rather than becoming a foundation on which to build a positive and hopeful life.

Religious teachings must mature to a point where a specific brand of religion does not feel bound to defend as literal history the stories of its tradition. Wouldn't it be honest and therefore better, to feel free to tell a child (or adult for that matter) that we do not know whether or not the events shared in a story ever really happened as told, but instead to emphasize whatever positive truth for nurturing the human spirit may be available in the story? It is typically true to say, "This is what the people who preserved this story believed at that point in their journey of life." It is much better to indicate that whether or not this story ever happened as told is not important, but the lesson of the story is important for consideration now, as it was then, even if common sense tells us that our opinion of that lesson should be different from the conclusion drawn by those who told and embraced the story many centuries ago.

Any Relígíon Not Better than No Relígíon

The story of religion gets worse! It is not uncommon for the child to be told about a great source of all evil, sometimes called the Devil, also known as Satan. The Devil, as the source of all evil, is at constant warfare with God, who is the source of all good. The Devil also makes a constant effort to get people to do "bad." In the mind of the child, the Devil is especially aggressive in his efforts to "get" the child. Fears, based on religious teaching, thus begin to take root in the child, on both the conscious and subconscious levels. These fears are often accentuated by parents who, having received the same kind of religious training as a child, use them as methods of control.

Please keep in mind that the methods used to teach religion to children are often quite sophisticated. The church knows how to use stories, songs, visual aids, drama, television, cartoons, and the latest technological tools of teaching. Incentives, such as prizes and gifts, are not uncommon. Techniques designed to build self-esteem, to create fear, and to persuade, are so common and effective that they smack of brainwashing. The impact of all of this can be great when utilized to share a healthy message or experience. It is heavy and dangerous stuff when it carries any kind of unhealthy psychological or spiritual virus or germ.

Just consider how the church uses what is taught small children as a lever of control! First, the church asserts itself as the final authority on what is right and wrong, both in terms of belief and conduct. Second, the church often asserts itself as judge of any who might question the rightness or wrongness of what it teaches. The point is often made that God speaks through the church and what we find difficult to accept intellectually, must be taken by faith. If questions are raised, such questioning is the work of the Devil. Third, anyone who persists in questioning, or who doubts, is regressing under the control of the Devil, and is thus rejecting God. Accompanying this teaching is usually the idea that hardship comes in this life to those who reject God. Furthermore, an eternity in hell awaits those who continue to reject God throughout their lives.

This is real leverage! "Believe what I say because I say it. If you don't you are bound for hell. Teach your children to believe what I have taught you, or they will be lost and bound for hell." When this kind of teaching is perpetuated from one generation to another, it becomes very deeply rooted. Not only is it difficult to break out of the "rut" of such theology, but it becomes very difficult for institutional or personal religion to be relevant in a world that is changing so rapidly. Creative theological thinking tends to be discouraged on every level of human maturation.

Religion As a Basis for Illness

Without going into elaborate detail, I wish to point out that many persons in the helping professions of Counseling, Psychology, and Psychiatry, have become keenly aware of damage done by such contradictory, and confusing, but extremely effective religious training. Many of the serious psychologically and emotionally based personal problems requiring treatment, have their roots deeply embedded in religious beliefs. Usually the beginning of such damaging beliefs are in childhood. Many who are able to escape psychological damage from religious teaching, do so by becoming religious schizophrenics in their expression of life. Religious expressions are made at certain times and in relation to certain circumstances. Secular life, including making a living, health, education, etc., is expressed in relation to a different set of rules. We may say on Sunday, for example, that we believe Jesus is coming back at any second, while on Monday we may buy an insurance policy worth $500,000 just in case — !

The church (institutional religion) also often does damage with its dogmatism. The dogmatic position of the colleagues of Jesus is what finally brought about his crucifixion. The dogmatic position the church tends to take on any of its beliefs often leads to damaging results. The closing of the biblical canon tends to say that God has said everything that God needs to say within the Bible. Furthermore, it indicates that God had no message for humanity for millions of years, that he took fifteen hundred years to say what he had to say, and since that time God's mouth has been sealed. Nonsense!

In an effort to support this "closed" point of view, we teach our children one kind of creation story as dogma through the church, and make no effort to reconcile that approach with what we learn about "process" and "evolvement" through scientific inquiry. Why is it so bad to acknowledge the possibility that biblical writers could only utilize the best knowledge available to them, and that we have since learned that God creates in a way different from what was once thought? Isn't the important message one that credits God with creation, past, present and future? Isn't it also a wonderful message that God not only permits us to learn more about how God works, but in many instances, gives us the opportunity to share in that creativity?

In what other area of importance to human concern has progress been made with that attitude? That is not the attitude we take when we need food, money, health care, or a higher standard of living. Little wonder institutional religion contributes to the world's problems! Perhaps it is even a greater wonder that the church has succeeded in contributing the good that it has.

Great Need for Positive Religion

Among the damaging positions of the church has been its insistence that God is in control of world events. This is consistent with its primitive interpretation of the death of Jesus. It is not consistent with the obvious ability God has given to human beings to change their minds and to change the course of "happenings" on every level in the world. Acknowledgment of this is not an affront to God by human beings usurping God's power and authority. It should be viewed as an expression of appreciation to God for giving us the high privilege of improving the world as a place to live, and of improving the human family as earth inhabitants.

The church has taught much about "the end of time." The world has heard of "Armageddon" and associates that with the last great battle and the end of the earth. Most prophecy of churches that carry a "prophetic message" is telling of a future doomsday. A major problem with such a message is its ability to be self-fulfilling. If God is in control and has programmed the world in a manner that assures certain things happening at an appointed time, then why bother to work at correcting its ills? If the religious doomsday message is true, why take the message that Jesus taught about the Kingdom of God on earth with any seriousness? The message of love which Jesus taught is capable of changing "hell on earth" to a heavenly experience. Why bother with working for improvement on any level, if the future is always planned and no change is possible?

Progress Is Evident

There is, however, reason to find considerable encourage-ment in the great progress experienced in the world on so many levels. It is true, however, that the challenges are very real and of great magnitude. But it is encouraging that the human family continues to make progress in so many important areas in spite of the blunders of religion and the other institutions.

The list that indicates progress is long. It includes every-thing that comes under the umbrella of human concern. Such areas include, but are not limited to health care, nutrition, edu-cation, child care, poverty, and even issues of war and peace. Isn't it wonderful that we have finally "fought" and "won" a cold war! The problems are not solved, but an opportunity is now provided in Eastern Europe for choices to be made and progress to be experienced. Perhaps the same opportunity will one day be experienced in every "nook and cranny" of the earth.

A Major Challenge to Religion

It is possible for religion to accomplish its purposes, while making a consistent contribution to the solution of primary world problems. Some changes from dogmatism will be re-quired. It is exciting to consider the possibility that the basic Judeo-Christian tenets of love for God and one another, can be-come universalized without threatening the basic tenets of other major religions.

Some fundamental universal beliefs are important and not impossible. First is the idea that regardless of our differences, human beings, without exception, have a common source. Sec-ond is the idea that all symbols used to designate this source are just that—symbols. The symbols, though important, must as-sume a secondary position of importance in relation to their in-tended meaning for different symbols may communicate identical truths to different minds. This means that everyone can respect the symbols of a religion different from their own, and feel a sense of kinship and appreciation for those who re-spond to symbols they may not fully understand. Third, there are certain priorities which all human beings must grow to embrace. Those priorities have to do with reverence for our source, respect and love for one another, respect for and preservation of the environment which produces and sustains life, and some general agreement on the meaning of these priorities in terms of specific applications.

A major but not impossible challenge! Given a shrinking world as a result of technological miracles in the areas of communication and transportation, the goal can be realized if it is viewed as a priority. The tools for this kind of change are now ours to use. This is the challenge of the "Third Plateau!"

Chapter V

Shedding the Shackles of Inhibiting Authority

The Bible and a Changing View of the World

I was afraid! I had depended on the absolute authority of the Bible for fifteen years—from my mid-teens to my late twenties. In it I had found a sense of personal security, a basis for religious belief, and the foundation for professional ministry. I was frightened because, with the advent of Sputnik in the Fall of 1957, the world was suddenly shrinking. Some of the streamlined biblical answers to important questions that had satisfied me and many with whom I shared them, were no longer adequate. Critical study of biblical development had caused me to understand the Bible as something other than a perfect revelation of God's total message to humanity. A strong urge to have consistency in my religious expression and a sense of security in life compelled me to reconsider what was once an unbending loyalty to a literal interpretation of the Bible as a perfect revelation of everything God wants his human family to know about life and how to live it.

What might happen to me if I actually permitted myself to think logically about my perception of religious truth? Does God permit honest scrutiny of "his word?" The answer to these questions frightened me. I developed heart palpitations, a spastic colon, and other physical symptoms of a troubled spirit. My knowledge of biblical content was considerable, and I developed a real sense of security in my ability to provide a meaningful and defensible interpretation of any part of the Bible. The fact is, I was frightened because I had absolutely no idea why

Jesus associated "truth" and "freedom" in his teaching. Unwittingly, I had become as shackled by a literal interpretation of the Bible as the peers of Jesus had become in their allegiance to Old Testament law.

Freedom from Biblical Tyranny

I have learned since, that I was far from alone in my fear of questioning the authority of the Bible. I am reminded repeatedly that many, within the church and apart from the church, suffer from the same fear.

The Bible is the basic book of our Judeo-Christian tradition. The Bible contains history. The Bible teaches. The Bible speaks with authority. It contains literature which intends to foretell the future. The Bible speaks of matters related to science, such as creation. Is the Bible a dependable authority on any or all of these? The answer to this question, which we come to accept for ourselves, is of ultimate importance to our religious "posture" in relation to the Judeo-Christian environment. Much of traditional Christianity has proclaimed the Bible as the inherent and inspired word of God. Those who accept this premise are thus placed under the tyranny of the Bible, and typically the church. It is challenging to become free from such tyranny.

It is therefore important that we evaluate our personal answer to these questions. Is our answer a result of careful study of biblical development, our experience, and our understanding of our world past and present? Is our answer one which is primarily formulated by those with whom we associate; i.e., is our answer primarily a matter of social accommodation and religious political expediency? Is our response one which was primarily established in our mind as a child, along with a wedge of fear which holds it solidly in place lest some unseen hand of judgment falls upon us? In other words, are we afraid to consider any other possibilities?

There are those who tell us that our response to such biblical questions must be "yes," as a response of faith. Such a view generally assumes the Bible to be the literal, inspired word of God. In this view, the mechanics of this inspiration involved the mental manipulation of the authors by God, in a manner that precluded their saying or writing anything other than "God's word." God spoke through them. In other words, each author became a tool of communication by which God "spoke" to the human family. A specific author may or may not have understood why he was saying or writing what he did, but that was not important. What was important was that he was a cooperative tool of communication in the hand of God. Had a given author not been totally cooperative with God and loyal to God's dictates, it must be presumed that God would have discarded this person as we discard an unusable pencil and secured another person who would do it "God's way." Those who embrace this belief in the literal inspiration of the Bible feel that we can be sure we have God's word, nothing more, and nothing less.

Are we justified in accepting the Bible as "God's inspired word" on this basis? If we permit ourselves to discover "truth" in the area of religion, in a manner different from the way we discover "truth" in most other important areas of concern, the answer may be "yes." If we are to be consistent in the methodology by which we determine "truth" or "fact" in any area of interest that is important in our life, then the answer is "no."

Discovery of "Truth" in other Important Areas

We can be glad, for example, that we have not relied on God to give us direction through the Bible, using the same technique of inspiration, to enlighten us in the area of health care. While religion is interested in the health of the whole person, and it often involves some level of "faith healing," most of us have sufficient knowledge of the progress made in health care in civilized societies to understand that it has not come by supernatural biblical revelation. Instead, we have learned much of what we know about the prevention and curing of a variety of human ailments through long years of observation, experience, experimentation, and study. It has been a long, slow process of growing understanding. Doctors have discarded theories and practices which have proved invalid and replaced them with theories and practices which are more useful. The more we learn the more we understand the limitations of our knowledge. Ideal health care is an evolving process of growing knowledge. It involves the practice of harmonizing our attitudes and behavior with the way we are designed and the intended expression of our lives as humans.

The result of our participation in this long and tedious process of learning and application has produced many desirable contributions to our existence: The prevention of some diseases that were once deadly; The ability to treat some diseases in a manner that brings a cure; The repair or replacement of certain "body parts" that results in improved quality of life and a longer period of quality life.

Much prayer and soliciting of God for instantaneous responses to health needs has been expressed through a variety of religious rituals through the centuries. Although there have been isolated reports of unexplainable "results," dependence on the religious ritual for good health has not been demonstrated to be "the way to go." If that had become a dependable source of health, we would have many "health chapels" and no hospitals. Such chapels might even be specialized to meet certain kinds of health needs such as Alzheimer's disease, cancer, transplants, and mental health, for example.

What we are learning is not that God is unconcerned about good human health, or that God is uninvolved in the process of human health, physical or psychological. We are learning that God is involved in a way different from what we once thought. We are learning that the "inspired ones" of biblical literature did not have all the truth about everything. We are learning that God is involved in a long, evolving process, which includes health under the umbrella of God's creativity. This process involves ways that we do not fully understand, but which are worthy of our best efforts in learning, thus continually adding to the level of our understanding. We have come to know this process by a very non-religious term — "education." There is a sense in which any time we learn anything, about anything, we are learning a bit more about God, through a growing understanding of how God works. In reality, this is education.

Another example of special significance to us is in the area of food. We are part of a human family that is growing in numbers. We live together on an earth home with limited resources. With growing numbers to feed and increasing stress on resources, we have reason for concern. We have learned through hard experience about the awfulness of famine and resulting starvation. We are learning that the problems related to human sustenance involve waste as well as food. For purposes of example, let's consider something that is of fundamental importance to each of us because it is related not only to health, but to the very possibility of human life, i.e., food.

It seems reasonable to assume that a loving and powerful Creator would always provide for the needs of his human creation. The Bible does portray God as the ultimate in both love and power. World history tells an unfortunate story of repeated episodes when portions of the human population suffered tragically, and were sometimes destroyed by starvation, as a result of insufficient food supplies. We can be assured that on such occasions a variety of religious rituals were brought into action with the hope that God would intercede with a loving response to his needy children. We can be just as certain that history tells a story of God's failure to respond to the needs of his children with an instantaneous supply of food. The "manna" story of the Old Testament is a delightful story, but we can be sure that a repeat performance by God, in a similar way, has not been known from that day to this.

I was a child during the depression and dust bowl days of the 1930's. My first memory of harvesting grain from wheat fields was one of surprise. My early experience caused me to believe that wheat was planted to: (1) "burn up" from lack of moisture; (2) be used as pasture because it was too puny from lack of moisture to bear seed; and (3) provide food for grasshoppers which moved in swarms just before grain was ripe enough to harvest. There were lots of prayer meetings in the Midwest where God was petitioned to send rain. God didn't respond with the kind of dependability which is required to keep food for a hungry population. Human beings were therefore forced to turn to a technique that would prove to be far more dependable than a miraculous, or even instantaneous natural response from God.

We already knew how to irrigate if there was a water supply. I never suffered from hunger as a child. My parents owned a farm where water gushed forth from crevices in the rock in what we called "springs." My grandfather had developed a system of moving water so that ponds could be filled with the spring water, and the pond water in turn could be diverted to gardens as needed. There wasn't enough water to irrigate pastures or fields, however, and so during the winter, "when the worse came to the worst," livestock survived on Russian thistles (known as tumbleweeds when they traveled across the prairie as they were driven by strong winds) which had been cut when green and salted down in "haystacks" for later use.

Water that comes from wells obviously comes from some underground source. Water that comes from springs obviously comes from some underground source. Concerned people began to reason that if a way could be devised to tap into the underground sources of water, large areas of cropland could be irrigated. Food could thus be plentiful whether or not sufficient water fell from the skies. We don't pray for rain anymore like we did during the 1930's. We drill wells, irrigate, and pray for other things in areas where knowledge is not yet sufficient to solve problems with the resources God has provided.

A Wonderful Lesson to Learn

The major religious lesson we need to learn from this is not that God is unconcerned. Instead, we need to learn that the biblical writers did not have knowledge of all truth, nor do we. It is reasonable to assume, however, that the quantity of our knowledge concerning our world far exceeds theirs. We need to learn that God is involved in ways other than what once was supposed. We need to learn that God continues to speak to us, but not in a monotone. We are forever challenged to "hear" the voice of God in a variety of ways and discern what it is that is being said. It is also worth noting, that as is true with children, doing for ourselves is beneficial for us in solving our own problems and producing the things we need. God provides basic resources. Our lives are enriched as we use those resources in positive and growing ways to reach more of our potential as human beings. If God were to give us everything we need, we would not grow to our potential, and we would be denied much joy and fulfillment in living.

There is something very wonderful about an understanding of God and creativity, as is being evidenced through a long process of evolvement. It suggests that we are part of the process. It suggests that we are also in a process of evolvement. It suggests that as human beings, we have the high privilege of working harmoniously with God in achieving what we need to achieve, and in helping God with whatever else it is that God is about.

A Common Sense Approach to the Bible

The Bible is thus an important book because it tells an important story about part of the process. It doesn't tell us anything, however, about the part of the process which came before the beginning of our Judeo-Christian tradition. We have to turn to other ancient historical sources for that, including archeology and carbon dating. It tells us little about other cultures that were contemporary with our own tradition. We must also turn to other sources for that. It tells us nothing about the development of other great religions as other cultures and civilizations developed their own symbols in an effort to relate to their source and existential medium. It is therefore clear that the Bible is limited as a record of history. This fact does not make the Bible of no importance. It simply limits its historical significance and thus suggests that it be considered only within the limits of its coverage.

As a teaching source, the Bible also is of great importance, but within the boundaries of certain limitations. It is acceptable to embrace the premise that "In the beginning God created the heavens and the earth." That teaches us something about the beginnings that we can accept or reject. If we accept the premise of God's involvement in creation, however, we still must deal with how creation occurs. Was it really a major effort on God's part, lasting one week, after which God treated himself to a day of rest? Is it possible that the limited knowledge of the environment of those who first wrote about creation, also placed limitations on their ability to explain how it was done? Today we are still seeking answers to this "how" question. We know it wasn't accomplished in six twenty-four hour periods. We know, in fact, that creation is still occurring, continuously. We work with God creatively in reproduction. We work with God in creation when we create ideas, and everything that comes from the ideas. Science tells us that creation was happening billions of years ago, long before modern humans came along. Astronomers tell us that creation is still taking place out in space. It is all a wonderful marvel, and we know very little about it. The great advantage which modern science has over the early biblical writers is that we acknowledge we know very little and are working hard to learn more. They thought they knew it all and were in awe of the completed "product." If they had known then what we know now! If we knew now what will be known two thousand years from now!

Even though the Bible has limitations as a teaching source, the resources it provides are wonderful. It doesn't teach us everything about God, but it does teach us some things people believed about God at a given point in our religious tradition. We now know that even on occasions when the Bible is very adamant about certain characteristics of God, that it is only telling us what someone believed about God at a given time. It does not mean that "this is the way God is." When I read how God is reputed to have said in the Ten Commandments, "Thou shalt not kill," and then proceeded to tell the Jews to kill certain people in the wilderness and in the Promised Land when they invaded it, I am glad to know that the Bible is not accurate in everything it says about God. This either says that God is inconsistent, or that he only wanted them not to kill other Jews. I don't like either image of God! What it really says is that this was an important perception which a certain group of people had of God at a specific time in their history.

The Bible emphasizes the importance of family. It teaches us wonderful things in the Ten Commandments about some basic behavioral patterns that are essential if any human society is to survive. It teaches us fundamentals about individual self-esteem and worthiness of being loved. It teaches us about the fundamental requirement of working at loving one another. It teaches about the need to respect life, and our environment as it teaches us to love God and thus hold in highest regard everything God does.

The Bible is a limited but wonderful resource. Much of what it teaches is wonderful. Some is not! It is inadequate in that it leaves the application of certain important basic principles to us. What, for example, does the principle of love mean in relation to slavery? What does it mean in the relationship of husband and wife? How does it apply to politics? What does it mean in relation to government? What form of government most readily adapts itself to an application of the principle of universal love? What do the two basic teachings of Jesus about loving God with all our heart, soul, and mind, say to us about the care of our body, mind and environment? How can the love principle be applied in international affairs? How can it be applied in a pluralistic society of religions?

Does the Bible teach anything that can help us in dealing with the problem of drugs? How about gangs? How about sexuality? How about AIDS? Are there principles taught in the Bible that apply to a primary dependence on the continued use of fossil fuels? How about the care of the ocean?

I suggest that most every concern of human beings and their environment can find some kind of helpful response through an effort to apply the principle of love to God/Creation and to humanity. The challenge is to search until we learn the BEST application, and then to adjust our attitudes, motives, and spirits to the point of behavioral application.

What is the biblical source of authority? Is it because occasionally in the Bible it says, "Thus says the Lord"? Is it because the Church lifts up the Bible as the final source of authority?

Authority is an interesting thing. Authority assumes and imparts power. Power gives either conflict or control. Prior to the Reformation, when Luther, Zwingli, and others, concluded that the Pope had far too much authority in both interpreting and "creating" the Word of God, they decided something must be done about it. They hoped to bring about a reformation within the church. Failing in this, they brought about a division in the church with the beginning of Protestantism. The "Protestants" effectively exchanged the authority of the Pope, for the authority of the Bible. Whereas the Pope had once held ultimate authority and power over their religious beliefs and practices, now the Bible became the "Holy Bible" with the same powers once usurped by the Pope. A major problem became obvious in the need for biblical interpretation. The priests or ministers could thus share this authority as they became "interpreters" for the congregations with which they were involved.

The biblical source of authority is the functional relevance of its teachings in relation to the principle of love acted out among human beings. Biblical authority regarding the place of women in organized religion has some problems using this criteria. Biblical authority in relation to slavery has some problems using this criteria. Biblical authority in relation to racism has some problems using this criteria. Biblical authority in relation to war has some problems using this criteria.

The biblical source of authority is found in experience as it related to the evolving process of human beings attempting to apply the principle of love. Contemporary human society is far ahead of the Bible in regard to relating the principle of love to women, slavery, racism, and war. I am not suggesting that we have these and all other related problems solved. I am suggesting that we are doing better as a human family than we used to do. I am suggesting that we know that we ought to do better than we are doing, and that is the prelude to doing better.

Can the Bible foretell the future? There are those who believe it is. From time to time someone sets a date when the world is coming to an end, based on some kind of biblical prophecy. I "grew up" on biblical prophecy. Most everyone "thinks" they want to know the future, but not many "really want to know." Because we think we want to know, prophetic biblical preaching is often very popular. I knew all about how the Second World War was going to end, before it ended, because the preacher told us in sermons. Was he right? Only in that the allies won? He was an optimistic man! The details of what would happen to nations were wrong. The prophecy of the immediate coming of Jesus to the earth for a second time were wrong.

The Bible should not be viewed as a book of prophecy. It is possible that if it came to be viewed by a majority of the world as such, the world might make the prophecy self-fulfilling. What a waste and shame that would be! This generation has more knowledge, more resources, and more technical ability, which can all be used to make the world more nearly a place of peace and prosperity, than has ever before been true. The major challenge of our day, and a religious one at that, is to work with God, utilizing the resources made available to us in a way that nurtures the creation of "peace, security, health, and good will, among human beings."

If biblical prophecy was all positive concerning the future, I would suggest that we "go for it." Because much of it is negative, it is important that we take it just for what it is — an immediate expression of discouragement and stress followed by a distant vision of hope. In a world of pain and injustice, a belief in a loving God is rationalized in a manner that promises to someday make everything right. It is thus believed that the love of God will be shown through the provision of a new heaven and a new earth.

Let's not give up hope for the renewal of this world. Let's believe that improvement is possible on this earth and work to that end. Optimism and rewards are more likely to be achieved if religious faith can be an impetus and encouragement rather than a detraction. The goal for which we all search and "pray" can be achieved only as we work with God through the tried and true methods of creativity and hard work harmoniously with the natural process of evolvement.

We live in wonderful and fearful times! How wonderful to live in a time when *God Talk* can truly be harmonious with what we learn about God's creation! The language we use on a daily basis which communicates thoughts and experience related to what we have come to learn about how God works is truly "God Talk." What a privilege for us humans to be able to invest our lives, with all the resources available to us, in such an eternal and valuable endeavor! What a thrill it is to be loosened from the shackles of inhibiting biblical (or church) authority! We need not be harnessed by the *God Talk* of long ago. We do need to add a sense of the sacred and an attitude of reverence to much that, too often, we view as secular or natural.

Part II

A Common Sense Application
Of Process To Basic Beliefs

Chapter VI

Religion As Ritual

It should be noted that when speaking of ritual the point of reference is the Judeo-Christian tradition. The principles involved, however, apply to any religion. In view of the contemporary world that is relationally shrinking as a result of advanced technology in the areas of transportation and communication, this matter of how ritual is viewed is extremely important. Both communication and transportation make the exposure of cultures, religions, and races to one another "the order of the day." If the world is to be a place of peace rather than conflict, it is essential that matters relating to religion and ritual find a common ground of acceptance and respect. Given the fact that most of us acknowledge our common parentage in "God," it would seem that this would not be a "tall order." In the real world, however, this challenge seems insurmountable. It need not be!

Ritual Required by God or Those Who Worship God?

On the basic assumption that all human beings have a common Source in God, it can be said that the basic question concerning ritual has to do with whether God demands certain rituals, or whether rituals in any religion evolve through the efforts of human beings to satisfy what they perceive to be the wishes of God. Does God need our rituals or do we?

If God demands certain rituals then it follows that a given formula for religious expression ought to apply to all people in all generations. If such were the case, it is rational to suppose that all people since the beginning of human history would utilize the same religious rituals for the same reasons. It might be assumed, in this context, that the older the religion the greater the likelihood that its rituals would please God.

If, on the other hand, rituals are a necessary expression created by human beings in their effort to relate to a God who is never fully known or understood by them, then it is reasonable to assume that rituals should change concurrently with changes in the perception which human beings have of God. This assumption is clearly harmonious with the manner in which progress is made in all other important areas of human concern.

Learning occurs in human beings in many ways but not as a result of supernatural revelation. As in learning about everything else, learning about God does not occur as a result of supernatural revelation. Learning about God is a process. We are made with a curiosity, and we are given tools with which to learn. Curiosity and intelligence keep us continuously in search of something beyond what we know and where we are now. A continuous search for greater knowledge about God and a focused effort to express life more harmoniously with God demands adjustments in the rituals which serve as channels of communication in worship.

It is clear that religious ritual comes into being as a result of human need rather than as a result of God's need or demand. God, for example, does not need human or animal sacrifice. The Old Testament indicates the practice of human sacrifice (the story of Abraham and Isaac for example) as part of ancient practice in the tradition of Judaism. The major Old Testament emphasis, however, is on the custom of animal sacrifice. We all agree that this is a step higher on the ladder of civilization than human sacrifice — especially if we or one we love is in line to be "the chosen one."

Is sacrifice, either human or animal, what God wanted, or was it what human beings thought God wanted? The answer is clear that both practices of human and animal sacrifice were an expression of human need at that point in human religious development. At the point of human development today, it is a matter of common sense to know that such activity does nothing for the needs of God.

Just as in the past, human beings designed rituals to satisfy their perception of God's need; we need to do the same today. A major difference, however, must be taken into consideration. Never before in human history has there been such an explosion of knowledge that has enabled us to learn so much in so short a period of time. What may have taken centuries in the past, may take only scores of years today. There is plenty of evidence to support the idea that this reality is accelerating.

It is important that we work hard in an effort to distinguish what it is that "God really wants/requires." It is not enough to assume that what human beings believe God wants in any culture and at any point in history, is the way it really is. We should consider ourselves to be on a journey of learning about God, in the same sense that gaining knowledge is a process in all other areas of human need and interest.

A Better Way

There is no indication in the New Testament stories about Jesus, for example, that he felt the need for either human or animal sacrifice. If he did, it certainly was not a point of either concern or emphasis. Instead, Jesus taught the importance of faith, love, relationships, and behavior.

The answer to the question as to whether religious ritual is a creation of God or of human beings is evident in our generation in a way that it has never been evident before. An intellectual basis of faith and religious expression enables one to see the process of evolvement in religious understanding in the same sense that it is seen in other areas of human life. Any other alternative involves either "blind faith" or "swimming upstream in the face of reality."

For reasons that I believe will become increasingly clear, it is essential that healthy religious growth is understood as a process. As growth occurs, some of the "old" is validated while some other "old" practices should be shelved with appreciation for their past contribution. As new insights reveal ways of understanding and expressing life that are believed to be harmonious with a growing understanding of God, the emphasis on specific rituals should change. Some old rituals will be reinterpreted. Some new rituals will be created. As human beings make progress in many other areas it is also reasonable to suppose that religious ritual will also be an area of healthy and meaningful change and growth.

If healthy religion is not necessarily the preservation of ancient rituals, then what can guide us as we move forward into an unknown but exciting and promising future? Old rituals should not be arbitrarily trashed. Reinterpretation should occur in all possible situations. New rituals will be a natural growth of changing experiences.

For purposes of example, let's examine three rituals related to the Christian tradition that are in need of change or reinterpretation. I speak of Baptism, Communion, and Church attendance/worship. Although church participation is not specifically viewed as ritual, for many, the act of participating in public worship is just that. The impact of the church on the development of western civilization has been major. If the church has made a positive impact in the past, we should be able to count on it to make a positive and effective contribution to human life in the future.

Baptism has been an important trademark for much of Christianity since its inception. Specifics concerning the absolute origin of the rite are not known. The work of John the Baptist, whom the Gospels indicate baptized Jesus, is the first historical indication of its importance in the Christian tradition.

Is baptism essential for healthy religion? Is it important to God that human beings be baptized? What is the correct form of baptism, sprinkling, pouring, or immersion? What about infant baptism? Is it possible to experience and nurture a vital faith without being baptized?

That which baptism has traditionally symbolized is essential to healthy religion at any time and especially as we move forward in a time with potential for human achievement never dreamed of before. Baptism, however, should be viewed only as a symbol of something which is much greater in value than the experience of baptism itself.

For John the Baptist, baptism symbolized repentance and turning away from behavior believed to be unacceptable to God. There is no shortage of that same need for the same reasons today! For Jesus, baptism symbolized an absolutely total commitment to God and to whatever became evident to Jesus as God's will/purpose/need in the expression of his life. For both John the Baptist and Jesus, baptism thus symbolized their participation in an expression and experience of life saturated in complete reverence for the Source and Sustainer of life, whom Jesus thought of as "Heavenly Father." It was this fact that brought Jesus to a point of emphasizing the loving of God with the whole heart, soul, and mind, as the first and greatest commandment.

John the Baptist and/or Jesus might have chosen a different symbol. Had they done so, we would be discussing that symbol instead of baptism. Baptism is only essential for healthy religion if a given individual or group of persons believes it to be a symbolic expression of their commitment in absolute reverence to the Source and Sustainer of their lives. Because both John and Jesus believed that behavior is important to religion, baptism also marked a point of beginning when persons would turn from old and unacceptable behavior to a "new and improved" way of expressing life.

There is plenty of evidence to support the idea that reverence for the Source and Sustainer of life is essential. There is plenty of evidence to support the idea that behavior that is harmonious with the ways of love and nature is essential. Without reverence, inadequate attention is given to the care and nurture of human life, all life to which human beings relate, and the environment in which all life occurs. It is an insult to God, not reverence for God, when we mistreat either one another or our environment. Both are priceless gifts from God to us. A major task in life is that we be responsible stewards of one another, our relationships, and the environment which makes possible the greatest gift that God has given.

The importance of baptism can be summarized by saying that it is important as a symbol to healthy religion in our tradition, only because we have made it so, and continue to make it so. That which it symbolizes, however, is extremely important.

The importance of the meaning of baptism to God is evident. The symbol of utilizing water is not important. That which baptism symbolizes is extremely important to God, and consequently to any healthy religion. A wedding ring is only as important to a marriage as a couple makes it. Fidelity in marriage, i.e., that which the ring symbolizes, is absolutely important. The same is true with baptism. Baptism at its best symbolizes the recognition of total commitment to God in absolute reverence. As such it is also typically a point of beginning, or acknowledgment of the beginning of such commitment.

The question concerning the correct form of baptism, i.e., sprinkling, pouring, or immersion, becomes a moot point. Which method is the best symbol for you? I was baptized by immersion because it was the custom of the community of faith in which I had my spiritual beginnings. I have baptized many by immersion, more by sprinkling, and none by pouring. The importance of method begs a similar response as questions concerning the basic need of baptism as a means of meeting requirements of God.

Infant baptism hardly fits the definitions used thus far. Infants have no behavioral inadequacies. They do what comes naturally until trained to do otherwise. Such training is the responsibility of parents by the very nature of human birth and nurture. Infants have no need to be reverent. The need for reverence is something that is learned. The teaching of reverence by word and example also falls in the category of parental responsibility.

It should be remembered, however, that much of the Christian Church came to accept the idea of the natural depravity of human beings. This belief continues to be held by much of the church, in profession if not in reality, and has traditionally been known as "original sin." It holds that human beings are "sinners" by nature and are thus born that way. Whether in or out of context, the Psalmist (51:5 KJ) laid the foundation for such a belief when he said, "Behold I was shapen in iniquity and in sin did my mother conceive me."

Concurrent with this belief, infant baptism was early believed to be important in securing God's favor on a child otherwise alienated from God because of is natural sinful condition. Such a belief ought to be considered to be as outdated as is the ancient belief in the need for human sacrifice. The belief that gave rise to infant baptism should be discarded. It can, however, be beautifully reinterpreted.

The need for parental responsibility in teaching a child reverence and commitment to the Source and Sustainer of life is absolutely important. Problems of children and youth in our society today make this abundantly clear. The ritual is not what counts. Good stewardship of a new interpretation of the ritual is what can really count. Either parents assume responsibility for the spiritual nurture of their children, or the human family pays the price in juvenile delinquency, deterioration of the family, and a frightening and insecure future regardless of the wonderful potential that the future might otherwise hold.

Infant baptism is a beautiful symbolic ritual which God does not need. It can be helpful to human beings in providing us a symbol of commitment to the principles of reverence for God and his creation, and to human behavior which is harmonious with our understanding of the ways of God. It is reasonable to believe that God does need our reverent and harmonious participation in life.

Communion/Eucharist

How can reinterpretation apply to the ritual of Communion? As we seek to move forward in nurturing an approach to religion that is intellectually harmonious with the best that we know about life, the ritual of communion stands in special need of reinterpretation, or perhaps, replacement.

Let it be emphasized that God does not need this ritual either. Surely there is no particular benefit to God in the wine, juice, bread, or wafers that are consumed. Whatever need there is for Communion is found in human need to symbolize something that is important to human beings in their perceived relationship with God.

The belief which Communion originally symbolized in the church, and the profession which continues to be symbolized, is really quite alarming. It is not alarming, however, to the mind that has been effectively conditioned to believe that truth is found by trusting the church, rather than by rational thought. The ritual was unquestionably designed to emphasize the sacrificial nature of the death of Jesus and appreciation to God for a willingness to give "His Son" as well as human appreciation for the willingness of Jesus to "give his life" as a ransom or sacrifice for our sins. This is an ancient and primitive idea that was okay two thousand years ago, but needs reinterpretation or change today.

How can it possibly make sense, apart from intellectual conditioning, to believe that God is in need of sacrifice by proxy! This, however, is the traditional meaning of this ritual in the church. In other words, the symbolism of this ritual is intended to be a celebration of a human/God sacrifice. How deep into the dark ages of human thought in relation to religion are we willing to stay?

Why does the church continue to teach such a horrendous thing? One can easily understand how the primitive mind might believe that it is the requirement of a vengeful God that a human being die as atonement for all human sin? In the beginning, this idea was central to the Christian belief system. The church has had plenty of reasons, but not the courage, to either reinterpret or retire the religious concept of sacrifice to the archives of religious belief, as Jesus seemed to have done. This belief was a distinguishing difference between Judaism from which Christianity came, and a new but growing Christianity.

Why was such a belief conceived, and why has it survived? Because such a belief was consistent with the general world view and beliefs held by other religions in the historical time when it was conceived. It thus made perfect sense then! Because the church has taught it as absolute truth for centuries, minds have been conditioned! Because of the threats of eternal damnation which the church has held over us for non-belief for centuries, Christianity has become, for many, a religion of fear! Because we have been taught since childhood that "Jesus died on the cross to save us from our sins," and because it is comforting to continue embracing such a belief at the same time that conversely, it is frightening to reject it as something which belongs in the past! Because the church has not been sufficiently creative to come forth with a good replacement belief that is harmonious with the way we understand our world and express our lives in our day! Because we have a number of other beliefs which have been critical to the Christian belief system in the past which will be challenged if this one is rejected! Because we have lacked the courage of an Abraham or a Jesus to step out of the norm exposing certain fallacies of our tradition and opening the doors wide to a search for religious truth!

Communion can easily be reinterpreted rather than replaced. Doing away with a ritual that has held so much meaning for so many, and that has been in place for so long, may be more traumatic than is necessary.

The elements of communion are wonderful whether they be bread and grape juice or bread and wine. United Methodists use grape juice instead of wine in deference to the conviction of John Wesley, its founder, that persons having alcohol problems should not be exposed to their "demon" in church. Because of the alcohol problems of so many to whom John Wesley ministered, he instructed his ministers to use the unfermented juice of grapes rather than the traditional wine.

Bread and juice/wine represent the heart of that which naturally supports human life. Grain and fruit are staples. They were common foods at the time of Jesus and they continue to be today. Life and the "staples" that sustain it are both wonderful gifts from God. One without the other would be not be complete. Because we are "fearfully and wonderfully made," the continual birth and maturing of "bread and wine" and the continual birth and maturing of human life is miraculous to us.

Communion is a wonderful symbol of thanksgiving to God for the privilege of life and all that sustains it. Communion is also a ritual which we can share together in thanksgiving as a corporate body again and again. In the same way that each of us is in need of the staples of life to sustain us, we stand in need of one another. The act of communion is an act of humility in sharing, and thanksgiving for the privilege. We give to one another. We receive from one another. We need one another. We have access to one another. A beautiful symbol of thanksgiving and renewal of commitment to the preservation of that which we celebrate is a good thing. Even reinterpreted, the sharing of communion today links us with our spiritual ancestors.

God doesn't need communion. We human beings need a symbol as a means of expressing both thanksgiving and commitment. Communion reinterpreted can do that.

Church Membership/Attendance

Finally, we consider the ritual of propagating the church itself. Without participation, the church ceases to exist.

Does God need us to attend church? Is the presence of God to be found more in the church than out of the church? As is true with the other rituals we have discussed, God does not need the church. Our church attendance is not something God needs. Instead it is something we need. It can be a wonderful aid in our efforts to live life increasingly harmoniously with God and all of God's creation.

Churches have been an important part of our developing society. Human history would be much different were it not for the fact of Judaism and Christianity. Contemporary western civilization would be much different were it not for the influence of Judaism and the Christian Church. Remove the fact of the Judeo-Christian influence from our society, and the future looks different.

But is the church ready to participate in the challenges and opportunities of a new century?

It has been said that when one enters a community, the highest values of the community are seen symbolized in the highest buildings. If there is truth in this, there is reason to observe our buildings of the past and the present with some concern. In early America the steeples on churches easily made them the highest. In modern America financial institutions occupy the tallest buildings in most metropolitan communities.

Has church attendance diminished in importance as a ritual of the masses because human need for spiritual nourishment has declined or because human beings in their search for spiritual nourishment have to look harder to find it in church?

Church attendance is sometimes viewed as a coming together of the "saints." Such a view assumes that these folks perceive themselves to be a bit better than those who do not attend. They are saved! They are "washed in the blood!" They are "bound for heaven!" They are "God's people!" Nonsense!

Such views of those who attend church often solicit the descriptive word "hypocrite" by those on the outside of their fellowship. Self testimony of holiness often is not harmonious with the view seen by others. Behavior often doesn't match up with profession. Many persons who are genuinely reverent in their approach to life are consequently discouraged from church participation because they choose not to be numbered among those who profess but don't produce.

Church attendance can be better viewed as a coming together of persons who are seeking to find a better way. Healthy church attendance does not testify of goodness or holiness, but of need. We need fellowship with "good" people. We need to learn better how to live. We need to understand better how to nourish our spiritual roots. In a world that is always challenging and often unfair and painful, we need the support of one another.

How wonderful it would be if the church could universally be perceived as a place where one could always be assured of learning some truth that would point the way to a better life! How wonderful it would be if the church could universally be perceived as an experience where one can be supported and supportive!

How wonderful it would be if when we attend church we could always hear a "message" that is consistent with what we have come to believe and experience about life in our day. It is an affront to the human intellect to assume a world view that is outdated except in our religious conversations. It is an affront to the human intellect to force people to listen to pronouncements that are outdated everyplace in our society except in church.

The mind and the spirit complement one another when one is in the best of health. It would be wonderful if church attendance would always bring about this wonderful result.

A "new" church is needed if we are to continue into the future with the best possible equipment to face the challenges and the opportunities before us.

In summary, let it be said that rituals can be empty and void of meaning. They can become empty habits which bring about a false sense of achievement. They can be an abomination to God!

On the other hand, if ritual is an authentic symbol which communicates an inner spiritual need, desire, or commitment, it will add to both the awe and the commitment of human expression in life. The new century promises much potential. A common sense approach to religion can help us obtain the realization of the promised potential.

The dawning of a new century deserves the promise of a new approach to religious ritual if spiritual growth is to keep pace with other kinds of growth as is now anticipated. Ritual is not changed by edict nor does an adjustment of ritual come quickly. Some ritual can be given a new and relevant interpretation. Some should be "dropped." Some should evolve from experience and understanding in the same way that traditional rituals came into being. Such thinking may be frightening to some. It will be refreshing and exhilarating to others. If religion is to have optimum meaning in a rapidly changing world which is characterized by an explosion of knowledge, ritual must evolve harmoniously with human need and understanding.

Chapter VII

The Biblical
Problem/Blessing

The Bible is "The Book" of the Judeo-Christian tradition. The Old Testament is the Scripture for Judaism. Both Old and New Testaments combine to form "The Book," i.e., the Bible for Christianity. It is often called "The Holy Bible" and is assumed by many to represent a direct communication to specific parts of the human family from God. It has been, and continues to be, the "glue of authority" that holds each of the religions of Judaism and Christianity together.

The Bible involves the work of approximately fifty different authors and was written over a period of about fifteen hundred years. It contains history, law, poetry, fiction, allegory, metaphor, promises, warnings, admonitions and prophecy. It is a best seller which is often bought for symbolic reasons rather than as a source of information. It is subject to a variety of interpretations and is often spoken of as "the word of God." It is truly a remarkable book.

The Bible is both a blessing and a problem. It is a blessing in that it is a common focus from which a variety of approaches to religion come. As such it provides information, inspiration, and a basis of faith for millions.

A Problem

The Bible is a problem in that it is subject to a wide range of interpretation. Beliefs are thus often encouraged which go far astray from common sense, good judgment, and the original intent of the authors. A recent news story told of a minister in the South who died as a result of snake bites experienced through the use of snakes in worship. This is not new. The Bible teaches that persons of faith can be bitten by snakes and will suffer no ill effects. Both common sense and good judgment indicate that this is not true except in rare circumstances on which we cannot generally depend. Some, without the use of common sense, continue to do foolish things in their effort to follow the admonitions of the Bible.

The Bible is a problem in that, in all cases, it has its roots in a culture different from ours and at a point in time when the level of knowledge about human beings and their earthly home environment was much less than is true today. The Bible is a problem in that it is often assumed to have authority in circumstances and ways which are not congruent with what we have learned to be best about life.

The Bible is a problem in that although it clearly contains contradictions, the aura and authority which is traditionally imparted to it, blinds people to its contradictions. Not "seeing" contradictions contributes to failure in the very areas in which human beings demonstrate their weaknesses to their own detriment. How, for example, can one attribute the commandment which says, "thou shalt not kill," to the same God who, on a variety of occasions, told the Jews to destroy other human beings. Why, if we are not to kill, is so much made of the story of the youthful David killing the giant Philistine, Goliath? Why, if we are not to kill, does the New Testament interpret the crucifixion of Jesus as a fulfillment of what God planned, and wanted to happen?

If we are to discover reasonable answers to these kinds of problems, we must find them through the utilization of a database of knowledge and by following a methodology similar to that which has been found to be useful in making progress in other areas that are important to human beings.

Process and the Bible

In the same sense that God should no longer be viewed as having literally created in the manner and time frame of the Genesis stories, the development of the Bible should not be viewed as the result of literal inspiration and perfectness as God gave his message to part of the human family. The Bible in itself is a process. It is a story of an expression of life by selected groups of people. It deals with spirituality and God, and tells about imperfect people who were themselves in a process of "becoming."

Although multitudes of questions remain unanswered about creation, we now know beyond any doubt, that creation is a process which continues to occur at this very moment. This is true from the micro world of cell division to the macro world in which the telescopes in space are "revealing" that universes are continuing to be created as far out as we can "see" and probably further. In the same sense that we think of an eternity of time, there may be an "eternity" of space.

We now know that all creation is not past tense, and that creation does not happen with the "snap of a finger." It is a process, which is often slow moving, in which a given "happening" is dependent upon many other "happenings" and which itself is also responsible for impacting other happenings which have not impacted it. A new island, for example, is presently being created by volcanic action to become part of the "Hawaiian Islands."

To put it simply and boldly, creation and the continual movement of life is never simple and is always in process of change. To put it in religious terminology, God is always at work, and our curiosity as human beings is always nudging us to learn more about what God has done, is doing, and how God does it. The term "science" should generally be applied to this phenomenon thus making religion and science "allies" as science becomes another source for learning about God's work.

Given the understanding that is generally accepted of "how things are" in the civilized and literate portion of the human family today, the interpretation of the Bible which is most helpful is one which is seen in relation to this kind of world. The world as perceived in the time when various parts of the Bible were being written only slightly resembles the world as we know it today.

The Bible can therefore be of much greater value to us when viewed as "history" than when viewed as "revelation." While it is true that the Bible as a whole provides an image of how "revelation" occurs, i.e., over a long period of time with the involvement of much human experience, it is not true that the Bible should be trusted in providing episodes of instantaneous revelations which ought to guide the understanding and expression of our lives today. In relation to our understanding of "how things work today," as I shall point out later in this chapter, one can rest assured that the experience of Moses in acquiring and giving the Ten Commandments was not a matter of instantaneous revelation. This is not withstanding the emotional and authoritative appeal which the image of God writing the Commandments with a finger of fire provides.

As history the Bible tells us how early people thought creation might have occurred. A sufficient database of knowledge had not been developed nor had the tools yet been created to enable them to understand creation as we do today. They did the best they could with what they had to work with, and in many regards, their insights were impressive.

The authors of the Bible did exactly what we do in terms of borrowing from others and the past. The creation stories in the Book of Genesis for example, are clearly not Hebrew records that can be verified, but were adaptations of creation stories from civilizations that pre-dated their own, especially that of the Babylonians. A major and important "spin" which the early Hebrews placed on their creation stories was the inclusion of the religious element.

The Bible can best be understood as the recording of a process of religious thought which originated in the minds of a specific part of the human family as it experienced life in relation to its time in history, place in the geography of the world, and experience of living.

Keep two important things in mind. First, during the process of biblical development, the authors did not know they were creating Scripture, and the only method of recording what their minds created was within the human mind itself. The thoughts they shared came from experience, observation, thoughts that had been shared with them by others, and memory. There were no computers, video tapes, audio tapes, books, or newspapers. The "recording" was first done as stories and philosophies were told around the campfires of nomadic peoples from generation to generation. As the process of the human journey unfolded, there came a time when other means of recording history and thoughts were available. With the development of written languages there came hieroglyphics on stones, writing on papyrus, scrolls, the printing press with books, and now all the wonderful means of recording and preserving ideas that are available to us today.

Second, the Bible is a product of human experience. Much of the human experience from which it developed was an experience of hardship and adversity. Consider some major episodes which impacted the lives of those whose contributions of religious thought eventually became part of what we call Scripture, i.e., the Bible: Abraham leaving the security of his family, religion, and culture and going to an unfamiliar place as he sought something better; the roots of strife within his own home as he sought to preserve his family line through fathering a child first with Hagar (the maid) and then with Sarah, his elderly wife; the friendly helpfulness of Egypt which eventually led to slavery for the Hebrews; the rigors of the wilderness "no mans land" as the Hebrews sought a "promised land" of freedom; the conquest of Canaan; the glory days of David followed by subjugation to the Assyrians, the Babylonians, the Persians, the Greeks, and at the time of Jesus, the Romans; and finally, the adversity in which the church was born with the crucifixion of Jesus and the persecution of the early church as it sought to take root in a culture of many religions.

The Bible, both Old and New Testaments, comes from a background of oppression in which "hope" always found a way. It is little wonder though that the last book of the Bible, i.e., Revelation, is a book about the future written at a time when it was hoped and believed that all evil would be destroyed and all good would be rewarded.

The multitude of inspirational resources which come from people who found a basis of hope in the midst of the kind of adversity from which biblical literature emerged is remarkable. If people living in those kinds of circumstances found reason for hope and thanksgiving, how blest and thankful most of us should be who live today. The Bible, as a resource which encourages faith and hope in the midst of the most difficult of circumstances, makes it a blessing which outweighs its "problem" aspects.

A Creator of Self-Image

The arrogance which is often evident in both Judaism and Christianity is unfortunate and inexcusable. The sense of self worth, however, which the Bible insists, for certain people, is commendable and is encouraged by both religions. The Old Testament insists that the Jews were a people especially chosen by God for a special purpose. The New Testament insists that the Christians took the place of the Jews as a "chosen people." Christians made this determination on the basis of the rejection or acceptance of Jesus as the Messiah. This level of arrogance is unacceptable. When placed in perspective with knowledge of "why" and with an emphasis on humility, it provides a partial answer to the "why" of human life. We are here because God wants us here! That is a simple but adequate answer.

The messianic concept was a concept which emerged when the Jews were historically at their lowest. Although they believed they were chosen by God as a special people among all the peoples of the world, they could not understand why they were so beaten up. Why should they be in Babylonian captivity? Why should their enemies be consistently victorious over them? If they were so important to God, why did God treat them thus?

In the midst of their affliction, there developed a hope that God would send a leader who would enable them to correct the errors of their ways, and lead them to victory over their oppressors. The title "Messiah" was given to this anticipated leader. Early Christians, including some Jews, believed that Jesus was this Messianic leader. Jews who did not embrace this belief were branded as non-believers by Christians. Christians thus rejected Jews and Judaism as "God's chosen," and assumed that role for themselves.

It should be pointed out that even under the umbrella of a religious arrogance there were times when a glimpse of God's parentage of all people peeked through. The book of Jonah is a wonderful story which was designed to teach the Jews that not only did God care about what happened to them, but that God also cared about what happened to the enemies of the Jews. The universalism of Jesus was shown through the biblical descriptions of his relationships with all kinds of people, rich, poor, well, sick, Jews, Samaritans, Gentiles, sinners and "good folk."

The message of Old Testament Jonah, and the universal spirit of Jesus, (and Paul for that matter) in accepting both Jew and Gentile were bright spots in a religious history that was otherwise characterized by an attitude of "we are better than they are because God loves us more than he loves them."

A great biblical gift to those oppressed by life is hope. The story of Adam and Eve emphasized a "fall" which was recovered through Abraham, Moses, and the Law. The inability of human beings to live by the hundreds of expansions of the law emphasized the need for change in the mind of Jesus and he emphasized love over law. The disappointment and surprise of the disciples following Jesus' death was followed by a belief that one day Jesus would return and finish what he had started. The failure of Jesus to return during the lives of the first generations of disciples following his death gave rise to the hope of a new heaven and a new earth in the future.

Among the great blessings brought to us through the Bible, notwithstanding its problems, is the gift of a reasonable sense of self-worth and a hope that things will one day be better than they are now.

Accepting the Blessing while Dealing with the Problem

How can the biblical problems be dealt with honestly, accurately, and constructively? Let's consider some possibilities.

First, let's assume that those who made contributions to the Bible were as sincere and committed to the task of sharing "word from and about God" as they could be. As normal humans beings, however, they could only speak from the context of experience and knowledge which was theirs or which was prevalent in their culture at that point in history. Whatever God-concept they may have used as a context for their utterings made perfect sense to them, and was in fact, a "common sense approach to religion" for them in their day. Whether it was the God of the mountain, of the wilderness, of the Promised Land, or whatever else, the theological point of view from which they spoke made sense to them. Refusal to either ignore or accept contradictions which are evident in biblical literature is therefore a matter of integrity.

Secondly, let's assume that the scientific and verifiable understanding of "how things were" in their day was far less sophisticated than our understanding is today. This is not to suggest that we, in our day, have even touched the tip of the iceberg in terms of what there is to learn. Given the fact that the persons responsible for the thoughts which now make up our Scripture were pastoral and nomadic people, it is fair to say that the science that was important to them was considerably different from that which is important to us. They had little concern about cloning, space, and genetic engineering. They were, however, greatly concerned about fertility, nature, and health.

It was wonderful for them to share their insights which were relevant and meaningful to them, and which were consistent with their understanding of how things are. We could not expect that they could have done more than they did. What they were able to do, however, good as it was, is not sufficient for the human family in our day. We should not just feel free to make adjustments to our interpretation of the Bible. We should feel obligated to do so.

Third, we should be impressed at the insights which biblical authors had into what made for good relationships among people and the "how-to's" of relating to God. It was this concern on which they were primarily focused in their religious expressions. If there was hardship, it must be because God was displeased in some manner. If this was assumed, the next question had to do with why God was displeased. If the answer was "because we have done wrong," then the next question had to do with what was done wrong. The same kind of reasoning and questioning occurred in relation to good things happening and why God would reward them thus.

Fourth, we should assume that in reality God worked then in the same way that God works today, regardless of how it was believed that God worked, and furthermore that God works the same today as God worked then. What we have learned about "how things are" and "why things are as they are" is that God does not intervene but works in very slow and processive ways that often include the involvement of human beings. Furthermore, it is becoming increasingly clear that God does not predetermine the future but that happenings occur in relation to other happenings which often are the result of choices made by intelligent, thinking, and reasoning creatures. Unfortunately the opposite is also true with persons or groups who are not good at either thinking or reasoning.

It is not likely, for example, that the beautiful story of God giving the Ten Commandments carved in stone on top of Mt. Sinai happened as it seems to have happened. In reality, the exposure which Moses had experienced as a Jew reared in the culture and religion of the Hebrews, and as an adopted Egyptian reared in the court of the Pharaoh, had equipped him with unusual knowledge of the past and present of that day. Furthermore, it is reasonable to assume that Moses had acquired considerable skills in organization and persuasion.

Moses realized that if he was to get the Hebrews from Egypt to the Promised Land, detailed organization and unflinching authority must be the order of the day. The commandments were therefore organized around the authority of word from God. They focused on allegiance to one God, and peaceful living among people who must find their security in and with one another. All the things which had been learned by the human family about common responses of human beings to one another were concentrated in the Ten Commandments. Moses proclaimed himself to be God's mouthpiece. The receiving of the Ten Commandments was therefore the fruition of centuries of human experience rather than a short term revelation from the God of Mt. Sinai.

Finally, and most important of all, this line of reasoning suggests that the learning and sharing of truth which relates to religious belief and all of living is not finished. Ancient church councils may have found it expedient in their limited wisdom to close the canon in order to control religious thought, but we must continue to expand our religious thinking in a manner that is relevant and harmonious with living and understanding in our day. In other words, we must, in different ways, continue the development of the general biblical idea of God, human beings, and the inter-relationships of them all.

The Bible is a wonderful source of history. It is a great resource for spiritual nurture. But it is not enough. The same spirit which inspired those who shared with us through biblical literature must be free to work through us to keep moving forward in our lives in our day. The Bible is a wonderful blessing and a challenging problem! We must be diligent in appropriating the blessing and responding in a positive manner to the challenge of the problem. This is a challenging and important task. We must be careful not to "throw the baby out with the bath." Equal care must be given to sorting the "chaff from the wheat."

Chapter VIII

Right and Wrong OR Sin and Morality in Process

ontemporary society is struggling with matters of "right" and "wrong," or using religious terminology, matters of "righteousness" and "unrighteousness." In some cases we struggle with the challenge of mustering sufficient personal discipline to do what we know to be right and to avoid the wrong. In other situations, we simply are not certain what is right and what is wrong.

Right and Wrong a Religious Matter

Among the reasons for the enduring strength of Judaism and Christianity has been an emphasis on the idea that some kinds of human behavior are right and some kinds of human behavior are wrong. Both have made major contributions to the development of human civilization because of this emphasis.

Both have emphasized that the standard of right and wrong is revealed by God. That is why the word "sin" has been used in our tradition to indicate wrong behavior while the word "righteousness" has been used to indicate right behavior. "Sin" and "righteousness" are both specifically religious words not commonly used in non-religious environments of communication.

In Old Testament biblical times, determining right and wrong was simple and straightforward. A personal God made arbitrary demands, or so it seemed. In fact, human experience to that point brought our spiritual ancestors to a point where it

appeared that certain things "paid off" and were thus determined to be pleasing to God, while certain other behaviors did
not "pay off" and were thus determined to be displeasing to
God. Undoubtedly some of what seems to be arbitrary on the
part of God was attributed to God by biblical contributors.

To persons interested in critical study of how the Bible
came into being, it is clear that the bible should be viewed as the
story of an unfolding process of growth in religious ideas in the
Judeo-Christian expression. The Bible is not only a result of this
process, but ought to also be viewed as part of a larger process
of religious growth. Unfortunately the predominant view of the
Bible is not that it is part of a process but that it is the beginning
and end of God's effort to communicate with human beings,
and they with God.

If the Bible gives evidence of an evolving process of understanding within it, and if it is part of a continuing process of understanding itself, then it is reasonable to suppose that ideas
concerning right and wrong should also be viewed as part of an
evolving process, rather than as absolute. The recording of historical human experience and the contemporary level of
knowledge from which we benefit today should also increase
our ability to discern right and wrong, righteousness and unrighteousness. Human experience can attest to the wisdom of
the "rights" and "wrongs" for a simple society as dictated in the
Ten Commandments. Society today is much more complex.
The database from which "right" and "wrong" must be determined is much broader now than it was then. The challenge is
considerable, both to discern and to do!

Morality anð a Process of Evolvement

Even through the rate of change has speeded among human beings, a slow process of evolvement appears to be "the
way things come to be" in relation to nature. There are certain
characteristics of life and its environment, such as creation and
change, however, which remain constant. There are clearly
some things in human life that do not change in the essence of
their importance. The sun must always shine for human exis-

tence. The rain must fall. Water and air are fundamental to our existence. The seasons must change. Love must prevail. Truth must forever be a virtue. In other words, all ideas of what is right and what is wrong cannot be forever a matter of interpretation, nor can they undergo essential change. On the other hand, there is so much change that is normal and desirous in life that it is important that we grow in our ability to distinguish what ought to be changed from what ought not to be changed.

Growth in human knowledge and power has ushered in a whole new challenge of determining right and wrong in areas that didn't use to concern us at all. In addition to these new areas of challenge, it is becoming increasingly clear that some old ideas of right and wrong need to be challenged, and some need to be changed. The religious ideas that major sins have to do with wearing jewelry, playing cards, going to movies, profanity, and other religious taboos of the past, must give way to matters of much greater importance.

The need for continual examination and re-examination of right and wrong adds complexity to human life, and especially in the area of religion. It is so much cleaner, simpler, and thus easier, if all matters related to right and wrong can be regarded as having been provided through the Bible as both absolute and eternal in nature. In other words, the temptation is to make matters of right and wrong known through a series of laws. Laws make it possible for behavior to be condemned or justified on the basis of "thus saith the Lord, Law, or Bible." Even this approach becomes complicated when an interpretation of the law is in question. It is for this reason that courts of law that transcend religious law came into being.

Legislated Morality

Most of us are more comfortable with the idea of law for the secular needs of our society than with an effort to legislate morality. "Legislated" morality occasionally becomes reality, however, for one of two reasons. Sometimes the propensity of human beings to press their opinions of morality on others results in laws on the books that, over time, become out-dated, and for practical purposes, unknown. It is more difficult to change laws than it is to make them. If the moral conscience or compass of individuals and a society are not sensitive and responsive to a reasonable standard of what is right and what is wrong, then for the protection of individuals and/or society, legislation is typically the alternative.

The greater the database of knowledge becomes for the human family, the greater the need becomes for us to always do right and not wrong. The greater the database of knowledge becomes, the greater the amount of power at human disposal and the more responsible human beings as individuals and as a family must be. With increasing knowledge and power, the matter of knowing what is right and what is wrong in all instances becomes increasingly complex and challenging. The more these factors are reality in human society, the more important it is that attention be given to fine tuning human understanding of right and wrong. The importance goes far beyond satisfying the whims of a concept of God. Carried to its ultimate end, it has to do with life and death, i.e., it has to do with the continued meaningful existence of the human race, and perhaps even existence at all.

Let's examine this matter from the perspective of our religious tradition and in relation to a common sense approach to religion for the future. Definitions will assume that "sin" is the religious word for wrong behavior and that whatever it may be, it goes against the highest purposes and potential which God has for human beings. Morality has to do with sexuality, but much more. Morality has to do with behavior that is right, i.e., harmonious and supportive of the highest purposes and potential which God has for human beings. Morality has to do with self control and decision making which is consistent with the "human drive for goodness."

The Ten Commandments

The basic common denominator by which right and wrong, righteousness and sin, has been determined in the Judeo-Christian tradition has been the Ten Commandments.

The Ten Commandments are included under two basic concerns. The first is a concern about the belief, worship, and obedience of human beings to one God. The second is a concern about human behavior in relation to other human beings.

The story related to the "revelation" of the Ten Commandments is a compelling story of God's interest in a specific group of human beings, i.e., the Jews. As they waited at the foot of Mt. Sinai, the story has Moses on top of the mountain in consultation with God. The consultation ends with God providing Moses two tablets of stone on which are printed the Ten Commandments.

What we have in the Moses story is the confluence and synergy of several sources of reality. Through his rearing with an emphasis on both Hebrew and Egyptian religion and culture as he grew up in the court of the Pharaoh, Moses had been exposed to a broad spectrum of history, philosophy, and practice. This was now coupled with the fact that Moses had assumed responsibility for the movement of thousands of Hebrews from Egypt, across unfriendly and uncharted territory, to a land which the Hebrew religion and tradition taught had been given to their ancestor Abraham as an inheritance for him and his descendants. But there was a problem of major magnitude. By the time of Moses the land was already occupied with a host of other peoples.

The successful consummation of such a challenge certainly demanded organization and focus on a common and single purpose. Moses understood this. In response he focused all of his ability and energy towards a successful response to this grandiose opportunity.

Moses spent considerable time on the mountain. In fact, he was gone for such a long time that the people concluded he was not coming back. They convinced Aaron, the brother of Moses in whose care the Hebrews had been left, to coordinate the making of an idol, i.e., a golden calf made from the jewelry which they had brought with them. It was the spectacle of hearing and seeing his people dancing around the golden calf that greeted Moses when he returned from the mountain. This was not an encouraging sight because it affirmed the breaking of the first commandment. Not a good way to start!

In spite of this inauspicious beginning, Moses continued to believe that, with God's help, he could accomplish the task. After appropriate reprimand and punishment by God, the story indicates that Moses understood more fully the importance of solidifying a focus on one God who would always be with this group of people as they traveled in dangerous places. In due time he set about creating an elaborate belief system which included rituals of worship, and a strict lifestyle. Moses taught the people that so long as this law of living and worship was followed, and the people demonstrated cohesiveness and a singleness of purpose, the goal of "The Promised Land" would be realized and their days in the land would be days of tranquility and peace as they basked in the favor of their God.

The second part of the commandments had to do with interpersonal human relationships. It was essential that the people not be permitted to be in conflict among themselves. Killing, stealing, lying, striving to get what each other owned, sexual unfaithfulness in marriage, and lack of respect from children to parents, simply could not be tolerated. Such behavior takes it toll on both family and society. For this reason the laws must be practiced by the adults and taught as primary values to children and youth.

Moses thus gave to his people a "law" which represented a basic common denominator which is essential for the survival of any society. The story becomes quite dramatic as God carved this "law" on stones which Moses was to present to the people. The "carving in stone" communicated to the people very quickly that these laws were not temporary. They should be considered to be valid forever.

Interpretation of these laws became increasingly challenging in light of specific situations. Breaking the original laws or the legal interpretation thereof brought about serious and severe penalties, which included the possibility of death. "An eye for an eye and a tooth for a tooth" was basic punishment for breaking the law. By the time of Jesus the "ten" laws had proliferated to over six hundred. Jewish religion had thus become so burdensome that Jesus felt compelled to bring about reform and thus set about to accomplish that regardless of personal cost to him.

In his efforts to reform, Jesus emphasized three major points. First, God should be thought of as a "Heavenly Parent," rather than as a judge waiting to "get his subjects." The law was thus softened but not destroyed. The presumption which accompanied the "heavenly father" idea was that of eternal and unconditional love which sometimes of necessity must be "tough."

Love/Want to Versus Law/Fear

Second, efforts to keep the law were important, but should be based on a desire to do the right thing out of reverence and appreciation to a wonderful "Heavenly Father," rather than out of fear that "God would get them if they didn't watch their step!" What a wonderful concept! How great it would be if everyone did "right" and endeavored to avoid "wrong," not out of fear of getting caught, but because they wanted to do the right thing. Jesus set about to change the "have to" to "want to." The forward movement of this process at work in the human species becomes increasingly clear! It is a major step from "doing good" or "refraining from evil" out of fear, to good behavior because of desire! When we want to do right, we are not "there" by a long shot, but the fact that we "want to" indicates progress in the process.

Finally, Jesus taught that all the laws could be encompassed into two, focusing on love for God and love of human beings for one another. Love, Jesus believed, could make the keeping of these important laws a pleasure because of loving desire. He took for granted that healthy human beings have a natural love for themselves. The goal of his life's work was therefore to educate and motivate people to a point of wanting to express their lives in love. Through a loving expression of life people would thus fulfill their responsibilities and wonderful opportunities for meaningful fellowship, with God and with all other human beings.

Some very basic, and common sense, questions need to be raised to properly understand the significance of religious belief to human behavior as it relates to our Judeo-Christian tradition.

When Moses taught the people that they should have no other gods before Yahweh, did that mean that Yahweh was to be the "main god" among several gods, or did it mean absolute monotheism, i.e., absolutely only one God? Although the former possibility may have been true early in Hebrew history, the Hebrew concept of God certainly evolved to a point where the emphasis was on one God. No advanced Hebrew belief system could tolerate belief in more than one God! This was especially true for Moses in his efforts to get the Hebrews from "point A" in Egypt to "point B" in the promised land.

Christians suppose that they have inherited and believe that they support this same monotheistic belief. There is reason to question this. Does the "one god idea" exclude the Christian concept of Jesus as human/god? One would suppose so! But not in the view of many Christians and/or Christian theologians both historically and contemporarily. Christians have made a gallant effort to justify the breaking of the first commandment by the development of a "Trinitarian" doctrine and other kinds of rationalization. The facts are evident, however, to anyone who can muster only a slight bit of objectivity. With the deification of Jesus, and the making of Jesus both an object of devotion to whom much prayer is offered, and as a god/human mediator between a holy God and sinful human beings, Jesus has certainly been put in a position of challenging God as "the only God." There is more than a little confusion about this matter among Christians. Most find it easier to identify with Jesus and so tend to use the terms of "Jesus Christ" and "God" interchangeably.

Is this a sin when measured against the first commandment? It would seem so. Is this what Jesus wanted? Viewing Jesus objectively from the point of view of the best information we have about him, sorting out the wishful thinking of the early church and flawless honesty, tends to indicate that Jesus had no such aspirations. History, i.e., the religious story, has attributed such aspirations to him because they support the primitive theology of the early church.

If this supposition is true, then what should be done conceptually with Jesus? A more comprehensive consideration of this important question will come in a later chapter. It is a reasonable and important question. Its answer is powerful and may very well be a difference maker to the future of human society.

The pressing question of this consideration, however, has to do with ways of defining morality and sin, right and wrong, in our own time. Jesus approached this question from the perspective of applied love, i.e., viewing love as a verb. How does one determine, in the world of our day, what is "right" and what is "wrong" in relation to the standard of "loving God with our whole heart, soul, and mind, and our neighbor as ourselves?" That is the definitive question.

The answer is often not as simple as it may seem. How does this standard apply to cloning? We have to figure that out. Time, experience, and focused consideration in relation to basic values will nudge the evolvement of an answer to this question. The answer will not come in the form of an instantaneous revelation from a God who functions outside the realm of that which is natural, i.e., a supernatural God!

How does this standard apply to abortion? We are in the process of attempting to figure this out. Unfortunately, abortion is such an emotional issue, on the part of those not faced with it as a personal option, that so much "heat" is often generated as to suppress rational consideration. Is abortion really the battleground where right and wrong, in relation to it, ought to be determined? The option of abortion would seldom need consideration if good judgment and self control were always exhibited in expressions of sexuality. It is on this battleground where wisdom dictates the expenditure of energy to determine right and wrong. If proper decisions are made here, except for rare cases, there is no longer a battle to be fought over abortion. Genuine and responsible love can solve that problem.

But what if good judgment and love that is both genuine and responsible do not determine behavior? It is not enough to say "if only," for the past cannot be changed. Is it better to respect life to the point of nurturing its continuance soon after conception, even if prevailing indicators suggest that it will be a life lived in a hell of agony for a variety of reasons? Is the fact of life the highest value, or is the likely prospect for a meaningful, healthy, and fulfilling life the highest value? Does each situation deserve a specific determination?

How does this standard apply to sexual relations outside the commitment of marriage? Is the entertainment and security value of sex without commitment sufficient to offset the dangers of disease, loss of self respect, unplanned pregnancies, family anguish, negative example for children, and general evidence of a hedonistic society?

How does this standard apply to drug use of any kind other than for medicinal purposes? Is an artificial "high," for whatever period of time, worth the slavery, senseless violence, dangers on streets and highways, out of control expression of life, and general waste of human life?

How does this standard relate to the suing climate that prevails in our society? Are whatever temporary values promised by dishonesty, positioning for dominance, fear of one another, and general disrespect for other human beings, sufficient to offset the plea of Jesus that we treat others as we want them to treat us and that our "nay" should be "nay" and our "yea" should be "yea?"

How does this standard relate to the strong emphasis in our society on "getting even" rather than getting our anger under control before worse harm is done? Is it really an evidence of human love and concern for other human beings when punishment is demanded even though there are plenty of reasons to suspect that the process of rehabilitation is underway, and that society is no longer in danger from the offender? How does one match this against the reported statements of Jesus that we should not judge one another lest we be judged and that we should pull the log from our own eye before we go about snatching the sliver from the eye of others?

How does this standard relate to capital punishment in a society where we plead for non-violence, but as a society we continue to make a public display through media reports of killing those who have sinned against us. If we want our children to grow up with a non-violent spirit, do we nurture that spirit by doing as a society what we ask our children not to do?

How does this standard apply to the multitude of challenges that face us as a world in competition and often in conflict? How does this standard apply to the multitude of moral and ethical questions that are presented by our recently acquired abilities in so many areas? Many things that once were simply considered to be in the realm of God's ability, we now find within the realm of human ability.

How does this standard apply to the matter of global warming? Is a change in climate brought about by the behavior of industrial nations a religious issue? Is there anything that is more closely related to the matter of stewardship of life and the environment which supports it? Probably not!

We may not like the prospect of determining "right and wrong" in relation to such weighty matters. Although we know we must reach conclusions in relation to these and other matters of morality we are an integral part of the process which is at work in moving us toward becoming more fully human. We might like to shift the provision of the answers to "God," but in fact we are entrusted to respond to the "nudges" of God within and among us, and to move toward conclusions. The process is often long!

The Ten Commandments no longer "cover the field." They were, and continue to be, important basic guidelines for human behavior. The law of love, however, is the only law that can guide us into becoming increasingly human in ways that are genuinely reverent toward the Source of life, and that respond harmoniously to the "nudges" of God toward loving relationships with others who are just as deserving and desirous of experiencing "the good life" as are we. Moral law with penalties is necessary for the immature. The law of love works at its best only in an environment of maturity, mental health, and commitment.

Common sense dictates that equal attention be given, in the present and the future, to carving out a general understanding of right and wrong that fits well under the umbrella of love for God and love for one another. This is "love" as a verb, i.e., the production of behavior that results in good consequences for all who are involved. There is no other way for the continuance of human existence, let alone the pursuit of the full potential of human meaning in life!

The spiritual challenge before us is both extremely challenging and absolutely necessary. The determination of "right and wrong" is sometimes easy. In a fast changing world where the varieties of human beings are being nudged to truly become a human family, the task is often difficult. The idea that it is often easier to do right and not do evil than it is to know the difference is sometimes true. There is much truth in the idea that we are more often punished by our sins than for our sins. The nurturing of a level of maturity and health that results in expressing life in love, and thus "doing right" because we want to rather than because we are afraid not to, is extremely important. Viewing the life of Jesus from a distant perspective makes it seem that he was able to acquire this maturity even though his life was brief. This can also be our goal of growth. The fact that we are afraid not to is extremely important.

Chapter IX

Punishment and Reward

The Judeo-Christian tradition has been heavily loaded with a belief that sin brings punishment and righteousness brings reward. The general idea has been that sin is whatever displeases God and righteousness is whatever pleases God. God is typically viewed as all powerful with some attributes also common to human beings. It follows then, that an all powerful and personal God would reward good and punish sin.

This belief is not unlike that commonly held by the religions in most primitive societies. Studies have shown a primary goal of primitive religions is to please the gods with the hope of gaining their protection and favor. Studies indicate ,for example, that primitive people who depend on fishing for their living, give attention to religious ritual in a manner commensurate with the level of danger believed to be inherent in any given expedition. The greater the perceived danger, the more intense the religious ritual utilized in preparation for it. Lesser dangers require less religious attention. Doing things believed to be pleasing to the gods is believed to solicit the favor and power of the gods assuring the success of their mission.

Punishment for Old Testament Jews was both personal and national. Personal punishment for sin might mean being stoned to death. National punishment might mean delay in entering the "Promised Land," or defeat at the hands of an enemy.

A Control Factor in Christianity

For the Christian, punishment is often perceived as lack of such earthly blessings as success, health, and wealth in this life, and hell for eternity after death. Reward is typically perceived as health, wealth, and happiness in this life to be followed with heaven after death. Jesus occasionally made reference to how things would be in the "after life" and told one of the thieves who died on the cross with him that the two of them would soon be together in paradise. This indicates that Jesus had a belief in life after death which included reward and/or punishment.

The church has traditionally emphasized personal reward as heaven, i.e., a place of no more sorrow or pain and where happiness is the order of every day. It has also suggested that persons will receive special rewards in heaven commensurate with the level of their good works here on earth. Among other goals of control, this aspect of the belief system emphasized by the church has traditionally been a major leverage utilized in the church's effort to raise money. During the middle ages the church capitalized on the sale of indulgences. The church taught that through indulgences the Pope could draw on the treasury of the saints thus remitting the temporal penalties for sin, not only for those yet alive but also for the souls in purgatory. This became an important source of revenue for the Pope and those favored by him. It was also an effective resource when funds were being raised to build large cathedrals in Europe. Tetzel is reported to have created a jingle to be used with fund raising which went something like this: "When the money in the coffer rings, the soul from purgatory springs!"

The idea of punishment and reward, especially related to heaven and hell, has been emphasized so heavily in the tradition of the church that many have supposed that the primary reason for Christian discipleship is to avoid hell and acquire heaven at the time of death. A famous sermon of the last century by Jonathon Edwards, entitled "Sinners In The Hands Of An Angry God," is a good example of the historical posture of the church on punishment and reward. Television evangelists, even those viewed as reputable, continue to use this methodology today.

Some Observations

A number of things should be noted about this belief. First, there ought to be an assumption that honesty is a virtue. It can be said in honesty that the church has taught as dogma for centuries that there is a heaven and that there is a hell, and that when we die we go to one place or the other. We have been conditioned by the church to believe this dogma as though we knew it to be true. In fact we must honestly admit that we do not know that this is true. Dogma implies truth without question. That is to say that it is accepted as "truth" because the church says it is, and what the church says should not be questioned. Even the raising of questions is frowned on by much of the church.

The embracing of such a belief is a matter of faith and choice. It is a product of teaching and the fruit of hope. It is not a matter of verifiable knowledge. If one chooses to embrace such a belief it should not be the determining factor as to whether or not behavior is good or bad in this life. The expression of goodness and the avoidance of evil should be determined on a much higher level of human maturity than the avoidance of eternal punishment or the acquisition of eternal reward. Trusting God for the future is a greater expression of faith than demanding to know details. Trust without details can be an honest expression, even when related to what happens after physical death.

Second, it should be noted that this belief comes from a personalized concept of God that imparts to God certain characteristics that are very human. Given the closeness of ancient peoples to nature and the literal smallness of their world, this is quite understandable. Nature is both wonderful and frightening, even in an age of enlightenment. It is even more so for persons whose world is small and whose local god responds with human personal characteristics.

Although our tradition has always viewed God as being of such a holy nature that there is a natural distance in the relationship of God and human beings, it has been supposed that God relates to us as we human beings relate to one another when there is an acceptance of a dominant and submissive relationship. The dominant one is in a position to reward or punish. The submissive one is in a position to please or displease. Reward or punishment for the submissive one is thus earned and rewarded by the dominant one, i.e., God. Such a view of the God-human relationship is both elementary and primitive.

Third, we should keep in mind that in our religious tradition, both Judaism and Christianity have their roots deep in adversity. Life was very difficult for both the Hebrews and the Christians during the time their religious views were being formulated and nurtured. The humility and difficulty of slavery in Egypt did not make for a positive environment. The rigors, dangers, and challenges of the wilderness were often overwhelming. Our spiritual ancestors survived only because they had strength which came from a faith that caused them to believe they could acquire their goal. For the Jews, the settling of the "Promised Land" was an experience of conflict and threat. The experience of being conquered by empire after empire was humiliating to say the least. For the early Christians, the constant danger of death and the experience of seeing friends and family killed for professing Christian discipleship did not contribute to a positive self image or hopefulness in life.

The Rootage of the Judeo-Christian Faith

Ours is a faith which has its roots in pain, defeat, and overwhelming challenge. Traditional Judeo-Christian beliefs were a life sustaining response to overwhelming negative factors in life. When life was "bad" the questions were asked, "why?" "What did I do to deserve this?" The answers gave rise to two pragmatic beliefs. First, life is difficult because it is not being expressed in a manner which is pleasing to a God who is in control of our destiny. Second, it is possible to receive God's forgiveness for our sins and have hope for a wonderful kind of future life that has eluded us in this one.

The Jewish faith evolved as a response to the rigors of life but contained a healthy element of thanksgiving for the blessings of life. This is evident in the religious celebrations, feast days, etc. of the Old Testament as well as in modern Judaism. Many of the Old Testament Psalms are expressions of this praise and thanksgiving.

The Christian faith evolved as a response to the oppression of religious law. It was nurtured in response to the persecution its adherents experienced at the hands of those who attempted to destroy it. It continues to be helpful to millions in the world who face formidable challenges. It has been less successful providing a theology for affluent societies which are on the growing edge of a knowledge explosion, because it is less experienced in this environment. Christianity is in the process of adjusting to the need for a theology that amplifies health and material blessings and instructing for a fulfilling experience of living through faith in partnership with God. This adjustment is neither adequate nor complete at the present time, but it is in process. In spite of the rigors of life in any age, you and I are living in the "good ol' days" and really are unable to identify with persecution of the past or that which is experienced in other places in the world today. It is a bit like adjusting to walking into the face of a strong wind, and then suddenly facing a "sheer" in which the wind immediately presses against our back.

One might extrapolate from these factors in our religious tradition that religious faith is a medicine for losers who, without hope for something better, are lost. One might also assume that winners gain the real values of life because of their own initiative and therefore do not need the support of a religious faith. If we find the way, religious faith can be as exciting for the affluent as it is helpful for the poor and persecuted.

Religious faith ought not be viewed as important just for persons who are "losing." The primary purpose of religion is the provision of strength sufficient to make the most of this life with appreciation and with the expectation that God has "okay plans" for whatever comes after death.

Ideas about the purpose of religion typically come either from individual observations or from what one has been taught by religious institutions. A case can be made for the idea that Christianity is often directed toward "losers" as a way of providing hope and enabling one to escape from despair. That message is consistent with "where we have come from" in the Judeo-Christian tradition. It is a message we should never lose and must always emphasize. It represents our rootage. It is not, however, the only or primary message of a healthy religious faith.

A Healthy Point of View

There is another side to healthy religious faith that deserves more attention than it usually gets. Healthy religious faith is much more than a "fox hole religion" designed for persons whose backs are "to the wall." It should, however, be adequate for that kind of situation in human life, should it arise, and much more.

A religious faith which is healthy produces no losers. It transforms those who would otherwise be losers into winners of some sort. If a healthy faith was embraced by everyone, there would be no real losers in life. The positive side of Christianity nurtures appreciative winners, not whining losers. The problem is that there has been so much emphasis on religious faith as a response to the negative side of life that many assume that to be the primary purpose of religion. The logical conclusion then, is that when life is experienced as a happy, productive, and successful journey without a background of faith, religion ceases to be necessary or important. The result in too many such situations is that too little emphasis is placed on the importance of religion as a response to the wonderful potential of a happy, healthy, and successful life. What might otherwise be an overwhelming appreciation for life with appropriate expressions of gratitude to the "Source and Sustainer" of life, is therefore diminished or becomes non-existent. In a worst case scenario, the "happy one" actually takes full credit for all the good things that come their way.

A common sense approach to religion places an equal emphasis on the two sides of life. It provides strength and hope in the face of challenge. It nurtures appreciation, reverence, respect and humility in the face of success and happiness.

Consequences

There is punishment for wrong behavior in this life. There is reward for right behavior in this life. Neither the punishment nor the reward has anything to do with heaven or hell. Neither is administered by a personal and all-powerful God. The current psychological term of choice which most accurately defines that which is often thought of as punishment or reward is "consequences." Some New Testament writers spoke of the fruit of behavior. Some spoke of reaping what is sown. Good behavior and bad behavior each has consequences, or fruit. Sowing is always in process. The harvest is sure to follow. Sometimes the person who sows is also the reaper. Sometimes persons and societies reap from what is sown by others. It is not a matter of a "personal" God handing out reward or punishment either in this life or in the future! A factor in human existence is that behavior and attitude both produce consequences.

Those for whom this suggestion creates emotional problems may find it helpful to attempt a "thinking" rather than a "feeling" approach to this matter of reward and punishment. Assume for the moment, that because of accumulated knowledge and its affect on our perception of who we are and our understanding of the environment which sustains us, that our concept of God should be considerably different from that of the ancients. This should be true because of experience that comes as a result of knowledge. We are not responding to a dominant "super person" bound to human characteristics. We are responding to a Creator whose creation does not wait for some future life as a time to dole out punishment or reward. Consequences may be immediate or they may be delayed. Neither is the punishment or reward given only to those who behave poorly. Reaping is experienced by those who have not sown. Planting in one generation may not be realized as reaping until subsequent generations. Jesus is reported to have said that the rain falls on the just and the unjust. It is not always clear who the folks are who behave in a way that is either right or wrong, but consequences are real either way.

Some examples may be helpful. Longevity of life is a common desire among us. We have learned much and continue to learn about the good things we can do to promote longevity. Health care is now a major industry which includes prevention of disease as much as treatment. What we are learning is that, though there are certainly limits beyond which we can not go, the length of life is not dependent on an arbitrary decision by God. It may have something to do with genetics or disease, but it also has something to do with how we care for ourselves, one another, and our environment. We have learned much and will learn more in relation to effecting change in the future of persons through preventing or healing disease and through genetic engineering. These multitudes of other consequences are the result of "good behavior."

Tragedy is often attributed to God when in fact God is not at all involved directly. Tragedy from nature means we have not yet learned, or did not apply what we already knew, to protecting ourselves from the power of nature. Standing in the path of a tornado says little about God, but it says much about the stupidity of the person who would do it. Death is the likely result and comes about through the consequences of a poor decision. Most automobile accidents are caused by human inattention or alcohol. Both are consequences of human behavior and have nothing to do with the activity of God. Many babies are doomed to an abbreviated or short life because of the behavior of one or both of their parents. The pain is just as real as though God inflicted it, but in fact it is brought about by human behavior.

We all benefit from good things done by others. We all suffer in some ways from bad things done by others. The more complex human society becomes and the more in number there are of us, the greater the impact of this phenomenon will be. Human experience is never totally independent but is always related to the experiences and expressions of others.

Determining Right and Wrong

There is another challenge! Wrong is not always clear, but often it is. Right is not always clear, but often it is. Human beings must always strive for clarity in understanding right and wrong if they are to experience the best possible consequences in this life. The matter of what comes after physical death should be left as a matter of personal choice in believing, and should not be considered as having any direct impact on behavior in the "here and now." Good behavior out of fear is better than evil behavior with or without fear. Human beings need to grow to a point of realizing the high value of goodness for the sake of goodness, and the painful and costly consequences of evil as a natural expression of life in this world. This may or may not be as we wish it to be. It is how things are!

It is this kind of belief system which should be emphasized in the minds of children from the time they are able to learn the concepts of right and wrong. Wrong behavior brings negative consequences in this life. Right behavior nurtures positive consequences in this life. There is no need to know about whatever may come after physical death. It is no more necessary for us to know now about the nature of immortality than it was to know about this life before we were born. The goal of healthy religious faith should be to encourage full and healthy participation in the wonderful opportunity of life that is ours at the moment. This philosophy, however, needs to be examined both from the positive and negative perspectives.

Morality Among Youth

In a recent nationwide survey by the Josephson Institute of Ethics, it was determined that dishonesty among teenagers has reached a tragic and alarming level. As reported in the Omaha World Herald, nearly half of the high school students and almost a third of the middle school students who participated in the survey admitted to shoplifting in the last 12 months. Seven of ten high school students and more than half of the middle school students said they had cheated on an exam at least once during the previous year. Ninety-two percent of the high school students and eighty-eight percent of the middle school students admitted lying to their parents. More than one-third of the students said they would lie to get a job. On the other hand, 97 percent of both age groups said it was important for them to be a person with good character. The scary part is that 91 percent of them said they were satisfied with their own ethics and character.

Although it is generally assumed that an increasing number of youth are opting for abstinence from sex, it is quite clear that the percentage of high school youth participating in sexual intercourse is high and that they see nothing wrong with it so long as they believe it to be "safe" sex. If this were not true, the controversy over the wisdom of making condoms available to school age children would not exist. A better way would be to emphasize "responsible sex" which brings us full circle back to an emphasis on sex within the boundaries of marriage. The wonderful rewards of responsible sex is evident. The high cost of sex not associated with a high level of personal responsibility is increasingly evident in human society.

The implications of this image of morality and ethics among youth are really quite sobering. According to the survey, they are saying that they lie, cheat and steal, and that they believe this behavior does not diminish their goodness as a person. If persons lie, cheat, steal and exercise little or no sexual discipline, what other major sins are there in which they might participate that will cause them to feel some sense of guilt for "falling short of the mark" of acceptable behavior? There are others, but the list is not long!

The frightening thing about this is what it is telling us about the general moral and ethical climate of our society. It says something to us about the matter of reward and punishment as a basis for religious faith. Consequences will come about regardless of how one rationalizes behavior. Religious faith should nurture behavior that brings good consequences and discourage behavior that results in negative consequences.

In terms of traditional theology, one would suppose that God would punish youth for their lack of right behavior. On the other hand, it would seem that God would reward them if they would "turn from their evil ways" and express their lives with right behavior.

Why do they think as they do? Have they no fear that God will punish them, or no sense of loss at the realization that God will not reward them if they would lie, cheat, steal and be sexually promiscuous? Whatever negative consequences they observe in others who do as they do is often submerged in favor of the "gamble" that "it won't happen to me."

The consequences of wrong behavior should be viewed as punishment enough. If behavior is sufficiently dangerous to society, however, society must protect itself against offenders. That is another reason we have a system of justice which includes jail or prison. Children must be taught that honesty, respect for the person and property of others, treating others as a healthy person wishes to be treated himself, etc. are among the highest values of life. If small children do not learn this, we need not expect them to behave on this level of conscience when they are youth. If they do not behave this way when they are youth, we need not expect that they will suddenly become good citizens when they reach adulthood — even if they become President of the United States. The greatest teachers of children are the adults whom children observe most closely. In most cases parents are effective teachers, for good, bad, or a strange combination of the two.

Where to From Here?

Goodness tends to be self-perpetuating from one generation to another. Evil behavior tends to be self-perpetuating from one generation to another. As rational and powerful creatures, however, we should know that it is possible for us to make course corrections at whatever point we choose.

Ours is a society which provides plenty of support for this aspect of a common sense religion. Many wonderful and creative experiences are available to the human family today in ways never before true. Good things are not the primary product of bad behavior. Many depraved and frightening experiences are possible within the human family today, on a level of frequency and ruthlessness that are scary to imagine. Bad things are not the product of good behavior.

At the heart of traditional Judeo-Christian faith has been the idea of good living with the end result of reward, and wrong living with the end result of punishment. There is need for nudging this aspect of our belief system step higher. Instead of supposing that God rewards or punishes behavior as a personal godly response, we need to understand that in very impersonal ways, the consequences of behavior are very much a part of how things are. Good things sometimes happen to bad people and bad things sometimes happen to good people! This is how things are! Examples are all about us!

Good things can come to people who behave poorly as a result of the good behavior of others, or just because of nature's ways. Bad things can come to people who behave right, as a result of the bad behavior of others. Social sciences and media teach us how the behavior of a few in an otherwise good society can have negative results for many. The message is just as clear about the rewards of good behavior.

The nature of life indicates the importance of goodness on a growing and massive scale. It also indicates the importance of reducing evil. A pain in the smallest of toes can create misery for the entire body! The goodness of a few can make life better for everyone!

A healthy religious faith will nurture an emphasis on the rewards of goodness in the here and now. A healthy religious faith will nurture an understanding of the consequences of wrong behavior now and for generations to come. Reward and/or punishment is not a matter for future consideration. Both should be viewed as products of our own creation in the here and now. Genuine faith will permit the future, after death in this life, to rest in the hands of God from whom the wonderful gift of this life has come.

What does this mean to us? It means that anything short of total attention to the expression of the wonderful gift of life "in the here and now" that God has given us, is an insult to God. It means that we should concentrate on expressing this life in the best possible manner and leave the future, after death, in the hands of God. It means that the focus of much religion needs to be redirected. For the sake of God's human family, the emphasis needs to move from immortality to perpetual learning about "right and wrong." It means that religion should be about the nurturing of spiritual strength necessary to bring about the natural consequences of right behavior.

The wonderful power for good which rests in human hands, and the frightening power for evil which rests in human hands, demands a course adjustment in the emphasis of religion!

Chapter X

Forgiveness—An Essential Challenge

Human beings are severely challenged, both in knowing the difference between right and wrong at all times in all situations, and in having the inner strength to always do right in relation to that knowledge. This is especially evident in an age when, in some instances, technological advances are far ahead of ethical knowledge of right and wrong in relation to the utilization of certain technology.

In a religious environment such as the Judeo-Christian tradition, this means that human beings often do wrong things either from lack of knowledge or from spiritual weakness. Sometimes we err because we don't know any better, and sometimes we fall short for lack of personal discipline and strength. Unfortunately there are also those times when we do wrong deliberately.

When human beings fall short of right behavior for whatever reason, someone is betrayed, harmed, or disappointed. That "someone" may be themselves, other human beings, or God. It may be all three.

Need for Forgiveness Is Universal

Most of us agree that no one is perfect. We are especially likely to experience total agreement among us on this point when we realize that "perfection" is a perception which is relative to a variety of definitions. Christians, for example, tend to believe that Jesus was perfect. By whose definition of perfection? Obviously there were many Jews and Romans who did not believe he was perfect, or they wouldn't have killed him as a criminal. Furthermore it is evident that no Christian since his contemporary disciples has had any first hand knowledge of how he really expressed his life in all situations. Even those of his contemporaries who knew him best did not know all about every activity and thought which was part of his life. This is not an attempt to discredit Jesus. It is only to say that perfection is a standard of conduct relative to those who define it at any given time.

The point is clear when observing the manner in which life is expressed by any human being that everyone falls short of human potential in some way in some situations, even when compared to the standard of perfection established by a specific group. It is not far fetched, for example, to question the rightness of Jesus' behavior when he is reported to have overturned the tables of the money changers in the temple. Did he do this in a fit of anger? Does this kind of behavior harmonize well with the idea that we ought to treat others as we want to be treated? If these questions are answered in a manner designed to protect the perfectness of Jesus, then the conduct of his disciples, past and present, should be judged less severely. If, on the other hand, Jesus is not defended for his behavior in this episode, one must suppose that on this particular occasion he showed himself to be very human indeed.

Because all human beings fall short in the eyes of some other human beings, we are all also challenged with how to respond when we are the one who is betrayed, harmed, or disappointed because of the behavior of another human being. Not only this, but when we "let ourselves down," we are challenged with how to respond to our own sense of inadequacy. Furthermore, we are challenged to determine how God (the Ultimate in the universe and human experience) responds when it is believed that we are behaviorally out of sync with what God is about.

Implications of Forgiveness

The Hebrews responded to this challenge in two ways. First, they made their perception of God's expectations for hu-

man behavior very clear through oral, and later, written law.
The behavior of people was judged in relation to the law. Judgment was consummated with reward or punishment. The ultimate punishment was death. The ultimate reward was
prosperity, many children, and the Promised Land.

Consistent with the inherent, biologically natural response
of life to avoid premature death, a means was sought and found
whereby "sins" that were believed to be worthy of the ultimate
punishment were forgiven. Forgiveness meant that the usual
punishment would not be applied.

Second, a substitute was created to take the place of the
judgment/punishment that was being withheld. This substitute was typically formulated in some sort of ritual practice,
which in the case of the Jews was primarily the offering of
something of great value to the "sinner." This offering might
vary in relation to the seriousness of the negative behavior or in
relation to the values of the sinner. When the law was given, the
Jews were primarily herdsmen. Consequently, when their sin
was gross, they were to offer a sacrifice of the finest of their herd
or flock. The idea was that "sin" always brings death, if not
death for the sinner, then death for something or someone on
behalf of the sinner. God, however, who loves his created children even though they do wrong, is thus shown to be willing to
forgive if a substitute life is given. In other words, God cut his
people "a little slack," but something else paid the ultimate
price for the "slack."

Forgiveness through ritual meant two important things. It
meant that God did not continue to hold the sin against those
who committed it. The usual punishment for "falling short"
was therefore avoided. It meant that the sinner was obligated to
do everything within his/her power from that point in time not
to perpetuate behavior that included the sin. In other words,
forgiveness implied behavior modification!

In time this approach to the matter of resolving the problem
of evil among human beings got out of hand. Jesus viewed it as
being out of hand. Instead of religion being viewed as a life giving source, Jesus saw some things about it that he believed diminished life rather than amplified it. The ritual had gotten out

of hand to the point where, for most Jews, it had become rote, and was therefore meaningless to God. Behavior did not change because of it. The emphasis was on going through the motion of pleasing God by ritual, with no strong effort to change how life was expressed.

There is every indication that Jesus fully understood and supported the need for change in human behavior. On the one hand he did not see that happening under the law. On the other hand he saw efforts to obey the law for the wrong reasons as something that made life a drudgery rather than a joy. It was for this reason that Jesus committed his life to changing the approach of Judaism from one of obedience to "law," with its consequences of judgment, to a life lived within the framework of love and its fruit. This, he believed, would bring about the desired result of human behavior being in harmony with the ways and wishes of God.

Jesus therefore emphasized forgiveness on the part of those who suffered from the imperfections of others. This, he believed, was consistent with the idea of God as "Heavenly Father." This was the kind of response he observed in those he perceived to be good and loving parents. It is likely that this was the kind of response he received from his own parents.

Jesus placed an equal and important emphasis on change in the way life is expressed when "sin" is recognized and forgiveness is sought. This "change" must include forgiving others. Jesus taught that God forgives us to the same degree that we forgive others.

Contemporary Society and Forgiveness

Ours is presently a society where the predominate mood is one of getting even at the least, and punishing as the ideal. This is true in spite of the fact that most of us realize that every last one of us has feet of clay. It can be said that the primary goal of many is not to express life in a manner that progressively demonstrates a desire to do more right and less wrong, but to do whatever seems to be in the best interest of the individual at the time. If what appears to be in the personal interest of the one doing the wrong, then the goal is to not get caught.

The mores of a society at any given time are typically the result of one or two things. They are the product of either an autocratic leader who may be a hero, or they may evolve as a result of human experience and human response to that experience. Moses and the Ten Commandments is a wonderful example of this principle at work. Moses was an inspirational and heavy handed leader who commanded the respect of his people. He brought together the basic beliefs, that he concluded he and his people needed, into a concise and definitive format which we now know as "The Ten Commandments." In fact, many of these commandments were insights which human experience had shown to be desirable and fundamental goals for any society.

In other words, a generally common consent formulates much of what a given society believes to be right and wrong. A generally common consent formulates the attitude of any society toward judgment and/or forgiveness in relation to wrong.

There is a factor in today's society, which has not existed previously to the extent that it exists today and which is having a powerful impact on our understanding of right, wrong, and judgment of wrong. Small groups of people who know each other well have always had opportunity to communicate with one another and thus impact the thinking of each other. There exists that potential today and much more. We share ideas with people we don't know except through the medium by which we communicate. This may be via telephone, computer, interactive television, Internet, and talk shows on either radio or television. Views are thus shaped through a variety of ways by which opinions are shared on a daily basis.

The impact of this new and powerful phenomenon among us is powerful. Not only do we have this tremendous power for a growing understanding of either right or wrong, but in a democracy we have developed the idea that we have the right to know and to be heard. We then elect persons to positions of power and authority whom we believe will carry out our wishes for the whole of our society.

It is this fact of contemporary life that has impacted minds in a manner that, apart from rare instances of exception, has nudged us into becoming a retaliatory, get even, and "punish to the full extent of the law" kind of society. We each hope that our behavior will not bring the wrath of society upon us. In other words, in whatever ways we do wrong, we hope we won't get caught. If we do get caught we hope we have enough money to secure a lawyer bright and slick enough to get us off.

Perhaps even more frightening, however, is the realization that even though we may be an upright citizen, we can be "brought down" through innuendo and falsehood. Once negative information about us is shared, those with whom it is shared often have no way of knowing the degree of its accuracy. In our society today, it is possible for good people to be brought down tragically and quickly.

Most frightening of all is what appears to be a growing tendency for persons to become a law unto themselves. Anti-abortionists, for example, are being represented in a growing way by persons who respond to what they perceive to be a problem, with a similar level of violence as that of which they accuse the abortionist. Gang warfare which is far too common in most of our cities is a demonstration of this phenomenon among youth. Drive-by shootings have become part of the daily news.

Rethinking Forgiveness

These facts and more are sufficient to indicate the importance of our re-thinking the meaning of forgiveness. Forgiveness is a value which should be considered with some level of high priority. Balance here is important. Cheap, easy forgiveness solves no problem. Meaningful forgiveness which involves an appropriate response from the one forgiven is of great value to the one forgiving, the one being forgiven, and to society as a whole.

What does it mean to forgive? The answer to this question has two parts. It has implications for the one who has been "sinned against." It has implications for the one who has "sinned."

To forgive means to attitudinally respond to the one who has done wrong, in a manner that does not require punishment or getting even. When one forgives, there is no longer a need or desire to "get even." In traditional Christianity the "law of forgiveness" takes priority over the Old Testament law of "a tooth for a tooth and an eye for an eye." On the religious God-human level, it means that natural consequences of behavior or attitude continue as a natural extension of the misdeed, but that God does not reserve "the real punishment" for us until some time in the future. The Christian interpretation of forgiveness means that, apart from natural consequences, we believe future treatment of us by God in relation to our misdeeds is as though we had not done them. On the human to human level, the meaning is the same. Forgiveness affects both attitude and behavior of the one forgiving and the one being forgiven. It is not easy to forgive when the harm done to us by the misdeeds of another are painful, enduring, non-fixable, and perhaps intentional. It is not easy to accept forgiveness when remorse for our misdeeds causes us to feel absolutely unworthy.

It should be said emphatically that forgiveness does not mean foolish and unwarranted exposure to danger at the hands of the one being forgiven. A basic purpose of law among us should be to protect us from one another while not denying the freedom necessary for us to share positively and creatively with one another.

Our society is presently being challenged with building bigger, better, and more numerous prisons in which to incarcerate those who are caught doing wrong, and to give greater attention to preventing the wrong. As we seek to protect ourselves from offenders, we should also seek diligently to determine the extent to which we, as a society, contribute to the creation of our own criminals.

This is a major challenge to which we are not yet measuring up well as a human family. It may be that, as a society and as individuals within the society, we are perpetuating the conditions that nurture the evolvement of criminal mentality. To whatever degree this is true then, how do we judge ourselves for creating criminals and after we create them find pleasure in getting even with them by the results of the judgment we hand down?

Values for the "Forgiver" and the "Forgiven"

As difficult as forgiveness may sometimes be for the one who has been "sinned against," failure to forgive for whatever reason only does greater damage to the one who has already been hurt. The absence of forgiveness leaves a vacuum in relationships which is typically filled with anger, resentment, hatred, and a desire to do something that is equal with or superior to the deed of the "sinner." The primitive law of the Old Testament attempted to equalize damage with the "eye for an eye and a tooth for a tooth approach." That means that both the sinner and the one sinned against each does the same thing. One just does it before the other. Jesus called his disciples to live on a level higher than that.

Equal or superior retribution solves no relational problems. One "wrong" is not neutralized by another. "Getting even" only makes a bad situation worse, regardless of how much the person who has hurt another may deserve to be damaged as much or more. This is not the way of love. It is the way of base human weakness which is at the root of the creation of the problem to begin with. It is not humanity at its best! It is difficult to imagine that this is the direction in which God is nudging the human part of creation!

Our society is struggling with this matter of forgiveness and how to deal with the sinner. Progress in this area is so slow as to be difficult to recognize. Indications of progress can be seen, however, in the fact that lynching and public retribution are not as common today as we perceive them to have been on the American frontier.

Just as we have support groups for other kinds of needs when people are "hurt," there is probably a need for support groups that will help persons with this matter of forgiveness. When forgiveness is difficult, there is a tendency to seek a way around it. One way is to revert, for the sake of convenience, back to Old Testament ways. Another is to act like we forgive when in fact we don't. A well known personality was asked if he had forgiven a former friend who had murdered his wife. The response was, "I am commanded to forgive." This is an interesting avoidance of the issue in both word and deed. It is also an interesting regression to outdated and primitive religious law over the law of love by a professed disciple of Jesus!

But forgiveness means something just as difficult for the one in need of forgiveness. It demands fixing that which has been done where possible. It demands no future participation in the same kind of behavior. Our society is working hard in many ways to assist with this challenge.

There is professional treatment available now for a variety of behavioral problems that was not known twenty-five years ago. In addition there are a host of "support groups" designed to respond to a variety of negative challenges which come into the experience of human beings. Such groups include, but are not limited to, alcoholism, drugs, gambling, and spouse abuse.

The point is an important one. Some kinds of wrong behavior can only be corrected by the individual who has engaged in wrong behavior. Some kinds of wrong behavior appear to become so much a part of what makes that person who they are, that change is only likely to occur with some kind of assistance. This assistance may come from professionals or it may come through the support and encouragement of persons who care without pay.

No positive contribution comes to human society or to individuals who refuse to forgive. The experience of forgiving is a universal need of God's human children. In the prayer which Jesus is reported to have taught his disciples, which we commonly identify as "The Lord's Prayer," the receiving of God's forgiveness is indicated to be contingent upon our ability to forgive one another.

Human beings who will strive to become as fully human as God must intend them to be, will on occasion, stand in need of being forgiven. There is no good thing which comes to an individual who has wronged another, and who is not inclined to either seek or accept forgiveness from the one who has been wronged. Having no conscience about having done wrong does not represent the highest level of being human. Neither pride nor self-abuse is sufficient reason not to seek and accept the forgiveness of others. Being fully human requires that when we have done wrong, we are remorseful for that wrong, that we have a strong desire to never do that again, and that we are willing to relate to the one wronged and who offers forgiveness, in a manner akin to what the relationship might have been had no wrong been done. Wrong behavior must be neutralized by ceasing to do wrong and by placing good behavior in its place.

Giving forgiveness is often a major challenge. Seeking and accepting forgiveness is often just as great a challenge. Changing behavior is a human potential which is just as challenging and often requires assistance from others.

God's forgiveness is a matter of faith but is very important. We will not receive a fax or hear a physical voice from God telling us that we are forgiven. In the Judeo-Christian tradition, we are taught to believe that God wants each of us to behave better in the future than is true now. We are taught that God's forgiveness is always available when it is sought with the intention of improving our behavior. God's forgiveness is fully known when we accept it by faith and forgive ourselves. Self forgiveness, i.e., the experience of no longer obsessing over our wrong doing and changing our ways, is critical evidence of our having accepted God's forgiveness.

Jesus is reported to have told Peter that if someone sinned against him seventy times seven times, he should forgive him each time. Jesus apparently believed that there is no sin which, for the spiritual and psychological health of the one sinned against, should not be forgiven. The point is not that we should foolishly overlook the transgressions of others, or ourselves. The greater emphasis here is on the negative consequences of holding grudges and/or hating. The other side of the coin has to do with providing an opportunity for the "sinner" to change his/her ways and in no way suggests that persons or societies should be placed in harm's way in order to provide an opportunity for repetitive evil behavior. Is it possible that the greater emphasis on responding to transgressors should be on correcting behavior and protecting society than on punishing in order to satisfy the human felt need for retribution?

An important element in an understanding of a God who loves unconditionally is that the only sin which God cannot and does not forgive is that of not claiming his forgiveness, forgiving oneself, and changing behavior from wrong to right. The important factor of a second chance is written into the expression of nature. When we cut our finger, the blood clots, the wound heals, and though a scar remains, we go on experiencing a full and wonderful life. We pollute our rivers and, given time and a change in our ways, the rivers heal themselves and we and they are given another chance. We pollute our air and, given time and a change in our ways, the air heals itself and we and they are given another chance. Forgiveness is a part of God's creative expression. It is written into the nature of things.

Forget the old saying about forgiving and forgetting. Forgiving does not mean to forget. The guilty person should never forget the wrong they have done or they might do it again. They should just respond to themselves and to others as though they have forgotten. The person who has been wronged can never forget that wrong. They should just work at behaving as though the wrong had never been done, but memory will serve them well as a protector against the same thing happening again.

Failure to forgive or to seek forgiveness results in persons being less than they might otherwise be. Bitterness, resentment and hate all take their toll on what a human being might otherwise be. Failure to seek forgiveness and change one's behavior turns what otherwise might be a beautiful human being into something less than human potential.

Wrong doing always has consequences. Scars are a reality of life. Forgiveness, both in giving and receiving, is a need that is always with us. It is at the heart of the faith we profess. It is an essential element in restoring self esteem, both for the one being forgiven and the one doing the forgiving. Forgiveness must be at the heart of the broad scope of religion if we are to make the future everything that it is capable of becoming.

Chapter XI

Human Life—A Spiritual Journey

Being Human

Past philosophies of what a human being is have tended to include a dualism which separates us into body and spirit. Considerable emphasis in the New Testament, for example, is placed on the temporal and evil tendencies of the flesh as compared to the eternal nature of the spirit. Under the general umbrella of this philosophy, the spirit has also been considered to be of a dualistic nature, i.e., an evil spirit and/or a good spirit. The essence of the mind is not clearly defined but seems to be a "floater" which can be associated with either the body, i.e., the brain, or the spirit.

A predominant contemporary view of what a human being is typically includes the idea of "body, mind and spirit." Most recent ideas, especially in the area of medicine and health, are inclined to emphasize the importance of not segregating the human being into parts. It is considered more important to view the relationship of each part to the other, thus treating the person as a "whole" being.

This more recent description of what it is that makes the human species different from other parts of the animal world, except for the spirit, emphasizes "degree" of evolutionary development more than "kind." Physical bodies in the animal world are viewed generally as basically similar, but different specifically, tending to adapt to their environment through a process of evolution. We do not consider the spirit of an animal in the same sense that we consider the spirit of a human being. We do not think of animals as having "souls."

We have discovered, however, that many animals are so similar in basics to human beings that it is possible for us to learn much about the human body through experimentation with animals. We have also learned that there are specific differences in animals and human beings. Even among human beings, limitations are inherent in regard to what can be learned from one "body" that can be applied to the knowledge acquired about another. This reality is evident in the near physical acceptance, but ultimate rejection of animal parts as transplants in the human body. It is also evident in the difficulties of rejection encountered when transplanting human parts from one human body to another.

A point at which there tends to be common agreement is in the idea that human beings have a spirit and animals do not. Even this supposition deserves to be questioned. Those who relate closely to animals discover that they do have very specific personalities different from that of other animals in the same species and that there is much to suggest that they also have an equivalent to what we call "spirit."

It could be argued that we prefer to think of animals strictly in terms of a dualism of body and limited mind without spirit, in order to maintain an idea of our own specialness. One day we may discover that the idea of human specialness is a good one, but that it is possible for different species to be equally special in different ways. It appears that we may be on the verge of reaching this conclusion through a growing understanding of the inter-relatedness and importance of species to the eco-system.

Could it be that human beings attain whatever degree of specialness they have through the way they respond to resources and opportunities? This response invariably has to do with "spirit." It has to do with morality. It has to do with reverence. It has to do with respect. It has to do with love. All of these, and more, are included under the umbrella of "spirit."

It does appear that we human beings are composed of "parts" of a "whole" and that each part is significant to the health of the "whole" but in a different way. This understanding can at least serve as a tool which enables us to understand ourselves better.

The Human/God Relationship

The idea of "parts" and "whole" in human beings is extremely important. The human spirit is of no less importance and significance to the "whole" human being than is the body or the mind. The fact of development and health of the "whole" is very much dependent on the "spirit." Jesus embraced the idea that God is "spirit." With that understanding his life was devoted to ministering to the human spirit which he viewed in relation to God as parent and child. He is reported to have spoken of God as "Heavenly Father."

A fundamental truth that we need to keep in mind is that we, as human beings, are in the process of creating other human beings, not just in body but in "whole." This truth is becoming increasingly evident in ways that go beyond the beginnings of human life. There is a tremendous need for us to grow beyond the idea of a God out there who is in control of everything that happens in the world. The idea of a God who predetermines things and events ought to be absolutely repulsive to us. There are a growing number of recent and clear indications that God has empowered us in ways that only a few years ago could not be imagined.

Human beings are just as much involved in the creation of other human beings as is God. This is true from the perspective of biology and genetics. It is true from the perspective of environment as it impacts social, intellectual, and spiritual development. Human beings could not create other human beings without God, and as things now are, God could not create human beings without the cooperation of human beings. One might argue that God could do things in a manner that is not now true, but the facts are that human beings are not created except through involvement of other human beings. It is just as true that human beings could not create babies without the "spark" of life which must be attributed to God.

The Responsibility Factor

Human beings know nothing and do nothing apart from the resources made available to them by their Creator. That knowledge should keep us very humble and reverent. Human beings are capable of accomplishing wonderful and good things because of these resources. When one considers the probability of resources provided by God, about which we now know nothing, such thoughts can be overwhelming in magnitude. This knowledge should cause us to understand the great need for, and value of, responsibility. Responsibility has to do with behavior which is impacted by the spirit!

We understand our role in the creation of the human body. We understand our role in the creation of mental potential through the creation of a body which is healthily nurtured, and an environment which provides opportunity. We realize that there cannot be a mind without a body, and we also now know that the beginnings of the body need to be healthy in order to assure the potential for developing a healthy mind.

These things are true before conception and birth. Because we have learned this, we are concerned that mothers do not smoke or drink during pregnancy. We do not yet know the extent of the impact which human behavior or health has on the sperm and egg that may eventually unite in the conception of a new human being.

The donation of healthy sperm and egg, and incubation in a healthy and wholesome environment is not the end of our responsibility. We have now produced a healthy human body. If this new human body is to grow into a healthy and whole adult, it must be nurtured. Furthermore we know that this new body is dependent upon the nurture which can only be provided by resources provided by other human beings and made available by God.

But what about the mind? A healthy body does not guarantee a healthy mind. In the same way that a body must be fed and exercised, the mind must also be nurtured and exercised, but with a different kind of food. Curiosity must be encouraged and challenged. Opportunities to learn about what has already been learned by others, and encouragement to be creative in building on that which has already been learned must be provided by others.

The importance of mental health and education is of primary concern in the world as we know it today. A recognition of the importance of these two factors is common to all civilized societies.

What we have also learned, to our chagrin is that a body and mind can be examples of health in terms of ability, but be capable of creating evil as well as good. We are often amazed at the intelligence and ability of the criminal mind. There is reason to suppose that environment is more responsible for this negative factor than biology or genetics.

We are part of a contemporary human society which is plagued by evil created by the human mind and brought to reality by human bodies. The robbing of banks is a daily occurrence in most urban centers. The world is challenged and confused by a powerful maniac known to us as Saddam Hussein. He is not the first nor will he be the last. Some propose his liquidation while others contend that there are those in the "pipeline" equally bad, or worse than him. Our children are killing other children. There are high school massacres. We hear of fourteen year old boys killing eight year old girls and hiding their bodies under their water beds. Our senses are paralyzed and confused as to how such monsters can "happen" at such an early age. We see video tapes of children assaulting and molesting other children on school buses. The home, which we idealize as a sanctuary of safety and love, has become in too many instances, a place where people are abused, battered, and perhaps killed. Cheap, degrading and excessive sex "sells" in our society and the minds of young and old are bombarded with it. Violence "sells" in our society and the minds of young and old are bombarded with it. As a direct result of the bombarding, too many of all ages become either victims or perpetuators of violence and degenerate sex.

Do these obvious threats to the potential goodness of human beings have anything to do with healthy bodies? Is evil nurtured by the healthy and the unhealthy? Do these obvious threats to the potential goodness of human beings have anything do with healthy minds? Evil is nurtured by the dumb and the brilliant, and the greater the brilliance, the more awful the potential of the crime.

Much wonderful emphasis today is placed on nurturing healthy bodies, and that is good. Much wonderful emphasis is placed on nurturing healthy and bright minds, and that is good. With all this knowledge and with all the wonderful opportunities for nurturing healthy, whole and good human beings, why do we have so much crime and unhappiness?

The Spirit Is Special

It has to do with the human spirit. The human spirit can energize any kind of body or mind to be either wonderfully good or terribly evil. A reasonable responsibility and opportunity to which sufficient attention has not been given is that of energizing the human spirit in a powerful and wonderful way for goodness. Let's not overlook the fact that much of this has been done. Our society and world is characterized by more goodness than bad. It is just that a little "bad" creates much pain and kills much potential for good even though good may be in the majority.

Let's start at the beginning again. Is there anything more pure and wonderful than a new baby? A healthy infant is like a blank page of potential. It can become wonderfully good. It can become terribly bad. It can become a strange and confusing mixture of both. What makes the difference? Environment! Those who create the infant, along with others who become part of the infant's life, provide the environment.

But environment is not all. Many examples indicate that two children can grow up in the same environment. They may be equally healthy and equally bright. One can become a powerful source of good. The other can become a powerful source of evil. This even occurs among persons of the same ancestry. What makes the difference? It is a matter of spirit.

It is spirit that makes the difference in both intensity and kind of life expression. Without a good spirit, an otherwise healthy body can be abused and neglected to the point of emaciation. Without a good spirit, a very capable mind can be filled with evil and degrading thoughts which prompt the kind of evil behavior which is a growing matter of concern in contemporary society. Spirit defies definition but it does not defy description. It has to do with attitude, desire, commitment, conscience, thought, intention, and a whole host of other human values. It affects relationships, appreciation for life and human behavior. The "seed" of spirit, as life itself, must be a gift from God. It is capable of being nurtured into something wonderful or evil, and many levels in between, including a strange mixture of both. The human goal throughout life should be that of nurturing the spirit into something increasingly wonderful.

We do not know the origins of the spirit other than to say its beginning potential is a gift of God. We know about conception as it relates to a body which produces a mind. The origin of the spirit, apart from understanding it as a gift from God, remains a mystery. This is not an unimportant mystery. What eventually happens through the body and mind is a matter of spirit. The spirit is fundamentally important in determining whether a human being adds to or diminishes goodness in the world, and to what degree.

Reverence, Respect, and Responsibility

The spirit is activated toward good in two ways. Both are evident in an emphasis on "reverence," "respect," and "responsibility." The first is most desirable and ideally should always occur. It is the nurturing of the spirit with attention equal to that given the body and mind by committed and good parents, from the time of conception.

The second is the next best thing and can "kick in" at any point in the continuum of life. It involves an intentional commitment to reverence, respect, and responsibility at a time later in life than childhood. It is a personal emphasis on the nurturing of the spirit at the initiative of the individual rather than the parents. The second is important because it provides direction for the balance of a specific life from whatever point in time it begins.

It has been demonstrated that a human being born in the absence of love can become less than a human being. This is true in degrees as indicated in those few, but too many cases, where a small child is completely isolated from contact with other loving human beings. Its body is fed. Its mind is left blank. Its spirit is not nurtured.

On those occasions when this happens, the entire "whole" of that person is affected. Neither body nor mind is likely to be healthy. There is no development of spirit which will make that person a pleasure to themselves or others. Such persons are less capable of making a positive contribution to the world.

Assuming that this situation exists in a matter of degree, depending on the level of neglect to the spirit, the importance of nurturing the spirit with love and positive reinforcement becomes clear. It is reasonable to assume that to whatever extent the nurture of the spirit is neglected, that human being is handicapped in relation to their potential for goodness.

Nurturing the spirit in love from infancy requires an emphasis on a number of factors. Jesus placed reverence for the Source of life at the top of his list of priorities. This automatically assumed an appreciation for life. He placed love and respect for others in a position of "close second." He assumed the conveyance of a hopeful and expectant attitude about the future from those who share their love with both God and other human beings. He assumed responsibility to be the natural result of reverence and respect shown in love.

Too many babies are made because of the love needs of parents, rather than because parents want to accept the responsibility and wonderful opportunity of sharing their love in the continuing propagation of human beings, i.e., God's human family. When children are created primarily in response to the love needs of their parents, it is less likely that the love, i.e., spirit, needs of the children will be fully met.

In a world as interdependent as ours, the creation of an environment which is dependent first, on the focused attention of the parent to the spiritual needs of the child, and second on the intentional and committed behavior and attitudes of others who impact the development of the child, is critical.

Institutional Challenges

In our present system the creation of this environment is most likely accomplished through a cooperative effort of family, church and school. The primary responsibility of the family is to provide a safe place for the nurturing of the child, physically, intellectually, and spiritually. The primary responsibility of the church is to assist the family in nurturing spiritual development. The primary responsibility of the school is, in cooperation with the church and family, to nurture the mind of the child. This is not a matter of any institution ignoring the responsibility of the others. It is best viewed and expressed as a team effort.

The church is always challenged to nurture reverence, respect, love, and hope. All religions have their roots in the level of knowledge, i.e., world view, available to them at the time of their "birth." Religion typically has difficulty adjusting to changing knowledge as it evolves. Consequently, with the passage of time, religion tends to lose its power in nurturing the reverence, respect, love, and hope which is required for a healthy spirit. Religion is weakened in relation to its healthy potential, to the degree that it is not synchronized with current knowledge and human response to the natural environment.

Activating the Spirit

The most desirable and healthy activation of the spirit results in a life-long journey of spiritual growth which is, at all times, in harmony with the knowledge and life experience of a specific place and time. The virtues of "the old time religion" should only be honored to the degree that it deals with truths that can be validated as eternal. There are some eternal truths. There are some "truths" that should not be considered to be eternal.

This "choice" approach to the activating and nurturing of the spirit is thus a process which begins with the parents in their earliest nurturing of a child, is continued by the child as it matures in responsibility, and continues throughout the span of a given life. This approach does not assume unusual and highly emotional religious experiences. Instead, it assumes life to be an absolutely wonderful and satisfying, continual religious experience.

Unfortunately, all children are not provided the opportunity for this desirable spiritual activation and nurture. This does not mean that those who are not so fortunate are "bad" people. They may become "bad" and too many do, but lack of adequate spiritual nurture does not automatically lead one into a life of sin and crime.

The story of Nicodemus is a wonderful example of the second way in which the spirit is activated. Nicodemus was a "good" guy, but his own lack of satisfaction in life indicated an absence of a spiritual spark that he needed and wanted. He sensed that Jesus had found the spark that he lacked but wanted. He went to Jesus asking how he could get it.

Jesus explained that the spiritual life is just as important as the physical life. Jesus placed the physical and spiritual on a common level of importance. Inasmuch as the religious environment in which Nicodemus was nurtured as a child and adult had not satisfied his spiritual needs, it was now important for him to start over spiritually, i.e., have a beginning in a spiritual sense in the same way that many years before he had a beginning in the physical sense.

The experience of Nicodemus is testimony to the fact that it is just as possible for religion to get in the way of spiritual development as it is for it to be a nurturer of spiritual development. Here were two men of very similar religious backgrounds. They were both Jews who had been reared in good Jewish families. They spoke a common language. They understood one another.

The major difference in Jesus and Nicodemus was that one had followed the "party line" without question. He had kept the commandments related to ritual and personal interaction. But he had no sense of closeness to his Source, i.e., God. The other had kept the commandment of personal interaction but had found much of the ritual to be empty of meaning. Building from what his religion had given him by way of ritual and belief, Jesus looked for and found a way of spiritual growth and satisfaction. He felt himself to be in partnership with God. Nicodemus had accomplished many admirable things in life, but he had not found a spiritual experience which gave him a sense of partnership with God.

Jesus was candid and clear in his remarks to Nicodemus. You can't capture what you haven't experienced in the past. You can, however, begin a meaningful spiritual journey now. It is like being born again—but in spirit. Nicodemus asked how this could be. Jesus explained that it was like other mysteries in life—the wind for example. You can't see where it comes from or where it is going, but you know when it exists.

The meaning of this story from the teachings of Jesus is that persons who have been deprived of spiritual nurture in the past need not be so deprived in the future. What one is now doing that they know to be wrong should be stopped. What one is now doing that they know to be right should be continued but with a new reason and purpose. The new reason and purpose is that good is done in partnership with God and as a means of contributing to the purposes of God.

This second way of activating the spirit is a matter of desire and faith. If the desire is present and there is a willingness to adjust one's expression of life to one believed to be consistent with the goals of God, then one is justified in believing that a new start has been made and spiritual growth can be expected from that point of decision and commitment. Paul explained it to the church at Corinth by saying "the past is forgotten, and everything is new."

Unfortunately, this second way of activating the spirit has also been tarnished by sincere but overzealous religious leaders short on understanding. The traditional evangelistic approach has assumed that there is no spiritual beginning or growth without a momentous change at some point in life after childhood. The evangelistic goal has therefore tended to be that of producing guilt and then offering an emotional experience of forgiveness and renewed commitment in exchange for the guilt.

Persons guilty of bad things can truly be converted in their way of viewing and expressing life. It is possible that persons who are normal in spiritual experience can be persuaded that they are inadequate and perhaps even bad, and thus be persuaded to seek this new birth experience. The only likely major damage in yielding to this kind of pressure—and it is pressure—is the development of an assumption that it is the only way, when in fact it is a way of spiritual beginning that is less desirable than the "natural" way.

Persons who experience the misfortune of becoming addicted, may find their "new birth" experience through "twelve step programs." This too should be viewed as a wonderful opportunity to move from a life of emptiness to a life of increasing fullness. It should not be viewed, however, as the only way, or as the best way.

Those who are spiritually enlivened from childhood should be glad and give thanks that part of their lives have not been wasted without spiritual nurture. They should have no sense of loss or guilt for not having experienced a "new birth." Those who have been neglected, or who have neglected the nurture of their spirit until later in life, should be glad that even though the past cannot be changed, the future can be much more satisfying as it is lived with a sense of partnership with God.

One way or another, full meaning in the experience and expression of human life requires an activating of the spirit. We have been taught that God is spirit. We have also been taught that, in some manner, we are created in the image of God. We are as much spirit as we are body and mind. Health for the "whole" demands healthy nurture of each part of the whole: body, mind, and spirit. A "Common Sense Approach To Religion" demands that among the major functions of religion is that of cultivating the kind of *God Talk* that makes sense and results in the nurturing of a positive and loving spirit in human beings.

Chapter XII

Functional Results of Spiritual Growth

The human spirit needs to be activated and nurtured from infancy, just as the mind and body must be nurtured. It can also be said that if the nurturing of the spirit is neglected in early life, in relation to the best time to begin such nurture, "the sooner the better" applies.

If Not Then, Now!

If the nurturing of the spirit does not occur on the same healthy level as is ideal for the mind and body in childhood, all is not lost. This has been, and ought to remain, a fundamental message of Christianity. The past cannot be changed, but the future can be affected by what is done in the present. Change is possible at any point in the continuum of life. At whatever point intentional nurture of the spirit begins, that life will be more harmonious with God's purpose for human life, and will be more meaningful for the individual experiencing and expressing it. A sudden interest in spiritual matters and nurture anytime after childhood is often described as a "new birth" and is thus the origin of "born again Christians."

Why such an emphasis on that which is spiritual? Why be concerned about "fruits of the spirit?" Increasingly the word is coming from those who consider themselves to be theologically conservative, i.e., fundamentalists, that they are "commanded" to bear the fruit of the spirit. Isn't this idea of living in response to "commands" precisely what Jesus endeavored to replace? The replacement emphasized by Jesus was an approach that satisfied God through the way life was expressed as a result of wanting to do so, not out of fear for breaking a commandment. If one must use legalistic language, it could be said that Jesus emphasized the "law of love," i.e., love, not law becomes the compelling factor.

Food, Clothing, and Education Are Not Enough

But to what end is this emphasis on nurturing the spirit? This, of course, is a question that is often asked about life itself. What is the ultimate purpose of life? Regardless of how either question is answered, most of us typically settle on three things which we believe to be of highest value in the experience of life. (1) We want our lives to be a long and happy experience. (2) We want our lives to be meaningful in the sense that we are making a lasting contribution to the world. We have a need, by our nature, to be "participants." (3) The recognition and approval of others for doing good things is important to us.

The first premise can be argued on the basis of all the energy which is exerted in an effort to create a vast variety of experiences that are designed to extend life and to help us in our quest for happiness. The second can be argued on the basis of the legacy that persons seek to leave for themselves and which they hope will be recognized by others as a meaningful contribution to the ongoing process of life. Memorials testify to this human need. Not only do we want the approval of others during our life, but we want them to remember us for a long time after we die. The third can be argued on the basis of the importance of recognition and status in social relationships. Every society has its own special kind of "pecking order."

A basic question for a society of human beings, which is primarily motivated by an attitude of "what's in it for me?" is exactly that. What's in it for the individual and for the entire family of human beings? Can one be happier when the spirit is activated, whether it be from infancy or a "new birth?" Can one find greater meaning in the experience of living when the spirit is in the process of being nurtured than when it is not? As persons who care about what is left by one generation for future generations, what is in this matter of spiritual nurture for future generations? In a pragmatic society, these are basic questions which deserve a thoughtful and intentional answer.

Although this technique is now ancient in the art of motor mechanics, one of the lessons I learned early from an uncle who was a mechanic by profession was that an automobile engine has an rpm speed at which it runs smoothest, i.e., is most at peace with itself. The speed is dependent upon a number of factors including the design of the engine and the speed at which it was "broken in." My Dad bought a '36 V8 Ford when I was eight years old. With the speedometer covered, my uncle could tell from sound and smoothness when the speed was 60 miles per hour. Given the nature of this car and the way it was broken in, the harmony of all its components was greatest at that speed. I was impressed!

Human beings are like that in many ways. We are designed with certain factors which nudge us toward a harmonic expression of life. The environment in which we live adds another factor of major proportion. How others around us live their lives is also of great importance to the individual. When we are living our life in the best possible way, and when those about us are doing the same, these two factors are likely to be at the point of their greatest harmony. Life then has the best opportunity to be at peace with itself, both on the individual and societal level. In other words, it is most likely to be "running smoothly."

We sometimes overlook the impact which serenity, or lack of it, in human society, has at the individual personal level. There is need, therefore, to consider the matter of what happens to the broader scope of human society as a result of the expression of our personal life. Although there are exceptions, in general, the serenity of an individual is somewhat dependent on the serenity of the social environment in which that person expresses and experiences life. Conversely, the serenity of the society is dependent upon the serenity of the individuals within it.

If, for example, banks were not being robbed, women were not being battered, children were not be abused and killed, drugs were not being sold or used, the needs of people were being met through their own productiveness and the caring and supportive interaction of society, there was never a threat of war, the tools of war did not require such a large portion of the national income, etc. etc., the general condition of human society would be one of peace and contentment. Taxes would diminish. Greater economic resources would be available to improve schools, child care, health care, and the general infrastructure which is so important to our society. Much more time and energy could be directed toward research and development of good things that would prevent much human misery from accident and disease.

If everyone was productively involved in making life better for themselves and everyone else, gambling would not be a business, the use of alcohol would diminish and drugs would be used only for medicinal purposes. Much time and energy now devoted to the neutralizing of negative factors could be committed to the promotion of positive factors. One is challenged to imagine what a wonderful world ours would be if this were the case!

If all parents were fully responsible for the development of their children on the physical, intellectual and spiritual levels, those in the teaching profession could devote more of their time and skills to the art of teaching. There would be no concern about safety in our schools, the court system would not be overloaded, and instead of increasing taxes to build more and bigger prisons, ways would be explored for utilizing or replacing the vast institutions of confinement which now exist.

A Worthy Goal

What I have described is a kind of heaven on earth. Jesus spoke of the Kingdom of God. In the "Lord's prayer" we pray "thy kingdom come." While I acknowledge that the challenge of such a state for the human family is one of major proportions, it is a worthy dream and goal. Attaining this goal to perfection is not likely. Attaining this goal to some degree and in an increasing manner is possible if people in general would see the vision and commit themselves to bringing it to reality. If it can happen to individuals, it can happen to a small group of individuals. If it can happen in a small group of individuals, it can happen in human society as a whole. If, through a process of individual and social evolvement, perfection is continually redefined, there is no end to the progress which the human family can attain.

It will never happen, however, as long as three general ideas prevail. First, it will never happen if persons do not take responsibility for their own behavior and accept the fact that their behavior either adds to the quality of life for themselves and society, or takes from it. Second, it will never happen if we don't believe it is possible and because of that belief, strive for it. Third, it will never happen if we continue to assume that the great system of reward and punishment for human beings actually exists "out there somewhere after death" and that this life is just a rehearsal for the "real thing."

Functional results of these three ideas as they now prevail are generally negative. They tend to work against the personal and social happiness. They prevent our experiencing the sense of fulfillment that we all want. Experiencing the "abundant life" of which Jesus reportedly spoke tends to be pushed continually beyond our reach.

Personal Discipline

Failure to take responsibility for one's own behavior excuses people who permit themselves to become satisfied with falling short of their potential. This is true even for those whose lives are controlled by anything other than themselves. When persons are obsessed or controlled by food, alcohol, drugs, sex, or anything else, including self centered religion, they should not be encouraged in an attitude which excuses themselves. Of course it makes one feel better to assume that they are an alcoholic because it is a disease and they just can't help themselves. No person needs to become addicted to alcohol or drugs. No person needs to become addicted to anything that becomes harmful through either excess or unnecessary use. More than one person has become addicted to alcohol or other drugs because they have yielded to peer pressure. Yielding to peer pressure is neither a disease nor is it in the genes. It has to do with the lack of personal discipline.

Much in our society places pressure on persons to yield to the wishes or behavior of others. The social environment in many high schools is conducive to such yielding to peer pressure, and it continues only because parents permit it and sometimes encourage it. It continues to prevail on college campuses because of the permissive attitudes of those who should know better. In other words, it is easier to "let them do as they please" than it is to take measures necessary to protect them from themselves.

Among the powerful evidences of spiritual health is the ability to control the expression of one's own life. Personal discipline, i.e., self control and freedom from addiction, are important values to both individuals and human society.

We are individually responsible for our own behavior. We are societally responsible for each other's behavior through what we encourage or condone in those too weak to discipline their own behavior. The complexity of life is revealed partially through the fact that we are both personally responsible for the way we live it, and that we share responsibility for the welfare of one another as well.

Increasingly, human society is permitting itself to sink deeper in the quagmire of excessive behavior that results from lack of self discipline on both individual and societal levels. Gambling is encouraged by legalization. Excesses in the use of alcohol, with all its negative spin-offs, are encouraged by a society viewing it as acceptable behavior for adults. Adults are watched closely by those not yet adults but who "can't wait." Delegated drivers is a major step forward in preventing deaths from drunken driving, but wouldn't it really be better if no one consumed sufficient alcohol to make their driving unsafe? We encourage sexual promiscuity by generally accepting it as another means of entertainment "so long as no one gets hurt."

Although the challenge is formidable, human beings can change any kind of behavior that brings pain and grief to the human experience. Change is possible and necessary on both the individual and social levels, but we must believe it to be possible if we are to accept the challenge and actually bring it to pass. A healthy "explosion" of spiritual growth would bring about such change.

A Renewed Emphasis in Religion

Religion must change its story. Persons are diminished when they are not nurtured spiritually beginning early in life. Spiritual nurture should begin with expressions of love and continue in additional ways as the child develops. Too much religion is a "cover-up." This is basic to a sacramental approach to religion. Sacrifices "cover-up." A belief that Jesus was given by God as a sacrifice for our sins is a "cover-up." God's love must be viewed as unconditional, but tough. "Tough" means growth in the way life is expressed. A healthy spirit assures an expression of life that is growing in goodness. Either a sacramental "cover-up" or threat or promise concerning the future should not be the goal of religion.

In reality, we don't know anything about what happens to the non-physical aspects of a human being after physical death. We do have freedom to believe anything about that which we choose. The promise of heaven as reward and the threat of hell as punishment should therefore not be a source of motivation for good behavior in this life. Human beings create hell for themselves and others here on earth. We are our own judges, and we bring upon ourselves and others punishment through consequences of bad behavior. We lay the foundation for wonderful rewards through the consequences of good behavior. It is not good when we rely on motivations brought about by threats or promises concerning life after death. It is a matter of wisdom to trust God in this regard, and let the future after physical death take care of itself. The potential of both good and bad in this life should be sufficient motivation to cause us to commit ourselves to doing something about the moral condition in which the human family finds itself.

All the good that I have suggested as possible is dependent on personal and social discipline. Whether or not all the bad in the world is obliterated is dependent upon personal discipline. Whether or not the great good of which we human beings are capable comes to pass is dependent upon personal discipline.

Christians tend to look to Jesus as the example for their faith. Unfortunately, too many Christians have been taught to believe that Jesus took their punishment for their wrong doing for them, and they can therefore do whatever feels good to them at the time and the "blood" covers their sin and promises them reward in eternity just for believing. What pure nonsense and what a blight of religious belief on human society! Think about the implications of such a belief! If it were not that such action would deprive everyone of religious freedom it should be outlawed! Such a belief diminishes rather than amplifies an understanding of the need for personal responsibility and discipline.

There is a wonderful story in the New Testament about the struggle in which Jesus engaged relative to taking control of his own life and living it as he believed he should live it rather than the way he was pressured to live it by the environment of his society. It is traditionally known as the temptation story. Jesus withdrew himself from others and went out into the wilderness, alone. That means he was struggling with the challenge of being what he wanted himself to be, as contrasted with becoming what others were encouraging him to be. Would he have made a wonderful priest? Would he have made a wonderful teacher in the temple? Would he have made a wonderful father? He could have been so many different and wonderful things had he been willing to conform more to the wishes of others.

What do you think Jesus would have thought of the polls and the power of the media which is ever present among us today? Do you suppose he would have thought the idea of determining right and wrong by public opinion was a good idea? Do you suppose he would have approved the idea of judging one another through the media even though information given to the populace was partial, erroneous, or conflicting?

Jesus was so threatened and challenged with the need for the approval of others that he went out into the wilderness by himself, alone with thoughts and his conscience, to determine whether or not he was willing to pay the price of freedom to say and do what he believed to be right.

One would expect, given the religious environment of the event, that the story would be spiritualized, and it was. The story teller saw to it that the story was told in a manner consistent with the general world view of people in that time. He was led out into the wilderness by the good (Holy) spirit. He was tempted by the bad (Devil) spirit. Jesus won! He concluded that he had one life to live. He believed that both he and the world could gain the most from his life if he lived it in harmony with the Source of his being, God. He was ingrained with the principles that determine right and wrong, and because he felt it necessary to transcend the law that was designed to enforce the principles, he was determined to express his life the way he knew it should be expressed. He left the wilderness after forty days as a victorious and committed person. He had determined to maintain control of his own life. He was in charge. This story is an ultimate expression of self discipline.

Later, in an effort to interpret what it meant to be a disciple of Jesus, Paul wrote about the "fruits of the spirit" to one of the early churches, i.e., the church in Galatia. One of the fruits of the spirit which Paul addressed was the matter of self-control.

Paul also spoke of other values as fruits of the spirit. God's spirit, Paul said, makes us loving, happy, peaceful, patient, kind, good, faithful, gentle, and self-controlled.

Just imagine what a wonderful world ours would be if the expression of these fruits in life was the goal of every person! If the human family was comprised of persons who are loving, happy, peaceful, patient, kind, good, faithful and gentle, we would think we were in heaven, wouldn't we? To whatever degree this goal is attained, it is worthy of our efforts.

This is not to suggest that the values of a good interesting job, a nice home, an attractive and congenial mate, a new car, early retirement, and perhaps — even a horse, airplane, or boat, are bad. It is to say that these goals should be secondary with the hope that these added blessings will come about as well.

Priorities are important. The fruit of spiritual growth should bring about a bit more heaven on earth for others as well as ourselves.

Chapter XIII

A Reasonable Basis for Hope

As is true in so many areas of life, the Christian faith is not without its contradictions. On the one hand it has historically been a doomsday religion. Its message has included the idea that the world is going to get worse and worse. Jesus will come a second time to "retrieve" his true disciples, leaving non-believers in the hell of their own evil environment. Two will be together — one taken and the other left. It has spoken of a last great battle, i.e., Armageddon, and finally of a new heaven and a new earth.

A Tradition of Hope

On the other side of the coin, the Judeo-Christian approach to religion has also always placed an extreme emphasis on hope. Notwithstanding the long tradition of defeat and bondage, Old Testament Judaism found hope in a belief in Messiah, i.e., a deliverer. In a similar manner, notwithstanding the severe persecution experienced by the early Christians following the death of Jesus, the first generation of the church developed the idea of a "second coming" of Jesus. At this time it was believed that true disciples would be rescued from the evil world, and those who had already died would be raised from their graves. Even though there were few ways the early Christians could find peace and security in life as a result of their religious faith, they held to the idea that if they were faithful, one day God would reward them with immortality and eternal rewards. They might lose for a while, but eventually they would win!

This hope for both Jews and Christians was bound up in a theology and world view that envisioned God on a super-human level and as being all-powerful and in charge. This world view encouraged the Old Testament Jews to ask "why?" when misfortune was continually their lot. The answer typically came back something like this: "We have all sinned and are wicked in our ways, BUT if my people which are called by my name will humble themselves and pray, and seek my face turning from their wicked ways, I will forgive their sin and heal their land."

The question for the early Christians was the same "why?" "If Jesus was the Son of God and if we are trying our best to be faithful and committed disciples, why does a loving God who has all power permit us to be persecuted, even to the point of death?" The New Testament answer was a bit different from the Old Testament response. Christians came to believe that persecution was their lot as a means of testing their faith. Their challenge, then, was to be faithful and endure to the end.

The question of "why?" Is not unlike that which is asked by many today in the face of situations, both world-wide and personal, which do not make sense in relation to a God who is loving and all-powerful. Do bad things happen to apparently good people as punishment because these folks just look good on the surface and God knows them deep inside? Are these folks really good, and is God just testing them to see how committed to Him they really are? Should bad things be viewed as punishment or as a testing of our faith? If people are genuinely good, and if they handle adversity well, will God one day respond in loving mercy and deliver them?

If one is to judge truth from history, neither the Jews nor the Christians were right in their supposition that one day God would deliver them, either because they changed the way in which they expressed their lives, or because they had passed the test of endurance in their faith. The Jews only recently have had a geographical piece of land that they could call their own, and that homeland remains under continual threat—it is not a place of serenity and peace. Christians have neither witnessed the return of Jesus nor have they been lifted out of this world with all its contradictions.

The hideous nature of crimes which human beings commit against humanity today is appalling beyond belief. Certainly the Jews have not deserved the treatment they have historically received by those in the world who have hated them. In theological theory, many Christians continue to find their basis of hope "out of this world" and at a later date, rather than in this world at the present time. The fulfillment of hope for either Jews or Christians has not yet been realized. Is there a real and dependable basis of hope for either or both?

Hope, and How We View the World

It is important to this discussion that we keep in mind the vast difference in the world view which provides direction for our response to "things as they are" today, as compared to the world view of any time period covered in biblical literature. In our religious rhetoric it may sound as though we believe in an all-powerful and loving God who can "make things right," but in reality we have discovered that God does not intervene or overpower the laws of nature in a dependable manner. That is to say that while it may occasionally seem that God works by intervention, there is greater evidence that such is not the case. This perception is typically a result of what one wants to believe and/or of inadequate knowledge, rather than a defensible observation of how God works.

Because of the truth in a realization that God does not work in the way we either want or once thought, the practical nature of human beings has forced us to learn and behave in a manner that indicates that God is very much at work, but in a manner different than we used to think. Although the concept is not widely accepted theologically, in most ways we have learned that we do best to express life in partnership with God rather than in utter dependence upon God. God's primary role in human life is to provide the experience of life first, then along with that gift comes resources, opportunities and challenges. How we respond in life to these resources, opportunities and challenges is a matter for us to decide. History attests to the fact that when we respond with gratitude, curiosity, and commitment, we learn wonderful things that can be appropriated in a manner which diminishes pain and evil, and promotes meaning and goodness.

God does not, for example, cause amputated legs to grow back, or paralyzed legs to work, in a sudden and miraculous manner. If such miracles seem to occur, they are the exception rather than the rule. The term miracle thus applies to what we do not yet understand rather than being an indication that God intervenes and performs a miracle. Because of this truth, serious research is underway to find ways of repairing damaged nerves, restoring mobility, and in a different way, utilizing the resources of healing which God provides for us, in order to bring about the desired result. Wonderful work has been accomplished in the development of artificial limbs which enable a person without a given limb to function as though all limbs are intact. A recent television story was told of a person who lost both legs as a result of climbing Mt. Everest and who, with new artificial limbs, returned to climb Mt. Everest again.

How God Works

There is overwhelming evidence to support the idea that God is at work in the way we utilize resources. There is minimal and only unusual evidence to support the out-dated belief that God miraculously and suddenly intervenes to correct the wrongs of the world.

It is now clear that the process by which God works often requires more time than we wish. Furthermore it involves the creative capabilities of human beings more than we once thought. Such new insights, however absolutely wonderful they are, should take nothing away from religious appreciation. In reality, they should provide a basis of hope for the future that "blows one's mind" and involves human beings in a wonderful, enthusiastic and fulfilling way.

Just consider some of the "hopes" that come from human history, and that are being fulfilled in our lives in our day, and which are testimony to the truth that God works differently than the Bible teaches and than we once thought! We are privileged to live in a time when more wonderful things are accomplished and experienced by more people than at any other time in human history. Thanksgiving should not be just a holiday that is celebrated once a year. Every day should be a day of "thanksgiving" for everyone of us. We are truly a "blessed" people living in a wonderful and blessed age.

Of course it is true that we live in a wonderful time! It also true that we live in a time when war is always on the horizon and can be a more hideous kind of war than humanity has ever experienced. Of course it is true that crime is an ever present danger regardless of where we live! Everyone is touched by crime in some way. Too many children in the world are abused, underfed, illiterate and unloved. Environments that were once safe for anyone are no longer safe for either children or adults. Our world is diminished by so many negatives that if we were to enumerate them all and obsess on them, we would be unable to enjoy the present or have hope for the future. There is plenty of reason to be negative about our world and its future.

Hope Essential to a Good Future

We also have plenty of reason for hope! The future, based on pessimism, is likely to result in more reasons to be pessimistic. The future, based on hope, is likely to result in more reasons to be hopeful. We can choose either pessimism or hope. Good things are almost always related to the fruits of hope. There are more reasons for hope in our world than there are for despair. Just consider an overview of the history of our ancestors in the faith!

At the time when Jesus was born things were at an all time low. Though the Jews had been taught that they were "God's chosen people," it certainly didn't look that way. They had been slaves in Egypt, placed in bondage by the Babylonians, and conquered by the Assyrians, Persians, Greeks and Romans.

Not only this, but their religion had been made a laughing stock in the eyes of the world by the Greeks prior to Roman domination. Antiochus Epiphanes, in an effort to make a loud and final statement to the Jews had symbolized his total disdain for the Jews and their religion by sacrificing a pig on the altar of the temple. The pig was an unclean animal to the Jews. Nothing more powerful could have been done to more effectively symbolize the powerlessness of the Jews and utter disdain held for their religion and ancestry by the Greeks.

Why would God let this happen to them? They were challenged to find a way to reclaim the approval of the God whom they believed had "called" them, and in whom they had placed their trust. Their religious faith provided a basis of hope which enabled them to recover.

This hope was based on two avenues of thought. One option included an emphasis on "getting back to the basics" and changing their ways of expressing life in a manner that conformed to God's will. The other option was to place their faith in a leader, i.e., Messiah, who, in the manner of King David of old, would lead them to freedom and glory.

In their efforts to "get back to the basics" and thus regain the approval of God, with the hope that such approval might bring with it peace, power, and prestige, they had elaborated the Old Testament Law to the point of oppression. They were not only in bondage to the Romans, but they were in bondage to their own religion.

It was into this kind of world with this kind of history that Jesus was born. With the life of Jesus one is able to see the two emphases that became a basis for hope. Some chose to commit themselves to the following of the letter of over six hundred laws. Some chose to trust the leadership of one who might be the Messiah, and who taught that "law" was not the way, but that love should be the motivating factor in human relationships with one another and with God. Even if one strips the story surrounding the birth of Jesus, as we have it, of much of the fantasy and supernaturalism which was congruent with the commonly held view of the world in that day, there is a remarkable lesson here about the value of hope.

Many of those who believed that their religion had become an impossible "demand" and burden were discouraged. As a result, many had developed an "I don't care" attitude in the face of such impossible religious demands. They were living immoral, sinful lives with the hope that through such living they could acquire some pleasure in a life that was short and painful at the best. "Eat, drink, and be merry" was not simply rhetoric for many, but was a way of life.

The biblical story which emphasizes the Messiah option is one of tenderness and beauty. Elizabeth believed that she would bear a child in fulfillment of a promise from God. She was so committed to her faith that she reared her child, whom we remember as John the Baptist, with the belief that he could make a difference in the world. He became a "strange one," retiring to the wilderness and living on locusts and wild honey. He made forays into the populated areas, however, in order to preach the dangers of sin and the virtues of repentance and change.

At about the same time, another woman, Mary, was so overwhelmed with her pregnancy in an unmarried state, that she also believed her unborn child was a special gift from God, different from and above all others. She committed herself to loving and rearing this child in a manner which would make it possible for him to fulfill the Old Testament dream of a deliverer "Messiah." He was therefore named "Jesus." Jesus and John had great respect for each other. Jesus appreciated the work that John did and, it is believed, became one of his disciples. John was so impressed with Jesus that he proclaimed him to be the true Messiah, indicating that he was not worthy to be compared with Jesus and that he wanted his work to prepare the way for whatever great things Jesus might do.

The "John and Jesus story" is testimony to the fact that even in times of great desperation, such as at the time when Jesus was born, the best of our religious heritage has always included a major portion of hope. The Jews have survived impossible odds because of hope. The early Christians and the church have survived impossible odds because of hope.

Notwithstanding the vast amount and hideous nature of evil in our world today, is there still a basis for hope? It has been said that without a vision the people perish. It can also be said that without hope for the fulfillment of a vision, the people perish.

In a world and at a time when God ought to be understood differently than in times past, what is the basis for hope in a predominantly Judeo-Christian society, and for that matter, for the entire world?

The New Testament teaches that Jesus is the basis of a dependable hope. But it teaches this in relation to a world view that is primitive in relationship to the general knowledge of today. The church turned Jesus into a sacrifice and has never moved from that position. The offering of sacrifices was consistent with the ancient world view but hardly fits with our understanding of "how things are" or ought to be, today.

Hope Found in Human Response to Life

Hope for the world is not found in a belief that Jesus "took the rap" for us. Hope for the world is found in the idea that all human beings are children of a creative God, and that through growth in love have the potential to become the kind of human creatures that God envisioned.

Reliable hope is not found in a belief that one day we will be lifted from our misery. Reliable hope must be based in a belief that we can do better, and that "better" is related to the teachings taught and exemplified by the founder of our faith, i.e., Jesus. It is not Jesus who saves us in some mystical and vicarious manner. It is the principle of growth in love that is capable of saving the human family from itself.

Resources that Produce Reasonable Hope

Our hope is found in knowledge. Knowledge is exploding all about us. It is like compound interest. The more we learn the greater the base from which we can learn even more.

Our hope is found in power. Growth in knowledge has provided us with power heretofore unknown to humanity. We have power to prevent many bad things. We have power to work with God in healing in ways never experienced before. We have power to cooperate with the natural world. We have power to create in ways never known before. We have power to destroy in ways too awful to imagine. We have power to communicate to more people, more quickly, with more ideas, than has ever been experienced in the history of the human race. We have power to get places faster than ever before, and we have power to go places we have never been before.

Our hope is found in love. Love can nudge us into becoming more responsible persons so that we use the power and the knowledge we have in positive and helpful ways. Love can make us caring and compassionate persons. Caring can enable us to respond to the needs of others in a manner that feeds a longing for peace not war. Love can encourage us to be participants in the positive and contributory aspects of life so that we find meaning through a sense of working with God to help one another. Love can make us lose reliance on drugs, alcohol and debauchery in an effort to find meaning in life. Love nurtures respect. Love nurtures appreciation and reverence for the great gifts of God in and to life. Our hope is found in our ability to teach our children about love, reverence, respect and personal responsibility.

Our hope is found in the human ability to change. If persons are nurtured in reverence and respect in a manner that brings about spiritual health, they can change whenever they choose. The past cannot be changed. The future can be affected by the changes that occur at any "present time." Our hope is found in the possibility of youth and adults who have not experienced spiritual growth to "be born again" and grow in spirit as they grow in wisdom, knowledge, and power. Hope is found in our ability to share this message and to encourage each other and everyone to claim it for ourselves and to encourage one another in it.

We are indeed free—free enough to save ourselves from ourselves—free enough to save ourselves for ourselves, for one another, and for the fulfillment of God's purposes for his human children. Human experience and a search for religious truth in this matrix of freedom provides a wonderful and dependable basis for hope!

Chapter XIV

"I Can Do That!"

Human life is filled with the need to make decisions on the basis of perceived values at a given time and in a given circumstance. Our response to a polar bear, for example, will be quite different when we view the bear within the safe confines of a zoo than if the same bear were loose on the city streets. If we are confronted by the bear on the street we suddenly recognize the highest value for the moment to be that of protecting our lives. Our flight reflexes "kick in" and you can't see us for dust! That same value exists when we see the bear in the zoo, but because we are not threatened, lesser values, such as taking a picture of the bear, may "kick in."

Decisions made at different times and under different circumstances may be very different, but be very right in relation to the circumstances at the time they were made. The decision of the early Christians to perceive of Jesus as they did was okay then, and we can understand the logic of their decision now. A decision to perceive him differently today is okay in relation to a view of the world that is entirely different now from what it was then.

Inspiration for Progress

Although the general rule is often broken, there is a tendency among human beings to seek the easy and more comfortable way. This is not all bad, and there are exceptions to the rule. Some persons, for example, are challenged by the nature of their spirit to participate in non-essential but difficult and dangerous activities. In general, however, we strive to find easier, safer, and more comfortable ways of attaining goals in life which we perceive to be important. The latter is the reason we don't walk everyplace we wish to go. When, as a human family, we grew tired of the most primitive means of transportation, either for ourselves or for items we wanted to move, we invented the wheel, we domesticated beasts of burden, we designed and built the steam engine, we mass produced the automobile, we created the airplane and now we explore the heavens with the space ship. We are always seeking an easier and more comfortable way of accomplishing those goals in life that please us.

The exceptions to this rule are illustrated in those few persons who commit themselves to the disciplines of training and the dangers of "living on the edge." Their motivation may be for the thrill of it, or they may also be motivated to experience danger for the sake of having an easier and more comfortable life as a result of learning from the dangers they experience. These are the persons who climb mountains because they are there. These are the persons who fly the space ships and experience dangers never before experienced by human beings. Some may be motivated by the prestige and public notice which may come as a result of their efforts.

Though only a few dared in the beginning, millions now drive automobiles. Only a few endure the hardships and brave the dangers of space flight now, but in the future many will likely participate in the exploration and challenges of space.

In many instances, the gradual change in the functional definition of conservatism, i.e., searching for the benefits of comfort and ease without the dangers, eventually comes to be viewed as progress.

What does this have to do with "Making God Talk Make Sense"? Most people are satisfied to embrace the easy approach to a belief/value system as it relates to God and religion. That which we reinforce to each other as "truth," and beliefs which have endured for centuries, tend to nurture comfort and ease. The conservative path of least resistance sometimes seems noble but is also often contrary to the spirit which has brought about whatever level of achievement is now being experienced.

Píoneeᴙs ín the Seaᴙch ꜰoᴙ Tᴙuth

Only a few along the way have dared to go beyond the traditional views of their religion and brave the dangers inherent in the "edge" of recognizing a changing understanding of truth. In our Judeo-Christian tradition, there have been only a few pioneers. Abraham was one. Moses was another. The eighth century prophets fit in this category. Jesus was another. Paul was another. After the canonization of the Bible, reformers such as Luther and Zwingli were of a similar but less radical nature.

Because of a rapidly "shrinking" world coupled with an exploding experience of knowledge, there is a major need for acceleration in progress in the area of a religious belief system that is harmonious with how we view the world in the 21st century. Although this is true in relation to most religions, it is especially true in Christianity. Given the predominance of Christianity as an approach to religion in our society, and the fact that it desperately needs an update in some facets of its truth, in this discussion we will confine our conversation to the Christian approach to religious truth and the search for ultimate meaning in life. There is a need to keep in mind, however, that when one part of a belief system is challenged, there are also tangent beliefs which require some kind of adjustment for the sake of consistency.

Without diminishing the impact and importance of Judaism as a foundation of Christian faith, it should be noted that to the Christian, no one and nothing is of more central importance as a basis of faith than what is believed about Jesus Christ. Had Jesus, or someone like him not lived, there would have been no Christianity.

Early, but not original, beliefs about the reality of the historical Jesus are centered around the Christmas story and the Easter story. Verification of this is seen not only in the testimony of the New Testament Scriptures, but in the increase of attention to religious ritual in the contemporary "Christian World" at Christmas and Easter. Attendance at religious celebrations increase to such an extent during these religious seasons that those who attend church only on these holidays, are often spoken of as the "C and E" crowd.

The traditional emphasis placed on attending church at these times testifies to the great importance given to the perceived nature of the birth and death of Jesus. As we think about the nature and importance of the traditional and typical Christian belief in Jesus and these two aspects of the historical life of Jesus, it is important to keep in mind the general manner in which the world was viewed in that day, and for centuries preceding and following the "Jesus event."

The Christmas story which celebrates the birth of Jesus comes to us only from the Bible. It is centered around a supernatural phenomenon. There is no secular recounting of this religious story, and considerable effort is required in utilizing sources that are not biblical to associate the events of the story with secular history.

Traditional Pivotal Beliefs in the Christian Tradition

The Christmas story is beautiful in all respects. It speaks of God's involvement in human conception and birth. It speaks of God's attention to the rich and the poor. It speaks from an environment of unconditional love and offers hope to the world. Furthermore, it fits neatly into the world view of that day.

The story tells of the birth of a baby who had no earthly father and was born from the purity of a mother who had never engaged in sexual intercourse. This kind of story was not unusual in that day and was designed to give credence to the authentic nature of a religious leader as having come "straight from God." Other religious leaders were believed to have been born by the same miraculous process and were touted as having the same ability to perform miracles as that demonstrated by Jesus.

In fact, we who are privileged to live in this modern age know much more about the process of genetics, fertility, conception, gestation, birth, and human development, than they knew then. Nevertheless, our knowledge of "life" is far from complete. The mystery of where human life comes from, how a fetus is "enlivened," and where human life "goes" at death, is just as great today as it was then. It is a bit like a flame of fire. From outward appearance its coming is a mystery, and where it goes when it "goes out" is also a mystery. We know about and understand the mechanics of conception and birth, but we are "in the dark" in relation to the impartation of life that makes the fetus more than a cell-dividing organism that develops in ways different from a plant. The essence of the spirit, the creativity of the mind, and the emotions of human beings all represent areas of minuscule understanding to us.

Though the processes involved in the beginning of human life are fairly well known and understood today, the origin of life that is repeated millions of times each day, is not. That is to say, that in spite of all the knowledge gained during the last two thousand plus years, the conception and birth of healthy babies is still a wonderful and awe inspiring miracle. Even a "virgin" birth does not top that! In that day it did. In our day it doesn't. It is quite possible to bring about multitudes of experiences of conception by technical virgins which grow into healthy babies in our day. We know how to accomplish this, and the mechanics are thus no longer miraculous. The process is often used though it is doubtful that it occurs with women who are strictly virgins. Even though we understand the mechanics of natural or "virgin birth," the matter of life and its beginning is a mystery to us. It remains a "miracle."

It is therefore possible for us to say now that the virgin birth is no big deal. In fact we should have been saying this all along. It is quite remarkable that even though the genealogy of Jesus in the first chapter of Matthew is given on the "Joseph side," rather than on the "Mary side" of his family, in the tracing of his lineage back to King David, the "virgin story" acquired tremendous importance. This contradiction was easily overlooked, however, and became important in the effort to establish the unusual power of God in this specific birth, and ultimately to establish Jesus as "The Only Begotten Son of God," believed to have had no earthly father. There are multitudes of committed Christians who are still willing to argue that one today, even to the point of viewing it as a necessary block in their foundation of faith.

This aspect of the Christmas story was perfectly acceptable for some at the time of Jesus and for many centuries after. It was consistent with the contemporary view of the world. It should not be acceptable nor viewed as necessary to establish the importance of Jesus in our own day. Jesus is important in our day not because of the nature of his birth, but because of the impact his life has had on human history collectively, and on the lives of millions of human beings individually. We celebrate his birth not because of the touted nature of its occurrence but because of the wonderful contribution his life made to the human family.

It should be noted that the same kind of reasoning can and should be applied to the biblical information about the ministry of Jesus, especially as it relates to the performance of miracles. All of this was consistent with the way the world was viewed in that day, and these stories were designed to establish Jesus as "The Son of God" thus giving authenticity to a new, young, and threatened religious movement. We are not less than we might otherwise be as disciples of Jesus, if we view Jesus as a very positive and hopeful person, a wonderful teacher and example, but void of power to intervene and change the course of nature.

This kind of thinking is also basic to an understanding of the resurrection story. The physical resurrection of Jesus makes little sense if he was simply to withdraw from the world which he hoped to save. The story about the physical resurrection made great sense, however, in relation to a great need for rationalization in the minds of the disciples of how death could have come to their leader, about whom they believed wonderful things, and in whom they had placed their ultimate trust.

The Savior Concept

In religion, as in other areas, we observe the impact of human nature. It is quite common for human beings to want something done for them, rather than to endure the discipline and pain of doing it for themselves. That aspect of human nature is basic to the "savior" concept.

There is a sense in which it is possible for the example of Jesus as exemplar to make him the "savior of the world." It is not that Jesus did something for the rest of the human family that they should not do for themselves. He did not offer himself as a sacrifice to satisfy the needs of an angry God as we have been taught. What Jesus did was to express his life in a manner, that if everyone else in the world expressed their lives in the same manner, would save the world from itself.

He was reverent, i.e., loved the source of his being and the environment in which he experienced life, and he sought to do nothing that would diminish the wonder and awe of creation. This reverence was at the top of his scale of value priorities.

He had love for his fellow human beings even if their behavior did not earn his respect. He sought to help other persons in the human family save themselves from themselves and one another. He did not seek to either get even or punish. He viewed resentment and hatred as wasted time and detrimental emotions. He taught the need to manage hatred constructively and wisely. This was the second priority on his list of values. He experienced deep hurt, even to the point of death, from other members of the human family, but he refused to seek ways of retaliation.

He wanted to live but was not afraid to die. He believed that the same love which brought about his creation and sparked the beginning of his life was the love that would receive him at the time of his death. This belief was fundamental to his faith.

He viewed himself as being part—and an important part—of the ongoing process of "what God is about." It was this belief in and about himself which provided Jesus with meaning and purpose. From this belief he extracted strength to continue on in the face of great adversity.

Can We Do That?

Now I ask you! If everyone in the world shared this same philosophy of life and involved themselves in life in the same spirit which we are taught Jesus involved himself, would the world not be saved from itself? It is in this sense and in this manner that Jesus is the "savior of the world." To whatever degree human beings, collectively or individually, express their lives in the same spirit which informed, inspired, and empowered Jesus in the expression of his life, "salvation" is experienced. To the degree that human life is not expressed in this manner, damnation in the form of negative consequences is the result.

It should be pointed out that this principle can be observed under the umbrella of any religion or no religion. It is not necessary to have heard of Jesus in order to follow the same principles of life. Words and names are only symbols. Behavior and attitude contributes to either the "lostness" or the "salvation" of human beings.

Did Jesus have to live as he lived? Although we have been taught to believe that Jesus was "sent," we need to develop the courage to assume that he was "sent" only in the same sense that we are "sent." In other words, Jesus had no more to do with his own conception and birth than each of us have had. We are not alive by our choice, but by the choice of others, and by the choice of factors such as the selection of the egg and the strength of the sperm which we do not fully understand. Although we are each subject to the influence and opportunities from many sources as we express our lives, the basic choice of what we each make of our life is up to us. We are the ones who choose to do what we will with what we perceive we have.

When Jesus stood before the crowd in the synagogue the day he started his ministry and announced his intention to fulfill the centuries old hope of his people for a Messiah who would lead them in deliverance from themselves, i.e., fulfill the prophesy of the prophet Isaiah, he chose to say that he would be that person. He did not have to say that. God did not force his tongue. He did not have to live as he did. He did not have to die as he did. He was not "sent" with only one possibility as to how he expressed his life or how his life would end. He is the one who said, "I can do that!" Because he chose as he did, and because he had the strength of character to express his life as he did, he became what he committed himself to become. The world should be thankful for that!

The world experiences salvation from itself to the same degree that others in the human family succeed in expressing their lives in the same spirit that Jesus expressed his. The degree to which Jesus becomes "savior" to the world is determined by the degree, both in quality and quantity, that any generation of the human family succeeds in expressing life in the same spirit in which Jesus expressed his.

This message is one which has universal significance. Whether one gives intellectual assent to historical reality of Jesus is not important to the salvation of the individual or the world. Whether one gives intellectual and spiritual commitment to the same spirit in which Jesus expressed his life is of absolute significance. Contemporary serenity and the future of the world is absolutely dependent upon this human choice.

A Matter of Personal Decision

God did not force Jesus to be "Jesus" any more than God forces us to become any specific kind of person. Jesus could have become a "Barabbas" had he chosen that course for his life. We have the privilege of the same choices that Jesus had in relation to who we become and how we express our lives. God provides life. God provides life with opportunity. We make the choices.

There is a wonderful "up" side to the two greatest Christian holy days. There is a misleading "down" side to the two greatest Christian holy days. We are misled if we believe that someone else, i.e., Jesus, is going to save us and the world for us, apart from our participation. It is a wonderful but erroneous thought to assume that Jesus was "sent" to save us from our sins. The celebration of Christian "holy" days tends to nurture that erroneous perception. We are also misled if we believe the ultimate goal of our faith is found in a physical resurrection. It is an insult to God, in the face of his wonderful gift of life to us, to live this life as though it were only a training experience for something better.

It is wonderful to be reminded of unconditional love. It is wonderful to nurture hope. It is wonderful to share in a loving, giving, and forgiving spirit with one another. It is wonderful to celebrate the great gift of children. We need "holy days" as symbolic reminders.

We also need "holy days" with a message of responsibility. As we learn more about the spirit which guided Jesus, we need also to learn how to apply that same spirit to the expression of our own lives in our world in our day. Holy Days can remind us of the need for our being responsible in doing just that.

Jesus in essence said, when faced with the challenge of the prophet in response to the needs of his people, "I can do that!" Jesus is a wonderful exemplar! It is through our following that example of spirit and behavior that salvation comes to individuals and to the world.

Chapter XV

The Ultimate Object of Devotion

R hetoric is one thing. Behavior is another. To what god(s) that we serve are we devoted? This is not a discussion about the functional displacement of any God in our value system by secular concerns such as money, social status or power. It is a specifically religious discussion about one's perception of the God/god to which one is devoted. In other words, whatever it is that we suppose we mean when we use the term "God" falls under this umbrella.

The Foolishness of Religion

The two examples which follow emphasize the importance of examining our "Objects of Devotion" and are very contemporary with this writing. Similar examples are available on a historical basis at any point in time.

Shortly before the turn of the century, Israel deported certain Americans, who as part of a cult, went to Jerusalem with their leader to initiate a shoot-out with Israeli police. They expected and hoped to be killed, thus fulfilling their vision of an apocalyptic transition to eternity at the turn of the century. Their leader professed to believe that God gave him messages and directed his behavior in a manner that provided direct mind and behavioral control over his followers. This kind of brainwashing and senseless religious expression is not unusual, but it is alarming. This is not the first senseless demonstration of this kind, and it will not be the last. To what kind of God are these persons devoted? The objects of religious devotion are very important to human beings. That to which we are truly devoted makes a major difference in the expression of human life!

Some attention has been given to the behavior of selected religious groups in relation to medical/health care for their children. A number of situations have been observed in which children died because the families insisted on depending on prayer alone rather than medical treatment in response to health care needs. In this day, a clear mind, free to use the best of human common sense, recognizes such behavior as abusive to children and an unwise and unrealistic expression of parental love and religious faith.

Such examples, when placed beside historical examples of the foolishness exhibited in our religious tradition, are not out of line. On a larger scale, such episodes as the crusades, the rejection of all science by the church, and the building of great cathedrals with the money of the poor, cause one to weigh the relative assets and liabilities of religion to human progress.

A Traditional Problem

The objects of devotion, i.e., gods which influence human behavior and attitude, have always been very important in the Judeo-Christian tradition. Moses, for example, was very careful as he assumed responsibility as a mouthpiece for Yahweh, to insist that no god would take precedence over the God to whom he re-introduced them. This was the God of Abraham, Isaac, and Jacob, and the God who would communicate to the Jews the manner in which they should express their lives in relation to every aspect of human concern. The very first commandment of the Ten is "thou shalt have no other gods before me!"

The Jews had problems maintaining devotion to this God of Abraham, Isaac, and Jacob because it was a God whose face they could not see and whose voice typically came in indirect ways. Even at the time that Moses was presumed to be on top of Mt. Sinai in communication with Yahweh, the people pressed Aaron, the brother of Moses, to permit and join them in the fabrication of an idol, i.e., a golden calf made from the jewelry they had brought with them from Egypt. This idol gave them something they could see and touch. It provided something to which they could psychologically impart a power which they could in turn believe would help them in their times of trouble and need. It was this spectacle, of the people dancing around a golden calf, to which Moses returned from the mountain top where he had put together the Ten Commandments, i.e., the basic common denominator of human behavior which must guide any society if it is to survive.

As the Jews settled in what they believed to be the land promised to them by this God, they had difficulty in not directing their devotion to gods of their neighbors in this new land. The worship of Baal, a Canaanite god which was depicted as a mighty warrior with a spear in one hand and a club in the other and whose special animal was the bull, was especially troublesome to the Jews according to much Old Testament historical and prophetic literature. It seemed to them that the worship of Baal worked for their neighbors. The worship of Yahweh wasn't working nearly as well for them, as they turned to agriculture in the "Promised Land," as it had worked when they were herdsmen in the wilderness. After all, Baal was the supervisory god of agriculture for the Canaanites!

Paul, in promoting Jesus as a representative of the Hebrew God to the Greeks and Romans, chided them for their many gods, including one known as "the unknown god." At the same time he attempted to introduce them to the Hebrew God who could not be seen and whose voice was heard only in indirect and unusual ways.

There is a major difference which ought to occur in our understanding of God as compared to that of our "biblical ancestors." The general world view which prevailed during the evolution of all biblical literature was such that unusual ways of hearing from God and a belief in unusual births for certain special people made perfect sense. What they could not understand about their environment, they tended to credit to some kind of spiritual force which was believed to be more powerful than they, and to which was given the status of a god.

Knowledge Explosion and View of God

In a scientific age which is characterized by an explosion of knowledge, we have much less need for the "unusual" as a means of explaining God and faith in God than has been true in past human history. Ancients explained natural phenomena which they did not understand by attributing it to the gods. The volume of human knowledge today is "only a drop in the bucket" compared to what there is to know. We have learned enough, however, to know that certain things are dependable and that many things have erroneously been credited to the expression of spiritual forces in the past. Weather for example, now has a very logical and understandable explanation apart from spiritual forces. The work of God among us is natural and the "usual" explains the work of God.

In the kind of age in which we now find ourselves, and in the kind of age which will undoubtedly unfold in the future, it is imperative that we return to the Hebrew concept of an "Object of Devotion," i.e., a concept of God, which is unseen and unimagined. It is just as imperative, however, that we move beyond the Old and New Testament concepts of an intervening God. This will require a "stretch" for some, but it is harmonious with what we are learning about "how things came to be," and why things "are as they are."

This means several important things. First it indicates that a point at which our God-concept needs to diverge from that of our biblical ancestors is in relation to our need for the voice of God to be heard in unusual ways. Contemporary knowledge of our marvelous universe is such that our ears need to be tuned to the voice of God as heard from that which is dependable, natural, and always about and within us. What a shame when God speaks and we don't hear!

Second, we need to examine the ways in which we have fallen into kinds of idolatry which are specifically different from, but functionally similar to, that which so often plagued our biblical ancestors.

Third, we must come to see ourselves as human beings who are not necessarily by our nature in opposition to God, but as capable of growing in our ability to experience and express life in a way which is increasingly harmonious with the nature and expressions of this unseen, but very evident, God.

The end result of a positive and effective response to each of these challenges will be a kind of spirit and meaning that will continually nudge us into a harmonious relationship with this unseen God, whose loving generosity makes it possible for us to live and to appreciate an environment which sustains us.

Concepts Should Fit the General World View of Any Given Age

In the "old" days, it was reasonable for persons with little knowledge of how the natural world functions to suppose that God either spoke through natural expressions that came only occasionally and were not understood, or through some kind of expression which seemed to go against what one typically observes in nature. We, for example, often see flash lightning in the clouds which makes it appear that the clouds are momentarily on fire. We understand the need for and source of lightning well enough to know that this is not God providing leadership in a supernatural way. The children of Israel understood, on the other hand, that they "were led by a cloud by day and a pillar of fire by night."

Unusual births were not uncommon in biblical interpretations of how special people had their beginning. Abraham was a special person. His son, Isaac, was reported to have been born to Sarah long after her days of child bearing had passed. Jesus was a special person. Some biblical writers, and especially the early church, felt it important to view his birth as unusual, i.e., born of a virgin.

Our understanding of conception, gestation, and birth is such today that the beginning of life is so awesome and the wonderful opportunity to participate in it both spiritually and physically is so wonderful, that we have little need for unusual, i.e., "virgin" birth, as an evidence of God's voice and work. The joining of an egg and sperm bringing about a human life, regardless of the methodology, is sufficient to indicate the wonderful creative power of God. If one wishes to "wonder" a bit more, he/she can contemplate the process which brought about the development of both the sperm and the egg and the reasons why each became what they are. Take such thoughts a step further and marvel at the great waste of both in relation to the negative consequences if there was not such waste. I doubt that we really need the "virgin birth" to indicate the presence of God in the creation of human life!

Exploration of space has enhanced the marvel that human beings have traditionally had of the universe. The ability to learn about both micro and macro universes has taught us that the voice of God is all about us. We just need to tune in with the expectation that some special message is coming our way!

God Today

There are those faculties within us that are related to mind, emotions, and spirit that are beyond our full understanding, yet are indispensable in helping us grow towards our capacity for being fully human, i.e., a human child of God. Consider the conscience! Consider moral sensitivity! Consider the desire for strength to overcome in the areas where we know we fall short!

The voice of God is all about us and within us in ways that are not at all unusual. God's voice may be heard in ways that are very natural and very wonderful. There is no longer a need for us to speak or think of God as "Supernatural." God speaks through creative expressions and natural phenomena. The fact that God transcends "nature" does not mean that God is not involved in it. Inasmuch as human beings are part of the natural expression, we need to be tuned in to God through the medium of which we are part and in which we can grow in understanding.

Sunsets, sunrises, the majesty of the mountains, the power of the sea, the wonder of plants that mysteriously come from a small seed and grow into valuable and sometimes monstrous trees, the curious twinkle in the eye of the small child, and the love of kin and friend—all these and much more speak of the presence and work of God. God speaks to us, through them, of his power and love. It is as though they are all encapsulated in a mystery about which we are curious and from and about which we can persistently learn. The awe and splendor of the presence of this unseen God is too marvelous for us to comprehend. Wow!

Approved Idolatry

Given a tradition that has placed such an emphasis on the avoidance of anything that smacks of idolatry, it is interesting that we have not become more curious and doubtful about the wisdom of the status we have given to Jesus and the Bible. Let's examine both of these from the perspective of idolatry and attempt to understand how this came to be! Keep in mind that idolatry always seems reasonable, and perhaps mandatory, to those who engage in it.

It should be clear that the intent of this book is not to destroy the importance of either Jesus or the Bible in the nurturing and nudging of faith for anyone. It is my intent to suggest that "we" have gone too far in attributing qualities of deity to both. They have become objects of devotion to an extreme that tends to limit important growth in our understanding of, and connecting with, the ways of this "unseen God," i.e., "the God of Abraham, Isaac, and Jacob." Could it be that the Bible and Jesus have become, to many of us, what the "calf" and "Baal" were to the ancient Hebrews?

Both Jesus and the Bible are very important to the development of the Judeo-Christian belief system, and subsequent religious experience. Although our devotion to the memory and knowledge of Jesus should be considerable, it should be much less than that given to this "unseen God." The only source we have for knowledge about Jesus comes from the writings of those who wrote about him after his death and, who at the time of their writing, had already formulated their idea of him as "the only begotten Son of God." Just as it requires a "leap of faith" to accept their premise, it also requires some extrapolation to reach the conclusion which I share with you.

I strongly suspect that if Jesus could know the status he has achieved across the centuries in the minds of millions of Christians, he would be greatly embarrassed. I suspect that he would exclaim in disbelief something like, "how in the world could they have arrived at that conclusion given the fact of my humble intentions?"

Why do you suppose that idolatry was such a major matter in both Old and New Testament biblical literature? The simple and most obvious answer is three-fold. First, anything which detracts from total devotion to the unseen God "in whom we live and move and have our being" diminishes our ability to harmonize our religious and spiritual life with the reality of "things as they are." We are unable to reach our full potential as human beings who are children of God when we persist in idolatry. Idolatry misdirects our attention!

Second, there is a tendency in human nature to desire something to which our physical senses can respond, as objects of devotion. If human beings are to harmonize with the objectives of God and thus enable God to achieve evolving goals that are harmonious with his nature, it is important to the ultimate purposes of God that human beings not be misdirected but that they be focused on that which "God is about." It is this kind of focus which fulfills the goals of God and brings the greatest meaning to human experience both on the individual and corporate level.

Notwithstanding the multitude of analogous lessons that can be learned from the life and teachings of Jesus as we understand them, his greatest contributions through his life include the following: (1) He understood God to be more involved in love than in retributional judgment; (2) He felt a relationship with God which was akin to, but surpassed that of parent and child; (3) He viewed religious law as helpful but as inferior to behavior motivated by love; (4) He wanted to share the wonders of his faith with all who were interested in taking a major step forward in religion and life; (5) He was so "sold" on his experience and the need to share it that he was willing to die in an ignominious manner rather than be silent about the principles which guided his life; and (6) the impact of his experience and commitment was so great on those close to him that the inspiration of his life and teachings transcended his death and became the basis of a new and powerful religion.

Devotion to Jesus is not alone in becoming a kind of idolatry within the Christian movement. The Bible has achieved the same level in the contemporary Christian scene. The idea that the Bible is a voice piece for God in which all truth is contained and which contains nothing but truth is fallacious. The Bible contains a wonderful record of the search for religious truth by certain individuals and groups of people. It shares many insights into human behavior and is a wonderful instructive resource in the "art of living."

In the minds of many it has become a fetish to which power has been imparted which is both false and misleading. It is not holy. It is not God's pride and joy. It is a wonderful resource and should be used in conjunction with other resources to determine how life should be lived and how the future can be more nearly what it ought to be. It is not a book of prophecy except as it is permitted to facilitate self-fulfilling prophecy. Interpretations of the Bible which result in cult groups that place a major emphasis on the end of the world and result in individual or mass suicides is clearly biblical nonsense.

The Bible should never become an object of devotion to anyone. As is true with Jesus, the Bible should be viewed as a resource from which to draw in our quest for harmonious living with the nature and purposes of God. Those who utilize the Bible as a valuable resource of instruction and inspiration for living do well.

Human Beings Less Than God

Finally, it is important that no human being be given a role which commands or receives our ultimate attention as an object of devotion. It is important that we neither diminish nor exalt ourselves or other human beings beyond being human. We are not, as some would say, "God with skin." Our importance to God as human beings is evident, for it is God who gives us life and provides the resources with which we are sustained. We are offspring of God and important in God's scheme of things. Idolatry in any form is dangerous, even self idolization. Healthy human beings are those who have a strong sense of reverence for that which transcends them in every way — for that which is responsible for their being.

There is a common perception among many "religious" people that "man" and God are in conflict with one another. If this is so, it is a one-sided battle which "man" will lose. One often hears about what "man" does, as being in contrast to what God either does or wishes to have done. We are not in conflict with God when we do good things that either accomplish something positive or satisfy our curiosity in a positive manner. Man works with God when he invents the fire, the wheel, the steam engine, the automobile, the airplane and all the devices we use in the exploration of space. Man is working with God in endeavors to promote health and healing. Man is working with God in exploring the limits of both space and technology. Man is working with God when he nurtures the human mind with that which is helpful and honorable and does not diminish others. This understanding instructs us to do all that we do with excitement and in reverent humility.

Partnership With, and Reverence for God Should Be the Goal

The idea that God and human beings are in automatic conflict with one another should be discarded. Instead we should view ourselves as creatures with potential. We are potential partners with God. We can do nothing apart from the provisions of God. God elects to delegate many awesome and wonderful opportunities and responsibilities to us. God provides the resources with which we can meet these challenges, and then continues to broaden our vision to potential accomplishments. The potential of human beings is beyond our wildest dreams at any given time in the continuum of human history.

It is important for human beings, because of their nature, to have an object of devotion that is above all else. It should be above self, other human beings, or any thing. This is what Moses had in mind when he made the first of the ten commandments, " have no other gods before me." It is what Jesus had in mind when he indicated the first command as loving God with our whole heart, soul, and mind.

In view of human nature and our growing understanding of how things are in the environment which creates and supports human life, a common sense approach to religion demands that our object of highest devotion be the unseen God who is responsible for creation and all that supports it.

The life that is lived in awe of its source, and in harmony with its resources, is the life that experiences the most meaning and gives back the greatest gifts. *God Talk* should have the development of this kind of life-experience as its primary goal.

Chapter XVI

The Mysterious Power of Faith

In a previous chapter I discussed the phenomenon of idolatry in our Judeo-Christian tradition. I suggested that Jesus and the Bible have become objects of devotion within the church in the same sense that the golden calf and Canaanite god of Baal were objects of devotion to many ancient Hebrews. There is therefore a need to return to a broader view of what might be meant by "one God" and the avoidance of creating a concept of God as either "personality" or "thing." Consistent with this view is the idea that God's response to human need is not released by the whims of a personal God as an answer to prayer. It is becoming increasingly clear, however, that power provided by God is demonstrated through human faith in dependable ways that are not yet fully understood.

The admonition to return to a broader view of God assumes a human inadequacy to fully understand the nature and purposes of God. It also assumes human ability to grow in knowledge and understanding about anything, including God.

This premise is based on the idea that we are always learning and the more we learn the more we recognize our data base of knowledge to be incomplete. In some cases what we have supposed to be true, we learn is not true at all. The ancients, for example, sincerely believed the world to be flat. They were obviously absolutely wrong!

It is becoming increasingly clear that learning about ourselves and our world is an evolutionary process. There is no reason to suppose that learning about God and other religious values is not also a process in which we sort and build, utilizing accumulated beliefs. This process of gaining dependable knowledge is true in all areas of natural phenomena and human experience.

Biblical writers repeatedly expressed concern about idolatry. Old Testament prophets were concerned that the Hebrews would worship idols. New Testament writers were concerned that persons recently converted to Christianity would become involved in idolatrous behavior with Greek or Roman gods. If Yahweh was so great for the ancient Hebrews, why be concerned? If Jesus was so great for the early Christians, why be concerned? One would suppose that, given the confidence shown in God in the Old Testament and New Testament, there would be no temptation to turn to other gods.

Why do we continue to pursue an idolatrous tendency today that has its roots so deep in our past? It is much easier to see the idolatry of others, past or present, than it is to see our own. It is also easier for us to explain the idolatry of Old Testament Jews on the basis of primitive minds, lack of knowledge about their environment, or even stupidity, (doesn't it sound stupid to worship a golden calf?) than it is to apply these same explanations to our own behavior. The question of "why" deserves an answer. Surely the answer involves some functional benefit which worshipers presume comes from devotion to idolatrous objects or persons which they probably do not "tag" as idols.

Although there are several reasons why idolatry is not desirable, the major reason is that it distracts us from discovering and growing in knowledge of the "Real God."

Faith in Idols Produces Power

But there are also benefits to be found in the worship of idols. Idols, to which power is imparted by the human mind, become a source for the generation of confidence. Mix a bit of imagination with idolatry, along with an occasional coincidental "proof of power," and the idol, in the mind of the worshiper, has power. Confidence in the power of the idol is thus generated.

Confidence is the basis of hope. If the Jews believed the golden calf had power to help them in their distress, they were better off than if they had confidence in nothing. The reason for building the golden calf was two-fold. They had lost confidence in Moses, and they had previously been taught that there was power in worshiping the golden calf. In other words, in the absence of something believed to be better (Moses), they returned to a faith in what had once been helpful to them.

The Jews were more likely to succeed with a belief in the golden calf, than with no belief at all. Faith is an important source of power even if it is placed in that which, in and of itself, has no power. Contemporary human beings are more likely to find power with a belief in Jesus as God or a belief in the Bible as a "holy book" than with no belief at all. The same is true for adherents of religions unrelated to a Christian or Hebrew tradition, and for the same reason. The power of religion is in the faith, not in the objects of the faith!

Is there really any evidence that Jesus or the Bible, in and of themselves, either together or alone, express any kind of positive power in the world today? Jesus does not stop war! Jesus does not stop crime! Jesus does not cure disease! Jesus isn't even alive today, in the way that you and I cherish the experience of life!

Close the cover on the Bible, and it is absolutely as powerless as a mail order catalogue. The Bible is only capable of staying where it is placed! It cannot open its own covers! It cannot change or impact human life without human interpretation of, and response to, its perceived message for that person! It cannot bring about change in inter-human relationships apart from human perception of its message! It cannot reveal God to us apart from human perception of its message! The only way the Bible has power is imparted through the perception of human beings.

Both Jesus and the Bible are useless to us except for the faith that we place in them, even if it is faith generated by an idolatrous kind of devotion.

In other words, all idols are without power in and of themselves. The power of any idol only comes from that which is imparted to it psychologically by human beings, and its power can be demonstrated then only through the human being who believes in it.

The power of much religion is not in the object or person which that religion lifts up as an object of its devotion. This includes the golden calf, Jesus, and the Bible. The power of all religion is found in the faith which it creates and nurtures whether the object of devotion associated with that religion is a person or a "thing."

The Judeo-Christian God Works through the Power Of Faith

Wouldn't it be wonderful to nurture a religious belief system, around an object of devotion which is a source of power in and of itself, and about which human knowledge is evolving, in combination with the natural power inherent in faith itself!

There are at least three things which must not be overlooked in this discussion of idolatry and faith. First, for those who make their religious faith an integral part of their lives, there is a tendency for them not only to "use" their religious faith, but also to defend it. Because it works for them, they are likely to assume that it ought to work for others also. This fact becomes the basis for fanatical expressions of religion as well as enthusiastic downgrading of other approaches to religion. Such persons are also often enthusiastic in the recruitment of others to their brand of religious faith. This is the reason for the proliferation of cults. This is the way Christianity got its start. The biblical book of Acts is a wonderful example of this phenomenon. The disciples of Jesus were excited about their new religious experience, and were so convinced that it was the only right way that the goal became that of making disciples for Jesus in every part of the world, beginning in Jerusalem, spreading to Judea and Samaria and then "to the outermost parts of the world."

Second, have you ever wondered about the contention of Christians that theirs is the only legitimate and acceptable religion. It is interesting that Christianity has historically placed

Judaism, which gave birth to Christianity, in the position of a second rate religion. There is a contemporary Southern Baptist movement which identifies its primary mission to be that of converting "Jews" to Christianity. It is called "Jews for Jesus." It is the position of this group that all Jews are "lost" apart from their conversion to Jesus as Messiah and Savior. Christianity has traditionally judged all other religions as not only "falling short" but as being false and damning. For centuries the primary goal of Christian foreign missions was the conversion of "heathen" to Christianity. Fortunately, most Christian churches are no longer guided by that philosophy.

Thankfully, most Christians respect Judaism as important for providing a basis for their own faith. Many mission efforts have also grown to emphasize the meeting of health, educational, and food needs more than the conversion of minds and spirits to Christian objects of devotion.

Finally, given the traditional Christian contention that a primary purpose of religious faith is to prepare us for immortality, and to assure that we inherit eternal life, have you ever wondered how so many other people in the world are "all wrong" while only certain groups within Christianity are "all right." The differences in expression of faith within the Christian family are many and broad. These differences often nurture distrust, disdain, competition, and sometimes conflict. The traditional arrogance of the Christian Church should not be overlooked!

How can so many different people have so many different approaches to religion and each find their specific approach to be so functional and meaningful to them? Are the adherents of all religions other than Christianity lost? Is God really condemning all Jews, Muslims, Buddhists, Hindus, and all other religions and any branch of Christianity other than the one to which we belong, to hell—forever? That is the historical and broad contemporary premise of many Christians. This is precisely what the author of Acts meant when he quotes Peter saying in 4:12, "...there is no other name (Jesus) under heaven given to men by which we must be saved."

God Is Not Relationally or Intellectually Provincial

Persons of healthy religious faith can take heart in the belief that God is not nearly as narrow minded as many people. The idea that all your Moslem, Jewish, and Catholic neighbors have an approach to religion that does not work for them, and that is dooming them to an eternity in hell, is absurd. There may be a better way for them, and there may be a better way for us. That "better way," however, should be the search of each person for him/herself, rather than through the efforts of others who choose to stand in judgment.

Given the smallness of our world, as defined in relation to communication, transportation, and the major changes which occur as a result of these technical achievements, major importance must be placed, not just on growth in our understanding of one another, but on our respecting one another in our differences, including differences in religion.

Doesn't it make sense, i.e., isn't it a matter of common sense to assume that millions of people are not wrong in their assumption that their specific approach to religious faith works for them? Are persons of all other religions stupid and only imagining the benefits which they perceive from their faith? If one wishes to contribute to a divided world in conflict, then one can afford to respond affirmingly to that question. If one wishes to contribute to a world that takes peace and the matter of loving our neighbor seriously, then it is essential that we deviate from out past religious attitudes and behavior, and consider some other options. The consideration of other options will include a genuine challenge for many religious people in that it will require learning, understanding, and acceptance of what makes other religions helpful to those who embrace them. The idealistic goal is that all religions emphasize the same intense commitment to learning, understanding, and acceptance of each other. When that occurs we all learn, accept, and respect the faith of each other.

Just Suppose!

Let's suppose that God is not proud about the name given to him/her. Let's suppose that the most important language to God is not English, Chinese, Japanese, Spanish, German or any other language that uses any kind of alphabet, but that the language which communicates with God is that of behavior and attitude, i.e., the language of the heart. Let's suppose that the very best of our concepts of God falls far short, and that God doesn't even care about that.

Let's suppose that the reason so many different approaches to religion seem to work for so many different people is because the power of religion is not found in the objects of religious devotion, but in the faith generated by that devotion! If we can suppose that this is true, then the umbrella of religion is broadened to include a wide variety of religious beliefs. No longer could the finger of humanity be pointed at Christians or other religions which encourage arrogance towards others. Out of mutual respect the message of division and disdain would die! Someone has said "he drew a circle that shut me out, a heretic, rebel, a thing to flout, but love and I had the wit to win—we drew a circle that took him in!" Although this is not a quotation from Scripture, it would make a good one!

It is the power of faith, regardless of the object(s) of devotion which generates that faith, which can become the circle that "takes others in." There must be certain commonalities to make this possible. In the broadest sense I suggest only three: (1) reverence for our Source and Sustainer, whatever name we use; (2) respect for creation which is our environmental home; (3) and functional behavioral love for one another which is demonstrated in mutual respect and concern.

If we are to make such a broad assumption, then it behooves us to examine reality and see if there is any empirical evidence to support this assumption, i.e., that the power of religion is in the faith, and not in the objects of devotion.

Faith and Growth

First, let's examine our own tradition. Keep in mind that at least the first half of our tradition was before Jesus. That is to say that Abraham, Isaac, Jacob, Moses and King David are as much in the Christian tradition as they are in the Jewish tradition. In the same way that we appreciate the Ten Commandments as being a very important and basic foundation on which to build an experience and expression of religious faith, we appreciate Abraham, Isaac, Jacob, Moses and King David as forefathers in our religious tradition who, because of their faith, dreamed a dream and kept it alive. We would not presume to conceive of God exactly as they did. We would not view the Ten Commandments as being sufficient to determine all matters of right and wrong in our day.

These heroes in our tradition, listed along with others in the eleventh chapter of Hebrews, had a faith that worked well for them at that point in human development. They were part of an early process which continues to this day. They, and their descendants were part of that process until Jesus made an "on course adjustment." Because of the nature of things involving continual change, "on course adjustments" are necessary in a wide variety of things. Seasons come and go, but they change. The sun rises and sets but at different times throughout the year. Human experience changes in relation to changes in human beings, the human family, and the environment in which human life occurs.

Jesus believed it was important for an adjustment to be made in the application of the law. It was one thing, for example, for the law to state "thou shalt not covet your neighbor's house, wife, manservant, maidservant, ox, ass or anything that is your neighbor's." As customs change, values also change. Slavery is now out so it is not difficult for us not to covet our neighbor's man or maidservant. Mules and oxen have less value and are valuable for different reasons now than they were then, so coveting those animals is not a problem either. But what does a blanket application of "thou shalt not covet" do to capitalism and the free enterprise system?

The point is that what has worked well in the past, either as admonitional guidelines or as absolute commands, may or may not fit the same way today as it did a few centuries ago. Regardless of need for "in course adjustments," however, the importance and power of faith remains the same.

Faith enabled Abraham to have the courage to move away from that with which he was familiar. Faith enabled Jacob to believe that if his family went to Egypt to "wait out" the famine, one day they would return to their homeland. Faith enabled Moses to believe that if he could get the Hebrews out of Egypt, he could also get them back home to the Promised Land. Faith that they were God's chosen people enabled the Hebrew people to survive captivity, occupation by other nations, existing without a homeland in the world, and the holocaust.

When Jesus sought to initiate a course correction, he was taking a major risk and he knew it. People do not change religious ideas quickly or easily. Political leaders, whether in religions or government, do not give up power easily. This is especially true when government and religion are combined. Jesus was a threat to the status quo in relation to a belief system. Jesus was a threat to the power of the religious leaders in his tradition. The possible consequence of such a threat was death, and he knew it.

It was faith which empowered Jesus, even though he knew the dangers, but felt compelled to go to Jerusalem for the Feast of the Passover. It was faith which gave him strength not to turn against his principles in an effort to save his life. It was faith which enabled him to face death on the cross believing that the good work he had started would continue.

We are challenged, as we move on into the future, to nurture, develop, and express our Christian faith in ways that are a bit different from that of our forefathers, including Jesus. In other words, in the application of our faith to life, a course correction is needed if we are to permit our faith to express itself with maximum power for good for us and for others.

The Functional Power of Faith

We need also to examine what we have learned from experience and observation. We have learned, for example, that a positive attitude, i.e., an attitude that is dominated by positive expectation, encourages much more happiness in life than does a pessimistic attitude. When we are positive and hopeful we enjoy life much more than when we are pessimistic and doubtful. When we are positive and hopeful, the contribution which we give to others through our association with them is one of joy and encouragement.

Growth in the art of medical science and health care has taught us the value of a positive attitude. The fact that patients who are positive and expectant recover from surgery and illness more readily than those without faith can now be scientifically supported. The nurturing of a positive attitude is now part of the process in nurturing health.

We have discovered the value of positive support from others, and now there exists a host of such groups designed to help persons get well. A few years ago the best known primary support group and twelve-step program was Alcoholics Anonymous. Today there are a host of such programs, including grief groups, groups for the treatment of a variety of addictions, and groups that respond to loneliness and other challenges to positive and productive living.

Faith, by its very nature, nurtures a positive attitude. Faith, by its very nature, suggests that something positive can come from any experience. There are those who believe that everything happens for a reason. This is a helpless and fatalistic view of life which needs to be discredited and discarded. Many things happen as a result of human foolishness or ignorance. There is no Master Mind or Super Power that wills misfortune on any of us at any time. God does not control our lives as many would like to believe.

This is not to say that good cannot come from bad experiences. In fact, the single most important aspect of the beginning of Christianity was the fact that broken, disillusioned, and frightened disciples found a way to make something good come from a terrible tragedy. The idea that God willed the death of Jesus is, and was, pure nonsense. The fact that both Jesus and the disciples were able to make good come from a tragedy which came about as a result of an expression of human depravity and meanness does not mean that this was God's plan. It does demonstrate in a powerful way, however, that faith provides the power which enables us to recover from major "jolts" that life sometimes brings, and that faith gives us an opportunity to create positive value from negative and tragic experiences of life.

The disciples could have cuddled their pain individually and/or collectively, and the world would soon have swallowed up the tragedy as the pond swallows the ripples created from a rock tossed onto its surface. Instead, because of their faith, that which Jesus started was too good to let die with him. A new religion took root and the world has not been the same!

Faith and Prayer

The fact of faith as a source of power is evident from a multitude of examples which are both historical and contemporary. But faith in what? The answer most often given to this question is probably "God." Does this mean that God is in control of everything? No! Does this mean that if we find ways to appease or please God, as is taught by most religions, that God will work things out for us? This is a common perception and is a primary reason why many choose to rely on prayer as a force to control life. The facts are that prayer often lets us down. We pray for our children's safety, and they are maimed or killed in unnecessary accidents which often involve the use of alcohol. We pray to be spared from disease, and we become a cancer patient. A multitude of prayers are never answered. Without doubt, more prayers go unanswered than are answered. Of course we devise ways of rationalization such as "sometimes God answers no," but such rationalizations do not change the fact of unanswered prayer.

Jesus taught the importance of faith in relation to both prayer and life. Prayer should not be viewed as a means of controlling the object of our devotion, i.e., God. What should be noted, however, is that faith seems to be a channel through which God works as we seek all possible resources of power.

An interesting thing about faith is that it demonstrates power regardless of what/who it is in which faith is placed. Faith, by its very nature, appears to incorporate power as part of its essence. Could that be the reason why a variety of approaches to religion work for those who embrace them with faith? I am suggesting that it is. Faith is the reason a variety of religions "work" for their adherents. A major channel through which God works is faith, regardless of the title given to God, or the group to which we profess membership. There is power in faith. The power of religion is in faith, not in the object of our faith.

There is a logical and reasonable conclusion to this argument. Faith in a "golden calf" is better than no faith at all. This certainly is not an argument for idolatry. Instead it is to emphasize that the most desirable goal in life is the placement of faith in that which does have power. Doesn't it make sense to suppose that if faith has power, which it does, even when it is placed in something that is powerless, that it is amplified even more when it is placed in something which does have power? The combined power of faith with a powerful object of faith should be the most desirable goal.

A practical application of this idea can be found in our relationship with a medical doctor or any other professional. Some healing good can be found in treatment by a doctor who is inept if we believe in that doctor (especially if he/she confines treatment to placebos.) The most healing good, however, is likely to come from treatment by a doctor who is knowledgeable, skilled, and has "state of the art" resources at his/her disposal.

Some powerful good can come from faith in a god which can be categorized as an idol. The most powerful good will come from a God who/which in and of himself demonstrates creative and remedial power.

The goal of religion at its best should be the nurturing of a growing belief in God, as God is witnessed and experienced in our world in our time. This, for example, is precisely what Moses and Jesus each did. Moses and his generation viewed the power of lightning and thunder as a powerful expression from God. Jesus was part of a culture in which the epitome of human devotion to a god was found in human sacrifice.

A view of God which is consistent with God's work as witnessed and experienced by people of a given society and at a given time in history produces a religion of functional power. This view combines the power of human faith and the observable power of God (Object of our devotion). It is a concept of God which progresses with the developmental process of persons individually, or of any society within the human family. Conversation about God within this kind of intellectual environment automatically makes *God Talk* make sense. It puts religious faith in the realm of everyday experience rather than in the realm of, what is perceived to be, occasional revelation."

Basic as this thought is, it is a "common sense approach to religion."

Chapter XVII

Nurturing a Functional Faith

Given the proposition that the power of traditional religion is in faith, not in the objects of devotion, two things become clear. First, the importance of nurturing a faith that is relevant to contemporary understanding of how and why things are as they are is evident. Second, a concept of God which incorporates some understanding of how power is expressed by God would be very helpful.

Understanding God

Human preference would be a personification of God in a manner that would enable us to understand God, at least as much as we understand one another. That still leaves a large segment of unknown! The ancient depiction of gods by sculptures and images combined with the contemporary need for symbols as aids in understanding and worship supports this observation.

Given the collective evidence of the magnitude of God's creative power which is now available, the Source of such power is clearly beyond current human understanding. There is no reason to believe that the human mind will ever be capable of fully comprehending the magnitude of everything that needs to be included under the umbrella of what is meant by the word "God."

With this in mind it is easy to appreciate the early Hebrew position that their God was a God of such wonders and magnitude that the best name was "no name." With this approach it is possible to use the term "God" in the best sense, with an understanding of its inadequacy and our inability to do better in explaining what we mean when we use the term.

If this "no name," "impossible to fully understand," and "description transcending" God is intellectually acceptable, then it is possible to suggest that a helpful connection can be made between faith and the object of our devotion. The object of our devotion therefore becomes that for which we have great admiration, and before whom we stand in utter humility and awe, about which we are able to understand little, and whom we hesitate to name because of the inadequacy of any symbolic name we might create.

Faith in relation to human beings and this "Source and Sustainer" that we call God becomes a vehicle through which Ultimate power is expressed and our powers are enhanced, but not in any absolute, complete, and always dependable way. The power of religion is therefore not perceived to be expressed through the intervention of an object of devotion. Instead we perceive the power of God through ways we understand to be quite natural. We appreciate this perception with a clear understanding that there is much about the "laws of nature" that we do not yet understand. These, as yet unknown "laws of nature," account for those "happenings" which those in need of an intervening God typically attribute to "divine intervention" and commonly call such "happenings" miracles.

The tendency of human beings to want a personal concept of God which permits divine intervention is the reason that there is the temptation to build Golden Calves, adopt the worship of Baal, deify Jesus, or impart eternal, inerrant, and supernatural power to a book, i.e., the Bible.

Inasmuch as all human efforts to attain a full understanding of the Ultimate Source and Sustainer fall short, and inasmuch as we have come to recognize the great power and value of faith, it behooves us to lay the major portion of the "God question" to one side and pursue a growing understanding of how to nurture a growing faith. It is not necessary for us to understand all the "how" of power that becomes available to us, at least not all at once. The learning of the "how" is a long process in which human beings have been involved since their beginnings. It is a process which is at work in the life of each individual, as well as in each generation. It is necessary that we learn how to acquire and use the power available to us in the best possible way. This is a simple but basic explanation of why education is such a value of high priority and should be viewed as being among the most wonderful blessings and opportunities that God provides us. The ability to learn and to build additional learning on that which has been learned by others and in previous generations as well as contemporarily is a significant contribution to that which makes human beings more than other animals. This "gift" should be appreciated as being of wonderful religious significance.

Faith and Power Then, and Now

A wonderful testimonial concerning the wonderful place in history of great persons of power is found in the New Testament book of Hebrews. These persons were perceived as great persons of power because of what they did, but they were able to do what they did because of their faith. The Gospels often indicate the importance which the writers placed on imparting miraculous power to Jesus in an effort to establish him as "God in human flesh." Those discourses typically emphasized what Jesus taught about the importance and power of faith.

One such episode has to do with the response of Jesus to a young man who was afflicted with epilepsy. The only hope available for one so afflicted in that day was through intervention and healing by God. Though lacking in medical information and treatment skills, they wanted the same thing in relation to this illness, and others, that we want. They wanted protection from it if it hadn't already occurred, and they wanted healing from it if they or a loved one was already afflicted.

We have learned that God does not intervene with such a disease because of religious rhetoric, i.e., prayer. We have also learned that God works through the human mind, human initiative, and subsequent medical knowledge and treatment. Epilepsy is thus controlled today much more dependably than in the time of Jesus, with or without prayer. If one judges from the dependability of results, we must reach the conclusion that God is more involved with the methodology of today than through the efforts of that day.

This comparison is a wonderful example of the difference in how they "hoped" God would work for them, and how we have learned that God actually works. Faith then, occasionally seemed to help the disease, but more often, it enabled those who were stricken and those who cared for the stricken, to find strength to "live with the problem" and not be defeated by it. It should not be overlooked that their hope and the general failure of prayer to activate God's intervention led to the contemporary solution and evident conclusion that God works differently than was once thought. Had prayer typically been effective in healing this disease, or any disease, there would be no reason for the expenditure of time and money to find treatments that do work.

Let's look at another example. The society of which Jesus was a part would have liked to move mountains, but they had no means to do it. Through exaggeration as a teaching method, and in an effort to make an important point, Jesus told them that faith could enable them to move mountains. We now know how to move mountains, and they didn't. We have faith that we can move mountains. Why does our faith work in this regard and theirs didn't? We know that mountains are not moved by faith alone, but by a combination of faith and action. Mountain moving action is now possible because of what we have learned and the power of technology that is available to us because of what we have learned. We have access to powerful earth moving machines and a variety of energy sources including the atom. They had none of this. The acquisition of the kind of assistance needed to go along with faith is our blessing as it was their lack. It has been a long and laborious process. Because of faith and the acquisition of knowledge, skills and resources, God is now involved in moving mountains in a way not known to that generation.

We have faith that we can move a mountain, not by divine intervention, but because of what we have learned or can learn. After we have learned enough to translate that faith into powerful action, then we set about to do it.

We know the great truth in what Jesus taught about a little bit of faith (like a mustard seed) being very powerful and much better than a lot of doubt. The effective message of this Scripture for us is not to turn all challenges over to Jesus believing that he can accomplish the desired goals. The effective message is that what we can accomplish as human beings is multiplied many times when we exercise faith. Common sense therefore teaches us that faith should be an integral part of religion and life. If we have faith, we will try — and sometimes succeed.

Faith And Partnership with God

How do we nurture faith in an age when much of what the ancients dreamed about happening through miraculous intervention by their God, we now accomplish? The fulfillment of these dreams does not come by praying that God will perform our tasks for us. Instead we have learned that much fulfillment comes from human beings working diligently with the amazing resources of creativity, power, and ability to bring about change. All these resources have their roots in the handiwork of a God who is so great that wisdom dictates the absence of an all inclusive name.

We need to become increasingly aware of the wonderful powers available to us as unfolding gifts from God. We need to understand that human involvement in the utilization of these powers does not make "God unnecessary" and religion therefore outdated. Instead it emphasizes the cooperative involvement which God desires between "us and him." The knowledge explosion and great power that comes from "state of the art" technology should in no way diminish our appreciation for God. In fact, such knowledge and power should enhance our experience of life as a religious experience in appreciation for the wonderful gifts God places at our disposal. Through the knowledge we gain, and the resulting power for which we become responsible, it should be easy for us to understand that God has not only given us the gift of life with all its wonderful spin-offs, but that God has made us with the capacity to express our lives as partners in creativity with God. This is wonderful! This is awesome! This is a truth that is so evident in our day, that every day should be a day of thanksgiving! It is a grave error to suppose that human beings do any wonderful thing apart from the gifts of God. The more we learn and the greater our capacity for doing, the more in awe of God we ought to be and the greater our humility should be.

The nurturing of relevant faith in our day requires much more than the reading of the Bible and prayer. That was effective in the time when human mentality was such that belief in an intervening personal God was relevant to human knowledge and power. God is now nudging us on to a higher level of perception and a greater sense of partnership with God. Nurturing faith in our day requires some adjustments in our thinking that are just as radical to us as the teachings of Jesus about moving on from religious law to relationships of love were to the people whom he taught.

First, we need to move from the belief in an all-powerful intervening God to an understanding that when it seems that God intervenes and performs a miracle, God is in fact, expressing his laws of creation in a very normal way for God, but in a way that we do not yet understand. At some point in the future when we have learned enough to understand, we will feel about that specific episode just as we now feel about many "happenings" which once were miraculous to human beings.

Keep in mind that for Jesus, the observing of a mountain one day, and the absence of the mountain at some later date, would have been a miracle. With modern technology and resultant methods, though the job continues to be technically challenging, "mountains" are now being moved without great fanfare. Not only are the mountains being moved, but in some instances, we are covering the areas where the mountains once were with concrete.

The mountain moving analogy is applicable to a host of examples. Included in these examples are such things as: "miraculous" means of communication to most any place on earth; "miraculous" means of transportation to any place on earth; the "miraculous" exploration of space which has only just begun; the miraculous observance of MICRO and MACRO universes at work; organ transplants, genetic engineering, and all related capabilities in the field of healthcare; the ongoing development of computers and the increasing dependence we place on them to think for us and control that which we want controlled; growing knowledge of weather, the natural environment and how human beings need to learn how to better harmonize with both; and a long list of other examples, many of which have not yet become part of our conscious realization.

Second, it is important that we move from a concept of a God who demands obedience to a concept of a God who invites partnership. All partnerships occasionally present the need for apology, change, and forgiveness. It is no different in our partnership with God. God never "screws up," but we do! Primitive faith had its basis in the idea of a God who could do things for us, and that this God could be persuaded to do things for us if we were obedient to his wishes and adored and praised him as we sought to be obedient to his every wish. Now we should understand that a harmonious relationship with God is the highest goal. We should further understand that falling short is part of the learning process. It was Jesus who taught us that God is more willing and eager to forgive us than we are to be remorseful and change our ways.

Contemporary faith should have its roots in the idea that everything has its basis in God, including life. We should understand that human beings cannot be or do anything apart from resources provided by God. We should further understand that it is God's nature to give great gifts, and so we are what we are, and we have unfolding abilities and opportunities as gifts from God. Every wonderful achievement that appears to have come from human wisdom and behavior should be recognized as a joint effort made possible by God, the accomplishment of which brings pleasure to both God and God's partners in human life, i.e., human beings.

Third, we need to make a course correction in our understanding of judgment and punishment. Prevailing religious wisdom suggests that behavior in this life is judged in the future by a "Great God in Heaven," in addition to whatever judgment and punishment we give each other here on earth. While a belief in future judgment may exercise some level of control in human behavior now, it is clear that it is not a sufficient deterrent to wrongdoing. This is a "mountain" which needs to be examined from a different perspective and removed.

It is important that we understand ourselves to also be partners with God in this matter of responding to the imperfections of each other. Human imperfections are "mountains" which need our constant attention. There are reasons for us to become concerned about the possibility that much errant human behavior comes about as a result of what was learned or not learned by human beings in the formative stages of their life. We teach each other and learn from one another. To put it in an exaggerated manner, there is a real possibility that as a human society, we contribute to the making of criminals. This thought is not to depreciate the great need for individual responsibility in the making of all decisions. It is to suggest that, given the strange combination of strengths and weaknesses in human beings, less errant behavior can be expected in maturing human beings who grow up in certain kinds of learning and relational environments. While the final responsibility for behavior rests in the individual, family and society contribute much to the kind of response made by persons influenced by that family and society. The emphasis should be much more on prevention and remedial efforts, while at the same time providing protection for society, than on punishment.

Negative human behavior, i.e., "sin," is therefore a consequence of sorts, which in and of itself brings about other consequences which result in a kind of judgment, i.e., punishment, to human beings individually and collectively.

This happens now and may continue through generations. It is not reserved as a judgment after the end of the world. Isn't it true that we feel some kind of negative consequence every time there is a bank robbery, rape, or death in the electric chair? We feel those things more specifically if we, or those we love, are the ones being robbed, raped, or put to death.

There has been recent concern about the deaths of white rhinos in Africa. Observation has revealed that they were being killed by out-of-control teenage male elephants who had grown up without the influence of older bull elephants who typically "keep them in line." The young elephants were without this older influence as a result of deliberate, but mistaken, human management decisions designed to solve a lesser problem. Those making the decision were without the knowledge at the time that they were creating a new and larger problem than the original.

Consequences are very much a part of "how things are." They do not represent a personal response by a controlling God. They are also an indication of "how things are." They are natural—not supernatural phenomena! We need to understand that and work harder in matters of prevention than we do in matters related to judgment/punishment and remedy. The latter is important. The former is even more important.

The Power of Faith Observed

Faith is nurtured by observing its power in the experience of others, past and present. Regardless of the level of knowledge and the primitive nature of belief in God, the power of faith is evident in the accomplishments of the ancients. We learn about this through the record of Scripture and history. We also observe it in the contemporary lives of those who experience great misfortune but rise above it and experience a meaningful and contributory life in spite of it—sometimes because of it. The idea that some good can always be made to come from any tragedy, regardless of how awful it may be, is at the heart of the genius of Christianity. The death of Jesus was tragic and unnecessary. He and his disciples made some wonderful good come from it.

Faith is nurtured by giving a religious value to all the wonderful things that we count on without recognizing their fundamental importance. We fear premature death but often fail to recognize what a valiant fight the human organism puts up in an effort to permit life to continue. God has placed remarkable healing powers in our body in addition to an immune system designed to give us life over all the enemies that seek to destroy us. We do not expect to bleed to death, for example, from the loss of blood resulting from a cut finger. The blood clots. The wound heals, and we go on as though it had never happened. Observation of such normal happenings which we tend to take for granted indicate how tenacious life is. Growing in that knowledge should be a source of nurturing faith.

Faith is nurtured through a growing knowledge of how much others know and are able to accomplish in their specific specialities of interest. Again, apply this principle to health care. Observe it in the unbelievable physical feats accomplished by athletes and those trained in saving others from danger. Faith is nurtured through observation of what wonderful things we human beings can accomplish through discipline, training, experience, and commitment.

Faith is nurtured by noticing, i.e., seeing, hearing, and experiencing how much more positive evidence there is in the world of God's great power and loving gifts than there is in negatives. Once we come to understand and accept the predominant positive evidence and influence of God in the world, it is easier to nurture faith than it is to diminish it.

Faith is nurtured through doing. Abraham had no assurance he could improve his situation but because he believed that he could and acted on that belief, he did. Moses had no assurance he could get the Jews out of Egypt and back to their promised land, but he believed he could and acted on that belief, and he did. Jesus had no assurance he could convince anyone that the law of love needed to be given a chance, but he acted as though he knew it could happen, and the world has never been the same.

Faith, Muscles, and Power

In the same way that muscles must be exercised if they are to improve, or even be healthy, faith must be exercised if it is to be nurtured and healthy. There needs to be much less religious rhetoric, and much more reverent, respectful, and loving behavior.

It is essential that the "doing" be done in a spirit of reverence, respect, and genuine loving concern for other members of the human family. The more we do in a spirit of reverent thanksgiving to God, in respect for God's handiwork and the good work of others, and with concern and love for the personhood of one another, the stronger our faith will become. With these ingredients, the "mountains" of humanity undoing itself can effectively be chipped away, and more people will experience what Jesus talked about when he spoke of the Kingdom of God on earth.

Given the great and urgent need for the human family to live with itself, the nurturing of a faith that produces a spirit of congeniality and love must be given high priority. Much of the religious rhetoric heard today is misleading, meaningless, and too often offensive. Given the need for human beings to behave as loving members of the same family and the wonderful ways in which the work of God is evident among and within us, there is no reason why meaningful and powerful *God Talk* is not an achievable goal.

Chapter XVIII

Prayer Redefined

It is a wonderful and encouraging thing when prayer is answered in the usual way that we have come to expect positive responses in other areas of life. It is especially encouraging when good things are thus accomplished. Unfortunately, more times than not, this is not true.

I am not suggesting that prayer be disbanded. I am suggesting that we refine the meaning of prayer and thus have a functional and common sense understanding of what is meant by "answered prayer." I am suggesting that prayer needs to be redefined in a manner which makes our expectations of prayer consistent with what we are learning about how God works in the wonderful world in which we have been placed.

Traditional Definitions

The church has traditionally defined prayer in ways that include the two main elements of praise and petition. The praise part is intended to have the functional result of getting God's attention in such a positive way that He will listen closely and respond positively to the petition part. The purpose of praise can range from simply symbolizing a spirit of reverence to an effort to "butter God up" in preparation for a response to the favors we seek. Just think about that for a moment! What kind of God does that suggest?

The functional result of the petition aspect of prayer has assumed that if we are in favor with God and believe that God is all powerful, prayer will so energize God that He will intervene in the usual workings of the world and give us whatever it is we seek.

What we would like, and what would make the traditional definition of prayer more acceptable, is for prayer to work more like the electricity in our homes. Electricity is so dependable that we are surprised when it doesn't work. When we flip the switch we expect that the lights will go on or off, and they typically do. We can count on it! When electricity is not available, we know there is a problem, but we also know that the problem can be fixed. The bulb can be replaced. The source of power can be repaired, and power can be restored.

We would like prayer to be like that, but it isn't. When prayer does work, we are typically so surprised and happy that we go about "singing God's praises" because He is the great "Answerer of prayer." We would also like it better if when prayer doesn't work, we could discover the reason for the malfunction and get it fixed in a way similar to the way electrical malfunctions can be fixed.

What Does "Unanswered" Prayer Indicate about the Person Praying?

Jesus is reported to have said that "everything you ask for in prayer will be yours if you only have faith." (Mark 11:24) The major problem here is that all of us who have ever engaged in prayer, in the spirit of the traditional definition, have had the experience of prayers not being answered. Millions have prayed for their son's safe return from war, and they have not. Millions have prayed for the healing of some terminal disease, and they have died. Millions have prayed for the necessities of life, and they have been denied. While we admittedly have no way of measuring the number of prayers that have been unanswered versus those that have been answered, it is probable that many more have gone unanswered than have been answered.

Does this mean that God does not answer prayer? Does it mean that not many prayers are offered with faith? It really means that there is a need for a new definition of prayer as well as a better understanding of how answers to prayer come about!

Jesus and Prayer

It is also reported that one of the most important prayers Jesus ever prayed in his life was not answered as he wished. It is said that when he prayed in the Garden of Gethsemane the evening before he was crucified, he asked for deliverance from the terrible ordeal which he sensed was before him. We have never been told how the writer knew what he prayed, inasmuch as the three disciples who went with him to the Garden were asleep at the entrance of the Garden as he went on alone and prayed. We are told, however, that his prayer went something like this, "My Father, if it is possible, don't make me suffer by having me drink from this cup. But do what you want, and not what I want."

The fact that Jesus was killed in spite of his prayer has caused the church to assume that God wanted him to die. Could the real reason have been that Jesus did not have enough faith? That would have been consistent with what we are told about his own recipe for successful prayer. Could it be that the understanding which Jesus had of the petition aspect of prayer, and the later teachings of the church about prayer, fail to represent the way God actually works?

It should be noted and not overlooked that the Jesus story indicates that Jesus made a marvelous response to this unanswered prayer. He rationalized the reason for his prayer being unanswered, "sucked it up," and made good come from a very tragic situation.

This description of the prayer of Jesus for the saving of his life is not a negative statement about Jesus. It is also not intended to be a negative statement about the early church. Neither Jesus nor the early church had any way of knowing better. What they believed was common sense to them. We should know better! We should also feel a sense of responsibility to make an adjustment in the definition of prayer. Unless we do, the typical approach to prayer is a negative statement about the contemporary church. The church ought to be teaching from the perspective of what is being learned about how God works. It is clear that God does not work by intervening as a result of praise and petition! When it seems that this approach has worked, it is clearly an exception rather than the general rule. Sometimes it is the result of an outright falsehood.

The fact that prayer has not produced the desired results for millions does not mean that prayer should be abandoned. It does mean that prayer should be understood differently than in the past. Why settle for "make believe" when a defensible and encouraging understanding is available to us? Perceived answers to prayer and the evident way God works should be in perfect harmony.

The typical and traditional explanations of why prayer does not "work" when it doesn't work are not adequate. It does not suffice to say that faith was insufficient, the one praying is a "bad" person, or that God answers "no." In relation to the statement of Jesus about prayer and believing, i.e., faith, one might conclude that a lack of faith is in fact the reason for unanswered prayer. Is this the reason Jesus died when he asked to be spared? We tend to think of Jesus as a person of great faith! This certainly isn't the reason the church has given. In fact, the unwillingness of the early church to use that kind of reasoning resulted in the development of a primitive theology quite different from the perception Jesus had of God as "Heavenly Father." It is a theology which requires a God who expresses his vengeance on people whose behavior or belief system is not according to His wishes. It is a theology that ties in neatly with the primitive Old Testament idea of God's need for sacrifice. It also provided the early church with an explanation of why the "Son of God" could be killed when he showed such promise as the promised Messiah. This theological explanation continues, to this day, to be the central theme of Christian theology. The fact that it is in direct contrast to the idea which Jesus taught of God as a loving parent, and that it has not presented an insurmountable stumbling block, is interesting to say the least.

Notwithstanding the great importance of a positive attitude, i.e., faith, and of the proper belief system, one is hard pressed to suggest that the prayer of Jesus was not answered because Jesus had a lack of faith, or in any other way, was displeasing to God. It is not unusual, however, when prayer is not answered for the assumption to be made that faith is inadequate, that there is something very wrong in the life of the one who is praying, or that God controls every life and has other plans or objectives for that person.

We should also lay to one side another simple but superficial explanation for unanswered prayer which states that sometimes God answers "no." This idea is consistent with the "God as parent" concept, because parents often need to say "no" to children on the basis of their superior knowledge of what is best for the child. Saying "no" thus becomes part of the parental training process and the children's learning process. While one can certainly make a metaphorical case for explaining unanswered prayer in this manner, it is not really very satisfying to know that God may arbitrarily deny our requests for reasons that are "good for us," but which we do not understand.

What Do We Know Today about How God Works That Jesus Didn't Know?

What have we learned in the two-thousand year period between the time of Jesus and today about how God works?

Consider the weather. We have learned that Jesus was right when he said that the rain falls on the just and the unjust. Even Jesus knew that God does not intervene in nature in order to punish the "bad" and reward the righteous. We have learned about "highs" and "lows." We have learned about "fronts." We have learned about "el niño" and "la niña." We have learned about twisters, hurricanes, clockwise and counter clockwise winds. We have learned about inversions, pollution of the air, and holes in the ozone layer. We have learned that the earth is round and that there is an equator. We have learned that when folks in the Northern hemisphere are having winter, the folks in the Southern hemisphere are having summer. We have also learned why these things are true. We have learned much more, and we realize that there remains much more to be learned about the weather. On the basis of what we have learned, we are now able to predict weather at given times and places in a manner that is very helpful though imperfect. Isn't it wonderful that God has provided the resources whereby we can learn these wonderful things about how this small portion of what God does works!

Surely all educated and sensible people have learned that God does not control the weather by whim and that praying about the weather is not going to change it. We learned during the dust bowl days of the 1930's that prayer does not change the weather and that we do well to learn how to irrigate from wells, rivers, and water storage resources during the periods when rain does not fall from the heavens. These facts about the weather ought to teach us, beyond doubt, that God does not work the way people used to think before knowledge enabled us to know better. Furthermore it indicates that God does not intervene in nature to satisfy human petitions.

Consider human health. I presume that no more prayers have been offered about any specific subject than have been offered about health. It is as clear today as it was centuries ago that a positive outlook, i.e., faith, is important to health and that faith provides wonderful assistance to whatever other legitimate treatment may be engaged for recovery from illness. The broad use of placebos in the testing of certain medicines, and the level of positive results from the placebo as compared to the medicine is testimony to the fact that faith is often all that is needed. Faith is important in releasing the healing powers of our bodies and minds! The fact that so many people do not recover from illness even though much prayer in faith has been offered indicates, however, that praying with faith is not enough. The fact that many people do not recover with the combination of prayer, faith, and good treatment also indicates that the best combination of treatment we know about sometimes is not sufficient to restore health.

The early church was so sure that faith and prayer were the answer to all health problems that the author of James indicated that the prayer of faith would save the sick. Some New Testament writers also believed that faith was sufficient to neutralize the effects of viper bites. Paul was believed to be a god by some of the locals of Malta because when a viper clung to his hand he shook it off unharmed. In their own misguided ways, there are religious groups today who handle poisonous snakes as testimony to their great faith. Some of them die.

In a redefinition of prayer, the whole idea of the great conflict between science and religion is discarded. Without changing the best techniques and intentions involved in science, it should come to be viewed as a religious endeavor. Without God's work, science has no objects of inquiry. Science ought therefore to be viewed as an effort on the part of human beings to learn more about how God does what God does.

As more is learned about God's creation, we are discovering that we are better able to utilize what we learn as a means of improving the quality of life for God's human children. Consider the matter of weather! Consider the matter of health care! Consider genetic engineering! Consider all applications of technology! Consider space exploration! Consider everything we have learned to this point and will learn in the future!

Prayer Redefined—Harmonizing with God

We have all seen the small child walk in the footsteps of an adult mimicking what the child perceives the adult to be doing. That is the way life ought to be for adult human beings in relation to God. Among the joys, challenges, opportunities, and purposes of life is that we walk in the footsteps of God and learn increasingly about the wonderful and awesome things that God is about. All of this, i.e., all of life, also carries with it major responsibilities.

In brief, an appropriate redefinition of prayer means that we work at bringing ourselves into a spirit and expression of life that is increasingly harmonious with the spirit and work of

God. This does not call for long, pious prayers to be heard by others in church or in the restaurant. Could it be that Jesus had a "grip" on this, and that is the reason he taught that praying should be done in the closet?

The greater the harmony between our spirit and the way we express our life, with the spirit and expressions of God, the more effective our prayers will be. Whatever we do that looks or sounds like prayer in the traditional definition should not have the goal of either petitioning or manipulating God. It should have the goal of bringing us more into harmony with the spirit and expressions of God. This kind of prayer is not only reasonable in relation to what we know about how God works, but it tends to prevent us from becoming over concerned and frustrated if we are unable to meet some kind of personal goal.

Does this mean meditation? Could be! Does this mean time alone with someone we love in silent, verbal, or active communion? Could be! Does this mean time in the mountains, or by the ocean, or helping cows calve, or being inspired by the twinkle in the eye of the very young or the very old? Could be! Does this mean being a "big brother" or a "big sister?" Could be! Does this mean getting so "carried away" in whatever it is we do to make a living or as a hobby that we forget the time and find full enjoyment in whatever positive endeavor we are engaged? Could be! Does this mean that when we come to the later years of life and are, as we call it, "retired," that joy is found in positive memories of the past and that such faith is inspired in the God who made us that there is no fear or dread of the future? Could be!

Does this mean that as we learn more about cooperating with the weather, responding to human health needs, tinkering with technology, engineering the genes, exploring the unknowns of space, or whatever else it is that we do by way of learning from and about God in order to express our lives more harmoniously with his spirit and ways, that this is prayer? Certainly it can be said that this is part of the most important kind of praying in the world.

Traditional prayer is primarily rhetoric. Prayer redefined is primarily behavior and accomplishment!

The other side of prayer is what happens on the inside of us that affects our perception of self, opportunity, God, and our relationship with self, God, others, and opportunities. Do I need to know about your prayer life? No! What one does in the closet is not the business of others. That aspect of prayer which is in the closet—or by the ocean—or on the mountain—or by the brook—or with someone we love—or in public or private worship—or with a book—should be appreciated as an experience which has the potential of bringing one more into harmony with the spirit and ways of God.

Infinite Possibilities of our Participation in "Answered Prayer"

When prayer is defined in this way, it becomes clear that as time is infinite and as space is infinite, the possibilities of prayer are also infinite.

One cannot participate in prayer, by this definition, without a growing sense of awe, and appreciation for, the fact and work of God. How humbling! How challenging! How wonderful!

Within the boundaries of this definition wonderful happenings occur. Life is lived on the high plain of a humble but reverent spirit. The "glasses" though which the human family views life become an image of optimism rather than pessimism.

International and interpersonal relationships improve and move increasingly toward the respect, concern for, and love mode.

Human health is improved both in terms of the prevention of unnecessary deterioration and remedial care.

Natural "disasters" which are important in the general scheme of nature become disasters for human beings on a decreasing scale of negative impact. We learn increasingly better ways of predicting, protecting ourselves from, and living with such disasters.

The human family assumes responsibility for controlling the population without overtaxing the resources of our earth home.

Sexuality is viewed as a sacred gift with wonderful powers of intimacy, self perpetuation, and joy.

Persons challenged in ways that were traditionally known as handicapped are empowered to find pleasure in life and make worthy contributions to it.

The level of personal and corporate responsibility increases, and the dangers of negative utilization of the power that comes from knowledge decreases.

The poor are empowered to become productive participants in life rather than slaves of the rich in their own ghetto.

All new powers such as communication, genetic engineering, space exploration, 2nd repair and replacement of body parts are recognized as having tremendous potential for either good or bad, and are thus utilized with the greatest responsibility.

Aren't all of these things, and more, what we typically pray for? Prayer, under the umbrella of this definition, literally changes things! Prayer, under the umbrella of this definition, changes the perception of life! Prayer, under this definition, increases motivation for good! Prayer, under this definition, moves beyond the arena of religious rhetoric and clearly indicates the experience of human life as one of partnership with God, certainly in time, and perhaps for eternity. Praying for others, under this definition, is not a way of "ganging up on God," but plants and affirms good thoughts about others, and creates of sense of family which brings a sense of comfort and causes persons to feel less alone in a time of need.

Our growing understanding of "the nature of things" lends little support to concepts of God which make petitioning a personality functional. On the other hand, growth in harmonizing with an understanding of God which comes from observing God's love and creative powers through and among us nurtures personal growth and makes great sense in relation to our functional understanding of "how things are."

Chapter XIX

Christ Among Us

Methods By Which Jesus Taught

One can become so enamored with the perceived need to protect certain symbols, rituals, and beliefs that the intent of the whole is not clearly understood. On the other hand, it is possible to paint with such a broad religious brush that the detail of that which gives power to a specific experience and expression of religion is not recognized. It is a bit like the forest and the trees. If one sees the forest only from the inside, the variety of conditions found among individual trees is a picture of both beauty and ugly. One misses the awesome beauty and splendor that can be witnessed from a distance. On the other hand, the realism of the forest is not experienced if one does not view it "up close and personal" as well as from a distance.

Jesus taught many things by words. The "Sermon on the Mount" is a splendid example of how he taught by words. The parables attributed to him in the Gospels are great examples of how he taught with words in a story form which often touched the emotions as well as the mind. How, for example, can one not be touched emotionally by the impact of a story like that of the prodigal son? After inexcusable foolishness, he is eagerly welcomed back into the family because of the unconditional love of parents who, in their heart, had never given up on him in spite of the arrogant rejection evident in his departure?

Understanding Jesus

The New Testament is composed largely of an elaboration of the word teachings of Jesus. These teachings were aug-

mented by the writers, with a theological interpretation of who
Jesus was, that is not necessarily supportive of what Jesus
taught, either in word or by his attitudinal and behavioral example. In other words, things were added which Jesus did not
or would not have said.

Jesus, for example, did not emphasize the importance of his
person and work in the same way that both came to be emphasized by the early church. It was the interpretation of those who
professed discipleship after his death that transformed him into
a sacrifice designed to take away the sins of the world. It was
the interpretation of the early church that transformed him into
the only access to the Creator of the human family and the
world. It was the early church that transformed the disciples of
Jesus into an exclusive and arrogant group that could envision
hope for the world, but only on their terms, i.e., believing in Jesus as they believed in him.

It is clear that the time came, shortly after the death of Jesus,
that what he had taught by word and example did not convey
the same weight of importance as the interpretation of his
teachings by the early church. Jesus was a universalist who
could communicate with, and feel for, the Samaritans, the Jews,
and Gentiles. Color of skin, cultural background or economic
class did not prevent him from viewing everyone as human—as one who could behave as a child of God. The church
was so determined to transform Jesus into a sacrifice for the sins
of the world that it found it difficult to hear anything else.

One misses the most important message of the Gospels if
only the individual "word" teachings of Jesus are noticed. This
is especially true as his message came from those who interpreted him after his death. One misses the most important message of the Gospels if one views the Jesus phenomenon either
only from a distance or "up close and personal." Both are important in the formulation of a religious system of beliefs based
on who Jesus was and what he taught by word and example.

The chasm of religious belief which separates persons,
sometimes in the same family, is not at all unusual. Throughout
the recorded history of the world families have been torn asun-
der, persons have hated one another, and wars have been

acclamations of those who followed and went before were encouraging and wonderful. By the end of the week, he had been frightened, challenged, physically and psychologically abused, spit on, rejected, abandoned, betrayed, lied about, and finally crucified to death. That is suffering — real suffering!

His response to what either he would not or could not change is both instructive and inspirational. Hopefully none of us will ever have to endure the intensity of the suffering he endured. It is desirable that we never have to endure any severe suffering for a long period of time. But in the event that we do, we need to receive both instruction and strength from the example left us by those who told the Jesus story.

Jesus found the options which were available for preventing the suffering that was clearly before him to be unacceptable. Given this, he was then faced with two alternate options. The most obvious would seem to have been the most natural. He could whimper and whine about the unfairness of life and of God, a process that would cause him to die a bitter and defeated person. The second option was the most difficult but most rewarding for him and for others who would choose to embrace his philosophy of life. He could endeavor to find some way of making good come from this terrible ordeal.

It is clearly the second option that Jesus chose, and the world has never been the same as a result of his choice.

The Jesus story clearly teaches that he believed God was with him, and within him, both in pleasant times and during times of suffering. It was this belief that made it possible for him to accept the suffering with an effort to make some good come from it.

You and I have the same need, right, and reason, to embrace the same assurance as that which enabled Jesus. God is available, both when his children suffer and when they do not. The nature of "things as they are" does not provide for miraculous intervention by God. Such availability can point us to enabling resources which may bring about change which disarms our fears. Without change it may also provide strength which enables us to deal with whatever it is that threatens in a constructive manner.

Chapter XXII

Life, Time, and Immortality

L ife is a wonderful gift. In the best of circumstances, we would like for it to go on forever. In the worst of circumstances, we would like it to end quickly.

A Primary Purpose of Religion

A primary objective of religion, and especially in the Judeo-Christian tradition, has been that of making life so good that one would want it to go on forever. Recognizing the inevitability of death, however, the goals have included the assurance that after death, life will continue forever without any of the elements that diminished its joy "the first time around."

The Old Testament author of Ecclesiastes preached the importance of enjoying life from beginning to end, but always with the realization that every behavior has its consequences, good or bad.

The Easter story has been one of hope in the tradition of Christians. One can imagine a group of disciples who were so totally devastated by the brutal murder of their leader and friend, that, irrational as it seemed, Mary Magdalene and others went to the tomb early on Sunday morning just to see if by some chance, it had all been a bad dream and Jesus was, in fact, still alive.

During the darkest days of persecution for the early church, life was made absolutely uncertain and miserable by those who sought to destroy the Christian movement. Christians needed to be guilty of nothing more than their religious profession and their life was endangered. It is the nature of life, however, to work hard at surviving, whether in the face of threats from our own kind, or in the face of disease. Consciously and biologically it is our nature to attempt to survive. That is the reason we have an immune system. It is therefore no surprise to know that, under the continual threat of death, Christians became very creative and found ways, including an attitudinal joy in martyrdom, to find a reason for hope.

Given the obvious fact that the Christians could not prevail against their persecutors, the deep desire for life to continue in some acceptable fashion nudged their attention toward a hope in immortality. In their minds, and harmonious with what they had been taught by Jesus, it simply didn't make sense to them that God would grant the wonderful gift of life only to have it snuffed out at an early age by someone who didn't agree with their religious beliefs and hopes. With this kind of hope and the real threat of death at any time, an emphasis on a reality of immortality "bubbled to the top" of their belief system.

The New Testament Book of Revelation is a hopeful religious response of faith to the inevitability of persecution and martyrdom at the hand of a ruthless enemy. "God's home is now with his people," says the author, and God "…will wipe all tears from their eyes, and there will be no more death, suffering, crying, or pain. These things of the past are gone forever." That is the hope of Heaven! That is the "stuff" of immortality which became associated with the central theme of early Christianity and prevails to this day. What was the central theme? Very early, the heart of the Christian message came to be that Jesus was unjustly crucified and slain, but that he rose from the dead the third day and after forty days ascended up into heaven to dwell with God eternally. Furthermore it was believed that this was the plan of God. The reasonable rationale then became that if God willed resurrection and immortality for Jesus, God also wills resurrection and immortality for those who commit their lives to him, i.e., to his friends.

242

A Physical Resurrection?

When one considers the likelihood of the physical resurrection of Jesus, apart from a hopeful faith typically associated with a belief system that is imparted to the human mind in a Christian culture at an early age, it is slim indeed. The physical resurrection of Jesus is unlikely because it is contrary to that which we observe about the nature of life, not occasionally, but billions of times and over a period of thousands of years. Regardless of how much we might think we want physical resurrections to occur, when physical death is established, the evidence is quite clear that it is not reversible. Furthermore, if physical resurrections became the norm, or even occasional, a host of problems would arise that have not yet been conceived.

If one would argue against the resurrection on the basis of the power of God to accomplish such a feat, however, that argument would be feeble. For the "author" of everything which we are coming to learn about the universe, resurrecting a physical body from death back to life would probably be no big deal. The more we learn about the universe and the life contained in it, the more complex and wonderful we recognize it to be. The author of creation must surely be capable of rebuilding what he has already built! A Creator who can create something as awesome and complex as the human body, and impart, as though from nothing and nowhere, a spirit that makes the human being different from all other animal creatures, though there may be physical similarities in the make-up of their bodies, can surely re-create a new and wonderful body from an old, worn out, or devastated body, if he were to choose to do so. It is not so much a matter of power and ability as it is a matter of "modus operandi." The matter of the physical resurrection really has nothing to do with the power of God. The power is ample. It does have to do with the way God works.

The problem with the argument for a physical resurrection is that the more we learn about the universe and the dynamic creativity which is occurring within it, the more impressed we are with the rhyme and reason that is part of it. Apart from demonstrating the wonderful power of God, and we don't need that kind of proof today, there is no need for either the crucifixion or the physical resurrection of Jesus. Jesus didn't "stick around" to help his disciples through the trauma of persecution. He did not assume a physical role of leadership that would protect the world and human family from the chaotic condition that much of it has been in all of human history. In other words, there is much more common sense evidence to support the idea that Jesus was not physically raised from the dead than there is to support the idea that he physically walked out of the tomb. Belief in the physical resurrection of Jesus can only be based on an irrational faith, weakly supported hope, and/or a sense of obligation to ancient beliefs of our religious culture. Such a belief, however, did put Christianity on the same power level as some other religions with which it was in competition in the beginning.

A Spiritual Resurrection!

If, however, one examines the resurrection of Jesus from a spiritual perspective, confirmation and support of that belief is readily available. The accomplishment of those early and weak disciples who were paralyzed from the trauma and nature of his death is absolutely amazing. What they believed and were willing to give their lives for as martyrs eventually brought their movement to a point where it prevailed over the mighty Roman Empire. Christianity, the religion hated and feared by the Romans after the death of Jesus, came to be embraced as the official religion of the empire. If history didn't testify to the truth of that reality, it would be hard to believe.

The spiritual resurrection of Jesus was so powerful and evident in the lives of the early disciples and in the lives of millions since that time that the world has had no choice but to take notice. In some ways much of the world has made adjustments to accommodate some beliefs which have to do with behavior and philosophy of life, to this "risen spirit" as demonstrated through the lives of human beings, past and since.

Take the churches out of the world for the past two thousand years and what do you have? On the negative side, you don't have religious wars with Christians attempting to kill those who believe differently from them. You don't have the Crusades. You don't have Muslims seeking to kill Christians or Christians seeking to kill Muslims. Who can imagine anything more disgusting and contrary to the spirit and teachings of Jesus than the Children's Crusade of 1212 A.D.! You don't have the ethnic cleansing which occurred in the Balkans near the end of the twentieth century. You don't have the conflict between Catholics and Protestants in Ireland. You don't have priests sexually exploiting children. You don't have ministers who bring disgrace to the human family and to their religious faith with their sexual exploitation of those who trust them. You don't have the church in the middle ages, or in isolated places in the world today, exploiting the poor in order to build giant cathedrals or provide lives of wealth for those in power.

On the positive side you don't have the institutions of learning, the hospitals, educational institutions and a whole host of humanitarian endeavors which have come to be so important and taken for granted in a culture that is heavily influenced by the Judeo-Christian religions. You don't have the countless millions who, after having reached a point of despair in life, have found a source of hope. There is no doubt that in spite of the negative "gifts" given to the world by the church, i.e., by those who have professed spiritual rebirth through faith in Jesus, the positive "gifts" far outweigh the negative. Our world is much better because of the spiritual resurrection. This in spite of all the evil that sometimes comes from hypocrisy and a convenient but weak and sometimes misleading belief system.

The world has been changed and, on balance, changed for the better because of the spiritual resurrection of Jesus.

Immortality?

What does this say about immortality? If one looks to the example of Jesus, and the impact of his brief life and ministry in the world, one must conclude that there is no basis of support for a belief in the physical resurrection of Jesus. The message of Jesus, as it comes to us, was one which recognized the value of the physical, but which emphasized spiritual values as far superior. One must also conclude that there is endless evidence of the spiritual impact which his life and ministry has had on millions of persons for the past two thousand years. Immortality needs to be viewed from a perspective other than the resurrection and reformulation of a physical body — either that of Jesus or our own.

If the immortality of Jesus is evident through his contribution to the spirit of human beings who lived after him, not just into the next generation, but in a continuing and evident manner two-thousand years later, is it not reasonable to apply that same kind of thinking to one kind of immortality for us?

One kind of immortality is indicated through the impact which human life has after that life has ceased physical existence. It is shown through the children, generation after generation. It is shown through the development of humanitarian institutions which exemplify a fulfillment of the admonition of Jesus to love one another. It is shown through the memory of persons and accomplishments that are carried from one generation to another. It is shown through whatever way an individual leaves the world a bit better when death comes than would have been true had that person never lived.

Wonderful as this kind of immortality is, it seems to have a "shelf-life." That is to say that, as good as that which an individual leaves to the world may be, it will one day be superseded by that which is deemed to be better. And that is the way life ought to be. Goodness should build on goodness from one generation to another and that in itself should perpetuate a kind of immortality which grows in quality.

While this kind of immortality makes sense and has good "rhyme and reason," the personal satisfaction which we derive from it is somewhat limited. We are glad to give good things to others in perpetuity, but we would also like an ongoing and endless hope for satisfaction ourselves.

There is a kind of immortality that occurs through our biological creation of children. Our growing knowledge in the area of genetics supports the idea of a kind of immortality in which we participate as we create babies from one generation to the next. This kind of immortality, however, is not particularly rewarding for those, who for whatever reason, do not experience the joy and responsibilities of parenthood.

Akin to genetic immortality carried on from generation to generation is the spiritual immortality of character. The absence of promoting one's biological immortality does not negate the importance of the immortality of influence. A goal of each human being, with or without the experience of parenthood, should be that of being a positive and growing influence on the young, both through the sharing of information, and especially through an exemplary spirit.

This thing called life is a mystery. Its beginning for any human being is the greatest example of a creative miracle. There is no egg, but from the dust of the earth comes the resources for the formation of an egg which holds part of the potential for new life! There is no sperm, but from the dust of the earth comes resources for the formation of sperm which holds the key to the beginning of new life from the egg! All sperm, no life! All eggs, no life! Join the two, and life for a specific person begins!

In the beginning the results of the union of egg and sperm seem to be little more than a "glob" of something, but with time it takes form and becomes a human body with a complexity that causes us to increasingly marvel as we learn more about it. But at some point a process begins which is just as miraculous, and without which the "glob" would continue to be just that—a glob. That body, however, grows and becomes a physical entity which experiences and expresses a spirit. The spirit is unseen and not measurable, but the impact on the behavior and potential of the body is tremendous.

And then one day, for a variety of reasons, and after a variety of lengths of time, the body dies and returns to the dust from which its original resources came. The spirit is like a flame on a candle. Once it was! Now it isn't! When it is no more, where does it go and, even more basic, what was its essence?

Trust and Time

These are questions for which we human beings lack the capacity to find satisfactory answers. Whatever answers we may believe to have rhyme and reason must be embraced by faith. Faith is sometimes right. Faith is sometimes wrong. Faith, in full bloom, translates into trust and is related to time. Neither faith nor trust is required in order to believe in that which is presently and clearly evident. Neither faith nor trust is required to believe in that which has clearly been reality in the past. It is the future of time that tends to create a problem for us. Can we count on God to be as wonderful, loving and creative in the future as we have come to understand an expression of his nature to be from the past and present?

Trust is related to time. Trust is not dependent on time that is past, or on time that is present. Trust is only of value when it is related to the future element of time. But what is time? It is measured in micro-seconds, seconds, minutes, hours, days, weeks, months, years, centuries, and millennia. But what is it? Time is and is no more. What is the difference in time and eternity? Is the experience of time in this moment different from what the experience of time might be one year, fifty years, and one hundred thousand years from now?

The response to these kinds of questions ought to lead us to a more complete understanding and acceptance of the great value of life in this moment. Right now is the same as eternity. The moment of life and opportunity which we experience now is no different than was true for a moment of life and opportunity two-thousand years ago. The moment of life and opportunity which we experience now is no different than it will be two-thousand or a million years in the future. This moment— this very moment— is part of eternity and as such is also part of our immortality. We should treat it as such! Life, time, and immortality!

If this time in which we now experience life is not utilized in a positive and productive manner, why do we long for immortality, i.e., life forever? On the other hand, if this time which is now ours to do something with is utilized in a positive and productive manner, is it not reasonable to suppose that there is an ongoing nature of life. Is there a kind of immortality, which is different from, and which provides greater personal satisfaction on our "wish list," than the kinds of immortality which do not involve the continuance of a specific personality? It is at this point that trust, as a product of faith, which ought to be a product of healthy religion, becomes extremely important to our view of the future and our experience of the present.

What We Think We Want

What most of us who insist on a belief in the immortality of the body and spirit really want is a continuance of life pretty much as we know it, in a loving and secure environment without the tears, suffering, stress, and finiteness of our present experience. In other words, we think God had a good idea. We would just like to see him improve on it a bit!

It was this desire by the persecuted Christians in the early church that brought forth the New Testament Book of Revelation. Not only did they want God to improve a bit on life in immortality, but they also wanted God, on their behalf, to get even with those who persecuted them. In other words, they wanted retribution for their enemies and reward for themselves. Given what they went through and the ability of human beings to be either extremely loving or extremely hateful, that may not seem like a bad idea. The Book of Revelation should not be viewed as a prediction of the future. It should be viewed as a wish list for a people who were being persecuted beyond imagination. They wished for the wicked and evil people who persecuted them just what it would seem they deserved, and just what the Book of Revelation promised them, i.e., an eternal hell where they would burn in a lake of fire and brimstone forever. They wished for themselves an eternal experience of heaven in the presence of God who would wipe away all tears from their eyes and in whose presence there would be no more death, suffering, crying, or pain.

Can you blame them? Can you blame us? What they wanted and what we really want is an eternal experience of living life with all the good things and none of the bad? Is it possible for life to be lived by the entire human family with this kind of experience? Can the human family live together, without bringing suffering upon themselves and one another? Logically it would seem the answer is "yes." Functionally, we give no indication that as a family we are willing to love one another sufficiently to bring this experience to reality.

If we can't experience all good in this life, then why not hope for it in the future? What we hope for and believe in, in relation to immortality, is of no negative consequence as long as it does not impact our expression of life now. That is to say that we should always hold the idealistic dream before us in this life, for this life. If twenty-five people can live together in love, why can't several billion? They can, but will they?

A major purpose in our life in the "here and now" must be viewed as the making of life better than it now is. That is what Jesus endeavored to do. That is our task. In many areas we have made wonderful progress. In some areas we continue to be dismal failures.

What we do know is that "this too shall pass." Each of us, and everyone we love, will, at some moment in time, die. What we really want is to be reunited with them one day in an environment of love, absolute fulfillment, with no suffering—forever. That is what we want. Some translate and detail that into a "happy hunting ground," or "a city whose streets are paved with gold," or "sitting at God's feet and enjoying the bliss of wonderful music forever."

I repeat, we should feel free to embrace whatever "wish list" of beliefs we choose, as long as it does not diminish or detract from what ought to be the primary purpose of our life. That goal should be the making of life in this world a bit better because we passed through it.

But what about the future? A goal of religion ought to be the nurturing of a level of trust in our Creator that there is neither paralyzing fear nor anticipation of destruction in the future. In other words, we have freedom to believe what we will about heaven or hell, but it is important that we not let those beliefs impact our attitude and behavior in this life.

The gift of a healthy religion that relates to life fully should be an evolving trust in our Creator. Greater faith is required — that is to say a more complete trust is required in God — to not know the future than to believe we know it. If we trust the one who has made the past and present possible, we need have no fear of the future. The opportunities for creativity, love, and meaningful experiences in this life are absolutely wonderful.

Trust in our Creator will not demand knowledge of specifics. It will not fear the future after physical death. It will not fear those factors in the future in which we have no input, nor over which we have control. It is no more necessary for us to know about immortality after physical death than it was for us to know about this part of immortality before our physical birth.

A Personal Message of Resurrection

Inasmuch as we have good reason, in trust, to commit our future after death into the hands of our Creator, we can therefore commit all our resources to making that part of immortality which we now experience, the very best that it can be. A wonderful lesson which we can each appropriate to ourselves, and which ought to come from a healthy religion, is that of personal new beginnings. We each fall short in some manner. We can be better than we are. We can be better stewards of what we have than we have been. We need new beginnings, again, and again, and again! Such new beginnings can result from benefitting from both our mistakes and successes of the past.

The symbolism of a healthy religion speaks of another opportunity, a new beginning, and a more hopeful and helpful life. It speaks of new life coming from death. Life does come from death all about us in the physical world. Plant life dies and becomes nourishment for seeds of new life. Salmon die after they have braved the adversity of swimming upstream and have spawned their eggs for the production of new life. Evidence is now coming to us that even in "outer space" there is the dying of the old and the birth of new galaxies.

The message of a healthy religion is not confined to a few who believe special things. Though it may come in different packages, it is a message needed and available for all. It is a message directed to all of God's created children who will hear it. It is a wonderful message for everyone to hear. It is a message of hope, trust, and immortality. It is a message to be embraced by each of us as we seek to make the most of the wonderful gift of life which is now ours.

Chapter XXIII

The Challenge of Choices—Theological

A mong the great benefits of being a child is that, compared to the demands made on adults, the need for children to make choices is quite minimal. This is true until as early as one year when they learn to manipulate their parents. Much of what appears to be the making of choices is actually an instinctive response. As age increases toward independence and adulthood, family and societal law and the making of choices in response to "law" become important factors. Most children learn the relative values of reward and denial at an early age. For an obedient child with a strong urge to please, life is quite simplistic until the pressures for alternate decisions, from outside the family circle, become reality.

For the very young, the following of one's instincts and obedience to the dictates of mom and dad keeps life quite simple. When one reaches an age of maturity where general issues of right and wrong are often related to God, many choices then become theological issues. When law is clear and the urge to please is strong, life is simple. When a "law" is questionable or questioned, and there is a need felt for alternate kinds of choices, life becomes more complex.

A child who strives early for independence adds complexity to life. This complexity is forced on both the child and its parents as a result of challenging the "law" of mom and dad. If, however, each generation was obedient without testing or questioning the law, and if each generation was satisfied to think only the same thoughts and make the same choices as their parents, progress would not occur.

Social Complexity and the Challenge of Choices

This analogy is also valid for adults in relation to the complexity of human society. When a given geographical area is sparsely populated, both the need for law and the pressure for making independent decisions that have to do with others is minimal. There is, for example, an agreement on which part of the fence indicating boundaries of property ownership will be maintained by whom. As long as the fence is kept in good condition and a reasonable effort is made by each owner to keep interests and activities within boundaries of ownership, law and decisions related to such concerns are not necessary.

In a simple society the Ten Commandments are quite sufficient. In a primitive society if everyone has reverence for God and seeks to treat others as they wish to be treated, the need to make many complex decisions, which are so important in modern society, does not exist. As the complexity of society increases there is a proportionate need for the making of decisions, by each individual, that keeps the interests of others in mind. The greater the numbers of human beings become, the greater the need will be for either understanding and cooperation or a profusion of laws.

Persons in simple or primitive societies did not need to make decisions related to many of our modern day concerns. They did not need to make decisions related to the internal combustion engine and its impact on the environment. Because there were not many of either people or cattle, they didn't even need to raise the issue of whether or not the methane released by cattle was sufficient to threaten the environment. In a simple human society, nature was able and permitted to take care of itself.

Although there are "pockets" on the face of the earth where a specific segment of society remains quite simple, in general we must think of the human family of today as being a global society. Not only is it global, but the present need for networking increases its complexity. Decisions made by any part of human society may impact the whole in some manner.

In modern society, change is occurring at such a rapid pace that it is not difficult for persons to encroach on one another without realizing it. care in making choices must also be exercised for example, lest the environment which supports all animal and plant life be threatened.

The Challenge of Choices in our Contemporary World Is Awesome

Just consider the magnitude of challenges in the world of today, many of which demand that we human beings make decisions. In some cases, not making a decision is in itself making a decision which may have far reaching results!

Today we are challenged with decisions related to such issues as the following: to clone or not to clone; to prevent conception or impregnate artificially; to initiate fertility outside the natural processes thus permitting couples to experience parenthood who otherwise would not, or deny them parenthood; to participate in the procedure of selective reduction, or permit human beings to give birth to "litters"; to build atomic, neutron, or biological weapons or run the risk of other nations having such destructive power at their disposal before we do; whether to "pull the plug or not pull the plug" in relation to our own longevity or that of a loved one; to permit euthanasia under any circumstances; or whether to resist ethnic cleansing. These are only serious examples of a much longer list of challenges related to choices to which we, as a human family, must respond.

The list is long! It is so long that not one of us as individuals comprehends its magnitude. Many are decisions which affect us, and we don't know it. Many are decisions which others must make for us because our knowledge or power of decision does not extend sufficiently in that specific realm. Of interest and concern to us all is the fact that the list does not shrink. In fact, as knowledge and power available to the human family increases, the list demanding the making of choices increases at a rate that is alarming.

These decisions are not only often associated with matters of morality, i.e., right and wrong, but they are matters which are associated with life and death. They have to do with the quality of life we insist on for ourselves and are willing to permit in the experience of others. They have to do with what is at the heart of moral, practical, and religious concern! They are theological issues!

The Need for Theological Beliefs to Evolve— A Matter of Choice

It should therefore not be surprising that we are faced with decisions concerning theological beliefs. Some sciences are known as exact sciences. In an exact science, the same procedure can be repeated again and again with dependable and predictable results. Human beings are not that predictable. Our knowledge about God is not complete. Theology has to do with an understanding of God, human beings, the relationship between the two and all possible spin-offs from that relationship. In the broad sense, theology thus encompasses the totality of life. In the narrow sense it deals with a specific belief system which then impacts responses to all areas of life.

Theology is one area where it may seem that we can either put off the making of decisions or simply ignore the need indefinitely. Does it really make any difference to us in this day whether or not the Trinitarian doctrine for defining God is factual or symbolic? The answer is "yes." Regardless of what we believe, God is what God is, and human beings are what human beings are! In fact, however, perception is often as powerful as truth. This is true even though perception may be wrong.

In other words, what we really believe about God and what we really believe about human beings make a tremendous difference in the quality of, and potential for, life. It makes a difference because if we really believe something, we behave in a manner different from what we otherwise might, whether or not our belief is defensible.

As is true in all other areas where the making of decisions is critical, sooner or later there is a reward to receive or a price to pay for what we believe. As my mother used to say, sooner or later "the chickens will come home to roost."

The relationship of what we believe theologically, that is to say, about God, human beings, and the potential relationship between the two, is directly related to decision making. In an exact science a decision can be made on the basis of our desire for a predictable outcome. We make a decision to plant and nurture a garden, for example, which is based on our desire to raise vegetables, which in turn may be based on our instinctive appetite for fresh vegetables. If all necessary ingredients are present, we can expect to reap vegetables.

With religion and the theology on which a given approach to religion is based, we choose, i.e., make a decision to embrace certain beliefs, either on the basis of convenience or on the basis of what appears to make the most sense to us. It is either more convenient to embrace a certain system of beliefs because our parents did, or because our spouse insists on it, than it is to embrace beliefs that make sense but run counter to prevailing teachings.

I am not suggesting that all traditional beliefs be discarded. I am suggesting that they be viewed as a point of beginning from which we are always seeking to move on to something more truthful and therefore better. This "moving on" recognizes that some beliefs will need to be discarded because they are no longer helpful and, in some cases are absolutely detrimental.

A God of Favoritism and Reward

The traditional view of a God who rewards certain behavior and certain beliefs with heaven and certain other beliefs and behavior with hell is suspect. A reasonable case can be made for the strong probability that this belief about God does more harm than good. Furthermore there is a real possibility that it is absolutely wrong. Nevertheless, a recent poll by the Princeton Research Center indicates that 76 percent of our teenagers believe in a "personal God who observes, rewards and punishes." (*Emerging Trends*, Vol. 21, No. 3, ISBN 3567890-1, March 1999) This is a God of favoritism and reward! This idea is not original with teenagers—it has been passed down from generation to generation for centuries. It is interesting that more youth are not in church if they believe in such a God!

Maturity teaches human beings that attitudes and behavior both have consequences. That portion of our lives over which we have control and about which we make decisions is affected by this knowledge. The literal idea of immortality, with heaven as a reward and hell as punishment, represents considerable leverage utilized by the church in its efforts to control the minds of its adherents. Some good is accomplished through the teaching of both children and adults through this mind control in relation to "right," "wrong," "consequences," and "hope." The integrity of such a belief needs to be questioned.

First, can it be substantiated? The answer is "no." A decision must be made, for whatever reason, either to believe it or not to believe it. The authority and teaching of the church is often involved in whether or not to be a "believer."

Second, does the good accomplished by such a belief system outweigh the bad or vice versa? One can certainly say, with supportive evidence, that much behavior modification has been accomplished for centuries by the promotion of a belief in heaven as an eternal reward and hell as eternal punishment. Some lives have been "kept in line" in an effort to gain the reward and avoid the punishment. It is this line of belief that gave rise to the Ten Commandments. Moses certainly accomplished much for his people then, and for the world since, through this simple and understandable law relating to human responsibility to God and to one another. Besides, who would dare say anything negative about the Ten Commandments? Jesus believed, however, that they are "second best." He taught that the commandments should therefore be subordinated to goodness as an expression of love. Through this kind of subordination, they were in fact, fulfilled.

Surely we cannot be proud of some of the "fruits" of this belief! Great Cathedrals, that we love to visit, were built in Europe during the middle ages by using this basic belief as a fund raiser to extract money from the poor through the loophole of indulgences. Many who have "lived like the devil" during their life, at its end have experienced "death bed repentance" which has at least given them some peace along with their loved ones, prior to dying. Such repentance, however, does not change the negative contribution they have made to the world throughout their life. The idea and application of the "last rites" is a further example of the belief in a God who administers eternal reward or punishment. Whether a belief in such remedial rituals does any good and whether or not it may contribute to much that is negative needs to be examined.

Weighing the Values of Beliefs

It is therefore reasonable to ask whether or not this belief about God and the ultimate destiny of human beings contributes more good or more bad to the human situation?

I am suggesting that it contributes more bad than good. First, it is misleading. Second, it is contrary to the Gospel message of a God of unconditional love. Third, it nurtures a life lived in either fear or arrogance. Fourth, it serves as a leverage of power for an institution that is struggling to maintain the integrity of its own power structure. Fifth, it nurtures a subconscious validation of violence as a means of relating to those who do not behave as we believe they should. There are more—you can complete your own list of negatives related to such a belief!

Another question needs to be raised about this general belief. Does this belief encourage an attitude toward life and/or a sense of responsibility to life that nurtures violence or peace?

It can be said without contradiction that it nurtures a belief in a God of favoritism. God loves me better than you! Why? Because I "believe right" and you "believe wrong." And so, holy wars have rootage. Christians kill Moslems and vice versa. Protestants kill Catholics and vice versa. Can any good thing be said about the promotion of a belief system that dictates believing in a God of favoritism?

A God of Favoritism Creates Dissension and Violence

This traditional belief about God promotes the idea of a God of violence. Do we need more violence than we already have? Do we need more violence than we have in our schools? Do we need more violence than we have on our streets? Do we need more violence than we have among those who have different ideas about "right and wrong?"

I was chilled while watching television recently as I listened to a Lutheran pastor who gives support to the bombing of clinics where abortions are performed. He justified his killing on the basis of preventing the killing of a fetus. He made no comment on the virtue of preventing unfortunate pregnancies as a means of preventing the need for even considering abortion. It is easier to kill than it is to prevent the problem!

Violence is part of our life; it is part of our entertainment; and unfortunately, it is part of our religious history and system of belief. If God does it, why can't we? If our nation does it, why can't we? If our State does it, why can't we? If killing is glorified on television and in the movies, why shouldn't we?

It was once okay for persons to choose this kind of theology because it was the best available. It made perfect sense in relation to the prevailing understanding of the world. It is no longer okay! Furthermore, it is a matter of choice. There is no need to embrace such an outdated belief system.

We each make a decision as to what theological beliefs we choose to embrace. We choose for a variety of reasons to either support outdated beliefs which made sense at the time they were conceived or we choose, as they did, to develop a belief system that is harmonious with what God is permitting us to learn about "things as they are."

An alternative belief system that makes sense in our world, in our time, is one which can afford to become unconcerned about immortality. Faith makes concern about immortality unnecessary. A healthy belief in and about God contributes to making this life sufficiently meaningful as to require total commitment with the result of absolute fulfillment. When we become totally committed to and absorbed by this life, there is no need or time for concern about immortality, and this life becomes better for everyone. Our belief should include faith in a God who is capable of handling the matter of immortality in a capable and wonderful manner.

This doesn't mean that we develop a belief system which denies immortality. It only means that we leave the future, about which we know nothing and over which we have no control in the hands of the Source of time, space, and life. It means that we are consequently free to give everything to, and extract everything from, this life that is possible.

Gloomy Predictions for a World Out of Control

Just consider what this belief system contributes of a negative nature to the insecurity and future of the human family. It assumes that God is in control of everything and that God has a time line. Under this umbrella, it assumes that everything that happens, happens for a reason, and that the reason fits neatly into God's plan. Included in God's plan is an end to the world as we know it. It teaches that there will be a great battle between the forces of evil and the forces of good. Evil will be destroyed along with the earth. There will be a new heaven and a new earth, and all the folks who "believed right" will reign eternally in the presence of God forever.

Predictions of when the "end" will occur are made on the basis of "revelation" concerning events that will happen as the end of the world draws near. One example of a sign is the prophecy that, "There will be wars and rumors of wars." So when has that not been true!

The negative point of this belief system needs to be made clear. It assumes that ultimate decision making concerning the future of human beings is made by God apart from human beings. Whatever decisions human beings make are predictable and fit neatly into this fatalistic plan. In other words, we human beings have no control in relation to the future.

Experience supports the idea that we human beings have more control through the kinds of decisions we make than was once thought. We might like to avoid responsibility, but we can't. God has given us the power, the ability, and the freedom to make critical choices. Our decisions make a difference.

Suppose that Change Can Nurture Hope

Would the turmoil and fear presently being experienced in America be as it is if different decisions had been made a generation ago? Would the predictable future of our society be brighter if different decisions were being made now?

Suppose that every generation of parents understood the heavy responsibility they carry from the moment they make a decision to create the possibility of personal parenthood. There is that about parenthood in any healthy environment that is romantic, wonderful, and awesome. Suppose that parents gave this responsibility priority over all other values, including their striving for status, wealth, and entertainment. Suppose that every parent who looked into the eyes of their creation saw the potential for saint or sinner, for citizen or criminal, and realized that a major contribution toward what that child becomes will come either from them or from those with whom they share parental responsibility.

Suppose that all parents really believed that their responsibility involves exercising sufficient control in the lives of their children to protect children and society from themselves until such time as children have sufficient maturity and wisdom to protect and promote the sanctity of life for themselves and for others.

Suppose that society determined that it has a primary responsibility to encourage and support parents in good parenting. Suppose that in relation to this understanding, society made a decision to oppose the glorification of violence in every form, even as entertainment.

Suppose that society viewed character development so importantly that certain principles would be agreed upon and taught in every school setting and supported by examples in the home.

Suppose that churches concluded that their task should be that of character development and the nurture of the human spirit, rather than "pie in the sky" ideas related to immortality. Suppose that all churches made themselves worthy of their calling and of wholehearted support of society.

Suppose that instruments of killing would be viewed with disdain by society in general, and instead of gun control being an issue of dissension among us, for the sake of innocents and children the availability to children of such instruments would be viewed with the same disdain as the sexual abuse of children.

Suppose that within the entertainment industry, whether movies, television or music, the glorification of violence and abusive sex will not be tolerated, much less supported. Suppose that all who make money from communication viewed the consequences of that which is communicated as of greater value than "the dollar."

Suppose that these and other worthy considerations had been reality two generations ago. Would our children live in fear of going to school or walking alone in our parks today? If we, the people, show ourselves unwilling to pay some price for the salvation of our children, where lies the hope of a future for our children?

The Challenge of Choices Is Not Easy

The weighing of values related to the bearing of arms and the killing of children may sound easy, but in a nation where the right to bear arms has been a building block in society, it is not easy. What freedoms are we willing to give up in the interest of human life?

Freedom of speech is a value inherent in our way of life. The news recently reported a judge unwilling to throw out a case where parents were suing a school district for denying freedom of speech rights to a youngster who was threatening to kill the principal.

One parent described the violent death of her child as being part of God's plan, not yet understood. What kind of theology is this? What a prime example of a need for a belief system that makes sense rather than parrots the teachings of tradition! God is not in control. God has chosen to share control with us, and a major share at that. The power of this control is evident through the decisions that we human beings make.

We are challenged with choices. The privilege of making decisions is part of God's gift to us that makes us human. Theological choices are only elective if we don't care about quality in life or about the future. But we do care about these things. It is not easy to move beyond what we have been taught or beyond where our parents are in their belief system, but we must.

The challenge of choices in relation to a theological system of belief is inherent in the nature of human life. To make good choices we must embrace the right values. To make the right choices we must have opportunities to meet our basic needs in legitimate ways. Both the present and the future are dependent on our response to the privilege of choosing what we will believe about God, about human beings, about personal responsibility, and about the potential relationship to both God and our fellow human beings.

Chapter XXIV

The Church—An Institutional Problem/Blessing

A Small Beginning to an Important Task

The history and duration of the church is impressive. Certainly it is today something that was never intended in the beginning, and especially not by Jesus. Jesus knew nothing of the church and had no intention of starting one. The brief reference attributed to him speaking about the church being built on the confession of Peter (Matthew 16:13-20) is presumed to be a statement added to the text at a much later time.

The church was not started by the disciples after the death of Jesus because they intended to "start a church," but they did want to share the gifts of Jesus with others. This, along with persecution contributed to the establishment of the first churches. The church was started in response to their need to find whatever security was possible for each other. Furthermore, the church came about through the need of the disciples to make sense from that which they had experienced together in relation to the friendship, ministry, life, and death of Jesus.

The church has evolved from that very small and functional beginning to what we recognize it to be today. Its impact on the world has been significant. Its impact on the lives of individual human beings exceeds comprehension. If you have been the recipient of any of the many wonderful blessings available through the church, you surely view it as a blessing. If your relationship with the church is such that you are confident in it as a channel through which you can express helpfulness to others, either economically or through other means of nurturing support, you surely view it as a blessing. The church is a wonderful resource from which we receive and through which we are able to share with others.

There are, however, reasonable questions which need to be raised and answered about the church as an institution. Often it has been and is a wonderful blessing. Sometimes it has been and is a problem and liability to human progress. The negative side of the church can be observed in those situations in which it has demonstrated a spirit of arrogance, involvement in mind control of individuals and groups, and regressive influence in the face of achievements made through non-religious efforts such as scientific endeavors.

The potential of the church to respond to the spiritual needs of human beings continues to be considerable. What the church is and what it becomes in response to the meeting of those needs is the current responsibility of those of us who are a part of the church as an institution. Its future is in the hands of those who are now in the process of determining its value through their observation of work that we do and the example that we are. Without participants, the church dies.

The Church as an Institution

Increasing complexity of human society demands the creation of institutions designed to meet the needs of both individuals and society. Outstanding examples of institutions in contemporary human society include government, education, health care, and the church. Each of these institutions make an important contribution to the welfare of the entire human family and individuals within it. Government provides order. Educational institutions provide an opportunity for learning in ways not otherwise possible. Hospitals and related health care entities provide both preventive and remedial response to the health needs of persons. Each of these institutions responds to specific human needs in a manner not possible if each person or family was dependent solely on their own resources.

The same is true with the church. The church provides a re-source of spiritual nurture for human beings in a way that is not otherwise possible. Human society, in this modern age, is so complex and interdependent that the contribution of the church to the spiritual nurture of individuals and society as a whole is very important. Without a healthy spirit, all progress in every other area of human experience and concern is diminished. In fact, without spiritual nurture and growth on both the individ-ual and corporate levels, the human family can become a dan-ger to itself and a threat to its future survival.

But institutions have their own unique characteristics and can easily assume a life of their own. The church is not immune to this specific institutional characteristic.

Institutional Dangers

The problem with any response to human need when it be-comes institutionalized is that there is an inherent danger that the institution becomes an end, in and of itself. That is to say that there is a danger for the institution to become so involved in self propagation that it ceases to function effectively as a re-sponse to the need for which it was originally created. This con-cern is especially evident in government, but it is clearly present in education, health care, and the church as well.

The primary goal of government should be order and secu-rity. The primary goal of education should be the provision of the best possible learning opportunities. The primary goal of health care should be precisely what the name suggests, the care of health for persons. The primary goal of the church should be the nurture of spirituality in persons of all ages.

A second danger inherent in all institutions is that they be-come so comfortable in doing the same thing in the same way that they fail to maintain relevancy as the rest of the world changes. That is a danger to which the church is especially sus-ceptible. It is easy for the church to become involved in many good things, and in its busyness overlook those things which contribute most to spiritual health. The nurturing of the human spirit is a major part of the responsibility for which the church came into existence.

Human Spirituality

But what is spirituality? Is it regular participation in certain rituals associated with religion, such as prayer and public worship? While religious rituals and practices may be helpful in nurturing and expressing spirituality, they can also become empty and meaningless exercises. Spirituality includes the recognition that there is that about us human beings which we call spirit. Spirituality involves emotions, but it is not contingent on emotional responses.

Spirituality is related to every other aspect of being human. It is related to that about us which is physical. It is related to that about us which is intellectual. It is related to that about us which is emotional. Without spirit, human beings would become something other than what we recognize as human.

The spirit has to do with attitude. It has to do with love. It has to do with relationships. It has to do with reverence for our Source. It has to do with respect for one another and the environment which sustains us. Although spirit is unseen, it has to do with everything about us that is seen and experienced.

When the spirit is not healthy, that about us which is physical is affected. When the spirit is not healthy, all our relationships are affected. When the spirit is not healthy, our attitudes about self, life, and each other are affected. When the spirit is not healthy there tends to be an expectation of receiving love without a sense of needing to give it. Both the joy and effort found in satisfying the love needs of others is therefore missing.

The importance of spiritual health is clearly evident. The primary task of the institution of the church should be that of nurturing spiritual health. To the degree that it accomplishes this goal it is true to its reason for being. To the degree that it fails to accomplish this goal, the reason for its being is diminished.

Spirituality, Religion and Superstition

Spirituality should not be confused with either religious profession or superstition. The term "religion" commonly implies an institutional relationship. There is much about religion that can easily become empty formality. There is much about religion which can easily become superstition, and there is much about superstition which can erroneously be interpreted as spiritual or religious.

Both of these dangers are clearly recognized in the Bible. Although it is clear that the Old Testament Jews believed that God had commanded them to observe certain religious rituals and practices, it is just as clear that the eighth century prophets concluded that these rituals and practices had become so empty, meaningless, and misleading that they were an abomination to God. Some of the New Testament writers became concerned that people, in their zeal to be "spiritual," were going off on harmful tangents. They therefore admonished Christians not to believe everyone who claims to have the Spirit of God.

There are many examples of church activities in church groups which are believed by that group to indicate the great depth of their spirituality which in fact indicate their level of foolishness. The handling of poisonous snakes, speaking in tongues, the total loss of psychological control resulting in trances, suicidal sect groups and practices involving the mutilating or sacrificing of the human body are all examples of practices believed by some to be associated with spirituality. In fact, they clearly indicate a sickness of spirit.

Much superstition in the name of religion is associated with the Bible; the use of incense, beads, and elaborate symbols associated with worship are just a few examples. Prayer, or the saying of prayers, also often fits within the realm of superstition. Giving to the church can also fit under the umbrella of superstition when it is done with a belief that God will show special favors to those who give either certain amounts of money or certain percentages of their income.

Spiritual Heroes

Human beings learn from one another. Human beings depend on one another. Human beings discover examples for their own expression of life in one another. All of this is related to what we often speak of as our need for heroes. A wide variety of religions have their heroes. Buddhists have Buddha, Jews have Moses and King David, Muslims have Muhammad, and Christians have Jesus and Paul. From these religious heroes, persons both learn about what it means to be spiritual in relation to that specific religion and how to nurture their spirituality.

Jesus can be, and ought to be, a wonderful hero to all professing Christians, both young and adult.

The message is clear that both individuals and the entire human family are in need of what Jesus had to offer. In relation to the broad spectrum of humanity, the principles espoused by Jesus are more important than the source. We really don't care whether the principles come from Moses, King David, Muhammad, Buddha, or some other respectable source. For those of us in the Christian tradition, however, it is important to learn all we can and emulate to the best of our ability the spirit of Jesus. It was his spirit which was basic to the belief system he taught and the example of how he expressed his life.

Believing "Right" About Jesus

If Jesus is to be a worthy hero whose memory can assist persons in experiencing and expressing their lives in the best possible manner, that which is believed about Jesus is extremely important. In other words, it is important to "believe right." The challenge is determining exactly what that means.

Believing right was fundamental to, and nurturing of, a sense of personal security in the life of Jesus. Everything experienced and expressed by Jesus had rootage in what he believed about God, about himself, and about all other members of the human family. If Jesus is to be the Christian hero, then it is at this point that one's expression and experience of life should begin. What is believed about God, about oneself, and about others is more than "just" important. It is absolutely basic to what we are about as persons, as a church, and ideally as a human family.

"Believing right" is not static. That is to say it is not an intellectual assent to some verbalized belief which stops with rhetoric. It is not a summit toward which we climb and, after reaching, sit down and enjoy the view. Believing right, has to do with how we express our lives. Believing right has to do with every good thing we human beings are capable of doing. The absence of believing right is related to every bad thing of which human beings are capable.

Fundamental for the Christian is what is believed about Jesus. The influence of the Christian religion for good has been impressive, both historically and contemporarily. There have been those lapses, however, when the history of Christian influence has not been such that we can take pride in it. There exist those situations today when it is not as good as it ought to be. Theology is a case in point. Most of the church is caught in a theology that is as outdated as the technology of the time in history during which its theology was formulated. Whereas the church has an opportunity to a be a leader in religious thought, it tends to cling to a theology that was viable in another day in an age gone by, while it resists the challenge of thinking new thoughts about the nature and work of God. This is precisely the problem which Jesus faced as he sought to bring progress to his own religion two-thousand years ago. Good products which served us well in the past should be remembered with respect and appreciation. Our perception of them should not become a mental and emotional prison which stifles further progress.

Among our tasks as disciples of Jesus is that of making the influence which we have on each other as positive as possible. Our task as a corporate group, i.e., as the church, is to make an impact on the world which is just as positive as possible. All of this is closely related to what is believed about the spirit of Jesus.

In general, both Judaism and the early church "screwed up" in how they finally defined who Jesus was and "what he was about." The Jews in general screwed up by not giving him enough attention. In not hearing the heart of his message, which is basically "love over law" with the same goals of behavior in mind, they missed an important element which might have become central to their religious teachings. "Obey the law from love of God, not out of fear of consequences."

The early church erred as they established a theology about Jesus which was considerably different from how Jesus viewed himself. This theology provided an explanation for the crucifixion, but in doing that claimed something for Jesus that he did not claim for himself.

The early church, as indicated in the New Testament, was dominated by "after death" and "other world" thinking. This was a natural response to a life "in the here and now" that was made absolutely tenuous and miserable by those who sought to bring an early death to Christianity. This "after death" and "other world" thinking, however, was not the dominant theme of the message of Jesus. The dominant theme of Jesus had to do with the human relationship with God, with each other, and human behavior.

The early Christians, on the other hand, embraced the idea that Jesus was God in human flesh and therefore ought to be received by the Jews as Messiah. Jesus affirmed his intention to fulfill the hope of Messiahship on the spiritual level, but this was not the central theme of his life and message. The Jews held that Jesus didn't fit the criteria for Messiah and so refused to give Jesus and his message the kind of attention it deserved.

In brief, the Christians credited Jesus with being more than he saw himself as being, while the Jews did not give him the credit that he was due.

The huge difference between what the early church taught about Jesus and that which most Jews believed about Jesus is unfortunate. Jesus did not intend to start a new religion. His desire and intent was to make Judaism all that it was capable of being and to nudge it from an excessive emphasis on legalism to a humane emphasis of doing good from the motivation of love rather than fear. The failure of the early church to believe about Jesus what he believed about himself is just as unfortunate as his rejection by Judaism.

The Great Debate—Conflicting Theologies

There has been, from the earliest days of the church, a debate within the church as to who Jesus was and how he accomplished what he did. This debate centers around two distinct interpretations. One approach emphasizes Jesus as one who did something to make us all right in the sight of our Creator. This "at-one-ment" is affirmed by "faith" and is something spoken of as the theory of atonement. The primary focus of religious life is thus placed on him as a mystical intercessor in whom we must believe if the intercession is to be effective for us personally. The phrase often heard in contemporary Christian rhetoric referring to this religious experience is "born again believer." Belief in Jesus as one's intercessor and personal sacrifice is believed to result in a new beginning, thus the phrase "born again believer." Sometimes the phrase "born again Christian" is used and thus tends to communicate a level of spirituality which is a step above that experienced by persons who do not embrace the "atonement" theological point of view, or who, for whatever reason, do not profess to be "born again."

The other approach emphasizes the behavioral side of what Jesus taught. This approach indicates that Jesus had a relationship with God which all persons can also have. It emphasizes personal responsibility in expressing life in a spirit of love for all other human beings. It emphasizes the idea that we have access to the same spirit of God to which Jesus had access. In other words, instead of "Jesus doing for us," he taught about a relationship with God that we can have, and demonstrated how the fruit of that relationship should be expressed in daily life.

A fundamental responsibility of the Church is to help us grow in our ability to "believe right" about Jesus and God. This "believing right" includes what we believe about Jesus as well as associated beliefs related to an everyday expression of life. The "Christian life" thus is informed, inspired, and empowered by the same Spirit of God which informed, inspired, and empowered Jesus.

The Church As a Source of Tension

There is a natural tension within the church between maintaining the institution, protecting tradition, and nurturing a religious belief system that is harmonious with present day knowledge. Contemporary knowledge of "how things are" is a wonderful resource to teach us more about what God is about and how God works in our present age.

Among the reasons why Jesus was crucified is that he challenged the status quo of his day and society. Had he not done this in the face of deadly opposition, Christianity would never have been born much less have made the positive contributions to the world from which we benefit. Established religion of his day feared that he might change the status quo. The human tendency to fear and oppose change is no less today than it was then, especially in the realm of religious belief and expression.

Important Considerations

How can the church help persons grow in spirituality in a manner that is harmonious with the world of our day? First, the church can help us avoid the religious schizophrenia syndrome. This is the experience of feeling compelled to believe something taught by the authority of the church when, in fact, it is contrary to both common sense and contemporary knowledge. In the same sense that the belief system of two-thousand years ago was concurrent with the general world view of that day, there is no reason why a religious belief system should not be concurrent with the general world view of our day.

Second, the church should view itself, and be viewed by each of us, not as an "end" in and of itself, but as a resource for the kind of mental stimulation and spiritual nourishment which encourages growth in those within the church which is then expressed outside the church.

The church should not feel the need, for example, to become involved as a political action group. If members have the best interests of other human beings in mind and are guided by principles which they believe to be harmonious with the "will and ways" of God, their political democratic votes along with those of their neighbors will respond to societal needs.

There is a sense in which the church should be to spiritual growth what the school is to education. The school is not responsible for all learning. It is essential, however, for one to learn how best to learn, and how to discover the best sources of learning. Much is learned in school, but nothing is more important than "how to learn." The church is not responsible for our spirituality. It should, however, be a resource for helping us nurture our spiritual growth.

Third, the church should help us "check out" the belief systems and behavior to determine if indeed they are harmonious with a healthy understanding of how God works. Everything that wears the cloak of religion is not in the best interest of human health or God's work. Much that insists on a presence of the umbrella of religion is an embarrassment to religion in general and to the church specifically. In fact, there is too much that carries the banner of "religion" which is, in fact, dangerous to human health and to the welfare of God's human children!

Fourth, the church occasionally gives evidence of being confused as to what its responsibility really is. Should its primary goal be that of entertainment? Much that is called worship today would fit just as neatly under the umbrella of entertainment. This applies both to television and public worship in local churches. Entertainment is pleasant, but that didn't seem to be the primary goal of Jesus.

Should the goal of the church be political power? Although there were those who feared Jesus might turn in this direction, he did not. The role of institutional religion in American politics today is both regrettable and frightening. A religious fanatic as President, for example, might present challenges to the welfare of our nation that would far exceed the negative challenges presented by any President to date.

The Conclusion of the Matter!

The church can be the greatest possible blessing, both to God and to God's human children, if its focus is on the spiritual needs of human beings. The church needs to be honest, whatever the reaction from other groups or individuals. We need to be taught to "believe right" in relation to all other aspects of our lives. We need the encouragement and support of one another in everything that is good and positive. We need the sanctuary of a loving environment where positive accomplishment is praised and where falling short is forgiven; where prevention of negative human behavior is a priority; where there is more interest in remedial reconstruction than in punishment; and where hope for better things in the future is a constant source of strength and motivation.

The church is now, and will be in the future, just what you and I make it. The church can assist us in our quest for an approach to religion that makes sense or it can nurture a spirit of "make believe" which makes a minimal contribution to the needs of the world. The church can assist us as we endeavor to grow in our ability to make choices which have critical theological implications. As is true with all human institutions, we would do well to focus on diminishing the ways in which the church is a problem and on amplifying the ways in which it is a blessing.

Chapter XXV

In a Nutshell!

Longer than We Think

L ife was much simpler when we could believe, with the best knowledge available to us, that the earth was created some six-thousand years ago as taught by Bishop Usher and that God created everything that exists in six days and rested on the seventh. This information comes from the first two chapters of Genesis with the reference to Bishop Usher found in the margins of many King James Versions of the Bible who, in the early seventeenth century, dated creation as having occurred in 4004 B.C.

What we have discovered by utilizing means of dating unknown to the good Bishop and much more accurate than any method available to him is that not only the earth but the human family has been in existence much longer than he supposed.

Human beings have always found it necessary to utilize the "tools" available to them. Among the wonderful gifts which human beings enjoy is that of being able to reason, think creatively, and build on knowledge that has been acquired previously. This process typically functions at a very slow pace but can seem to have been accelerated in relation to certain things at certain times. The gaining of technological knowledge is part of what we now speak of as a "knowledge explosion." That suggests acceleration! We become quite aware of this when electronic units purchased only a few months previously have already been superseded with something more sophisticated or better. We become aware of this with the changing and more effective procedures by which health needs are treated. We become aware of this when we are no longer confined to the bonds of earth but go charging off into space.

It is also reasonable to suppose that different tools are available to us than were known by the ancients in relation to an understanding of how the universe came to be. This means that we come to understand a bit more about the creative work of God. As we grow in understanding about this fabulous creation we also learn more about God.

We should therefore have some religious beliefs that are somewhat different than those of centuries ago.

As indicated earlier in this book, the Bible has shared much wonderful information, but it has also been a stumbling block. Contradictory to its great value in nurturing religion, it has also slowed down the process of progress in religious understanding. This is not through a fault of the Bible. It has occurred because of the status accorded it by those in religious authority and then by the populace in the Judeo-Christian tradition. The Bible is a wonderful book and shares much God Talk from Judaism and Christianity. It should, however, neither be an object of worship nor should it be viewed as an absolute and dependable source of truth for all situations in contemporary human life.

What one truly believes at any given time makes a difference in that person's attitude toward life and the manner in which it is expressed. Hence it is important that professed beliefs reflect our best knowledge of truth at any given time. Many religious beliefs are based on timeless truth, but many are based on truth as perceived thousands of years ago. We "know better" than many professed religious beliefs today. The best religion promotes a belief system that is consistent with the "state of the art" truth at a given point in human history. God Talk ought to reflect the broad scope of this up-to-date truth as well as beliefs that have stood the test of time.

Ancient God Talk is not holy or sacred because of its age. God Talk can nurture that which is holy and sacred within and among us when it expresses reverence for our Source, Love for one another, Respect for our environment, and Responsibility for personal behavior and attitude. Such God Talk should be communicated in a manner that is both common sense and up-to-date. One should not need to take a special course in religious language in order to understand the religious vernacular of the day.

Human beings are much more privileged in relation to God than was once thought. The Old Testament emphasizes the need to be obedient to the law. The New Testament emphasizes love and faith, indicating that good behavior is a fruit of both. Given the knowledge that has been gained from that time to this, the recent explosion of knowledge in which we share the many wonderful things human beings are now able to accomplish that not long ago they could only dream about, it is therefore becoming evident that our relation with God should be viewed from another perspective. This is not to say that those timeless elements of values which come from the Old Testament are no longer important. It is to say that we do better than "obedience" if they are automatically fulfilled through hearts of love and commitment to the very best that we know.

We need to recognize that given the contemporary level of knowledge, we are much more honored by God than we once thought. It is not presumptuous to view ourselves as potential partners with God at God's invitation. This is not an effort to "play God." It should be viewed as a noble, appreciative, and humble response to a magnanimous invitation from God which adds value to life. Such a lofty privilege should nudge us all in a growing spirit of reverence for our Source. We should grow in respect for all of God's creation in which we have not shared, as well as in that in which we do share. It follows then that the values of love for God, self, and one another should be high priorities in our commitment to growth. It also follows that in addition to helping one another all we can, we must also take personal responsibility for our own growth and behavior.

If God controls the world, as is often suggested by religion, he is doing a poor job of it. That is to say that if God's work is evaluated by the principles and values we believe to be consistent with the nature of God, then he is doing a poor job. The contradictions in human life do not indicate a loving God who is "in charge." On the other hand, if God has relinquished "being in charge" by virtue of the great responsibilities shared with his human creation, then that means personal responsibility for human beings takes on an amplified meaning. Life today does seem to indicate a challenge to work in partnership with a loving and powerful God. The human family is "nudged," not "controlled" by God. In some way, not fully understood by us, human beings are challenged to grow in understanding of what it means to be in such partnership and in an ability to express life in that spirit. Meaningful God Talk can assist the spiritual evolvement of human beings toward that end. In addition, life can thus take on a whole new and wonderful sense of excitement and fulfillment. Can you imagine being in partnership with the greatest "inventor" and "employer" that ever has been or ever will be!

The best religion does not "spoon feed" its adherents. Instead it leads them in a progressive manner toward something better and more wonderful than they have previously experienced or expressed. Religion does not become a segment or an adjunct to life. Within the need to talk about it, religious understanding and faith is at the heart of life. It is part of everything which goes into what a person is and does. God Talk, as a language of religious communication, should progress in harmony with this evolving experience.

There is that about institutional religion, i.e., the church, which tends to insist on the authority of the past even though the past is no longer in harmony with the present in relation to knowledge, culture or potential. For that reason "new" religious ideas are typically met with opposition and the messengers who bring them are often rejected. Some Old Testament prophets, Jesus, and many people of faith in a variety of religions throughout history have experienced this fact with much pain or death. We are each always challenged to keep an open mind that will enable us to avoid being allies in spirit with those in the past who rejected what we now cherish as truth. A closed mind is not a friend of religious progress in the same sense that a non-selective mind is an enemy to the retention of truth that should be viewed as eternal.

Institutional religion should not maintain symbols as sacred forever. Symbols are a means of communication. They are God Talk. Some symbols that held meaning in the past because they came from the past are no longer meaningful. They no longer reflect that which once was a matter of common sense. Slow though the process may be, there needs to be creative freedom and encouragement for the development of new symbols which communicate to and from people at any point in human history. There is much better symbolism possible, for example, than "the old rugged cross."

What does this approach to religious experience in the Judeo-Christian experience offer? It offers appreciation for, and edification from, the past. It offers instructive material that is not static but is foundational in a progressive manner, and that nudges us on to perfection with the realization that the goal will never be fully attained. As we move closer to it, it moves further from us.

It offers faith in the strength of our partnership with God and nurtures a sense that God loves us, wants the best for us, and provides resources which, if utilized, can help us become more than we ever dreamed. God is "on our side" in this matter of life.

It offers hope for the future that is not based on predestination, but is based on confidence in the teamwork of God and us to make the world an increasingly better place to live rather than for it to be doomed to a deteriorating home for the human family.

If offers strength, knowledge, and positive expectations for the challenges that we face at any given time. It nurtures gratitude for the sciences, realizing that they are never absolutely right or complete, but are capable of improving their abilities and thus enabling us to accomplish more in our partner relationship with God.

It offers a religious experience and the opportunity for religious growth that requires neither idols nor non-adjustable authoritative Scripture. It looks for communication from God, not just in helpful words from the past, but in contemporary wisdom, the handiwork of God in nature, and the creative wonders of the human mind.

It offers the need not to know about what happens after physical death. The lack of a need for this kind of knowledge leaves us free to make the very best we can of this life. Faith in forgiving love enables us to give full attention to this life without either paralyzing fear for the future or regrets for the past. We are thus not always hoping for something better in the future after death. Instead we are striving for and expecting something better in this life. It offers us a serenity about death that takes it out of the category of being a natural enemy and places it in the category of being a natural experience. Death is viewed as an enemy only when it comes in an untimely and/or unloving fashion. Premature death is an enemy because it cheats us out of a reasonable expectation for longevity, and the world is cheated out of what we might otherwise have contributed to it. Death that comes from painful disease, tragedy, or at the hands of another is an enemy because it inhibits or prohibits life that has a right to exist, taking and giving, without suffering.

It offers a faith that the same God who arranged for life before we were born when we knew nothing about it is capable of either giving us a rest, providing us with something more wonderful than we have yet experienced, or bringing us into an experience not yet known to us or imagined by us. In other words, it is a faith which encourages us to trust God for the future and thus not detract from our working relationship with God in the present.

Among the earliest prayers that I learned as a child was this: "God is great, God is good, let us thank Him for this food. By His hand we are daily fed, let us thank Him for this bread." The greatness and goodness of God is demonstrated through the gift of human life and the arrangement that permits, yea invites us, to work in partnership with God. God provides the resources from which we can build life.

God Talk makes sense because in the environment in which we "live and move and have our being" (as Paul quoted the Greek philosophers), it is common sense!

Appendix I

I have selected work from four recent authors who have explored the meaning and implications of Process Thought as it relates to Christianity for inclusion in this appendix. *Process Thought And Christian Faith*, by Norman Pittenger, is an example of how some theological writers are taking the need for relevance in theological research seriously.[1] Pittenger draws heavily on the works, and interpretations of the works, of Alfred North Whitehead. He also shares views related to the works of other "Process" writers.

Pittenger's concern in relating Process thought and Christian faith is explained when he says:

> In any event it is plainly the fact that the way in which Christian faith has been and is being presented in many quarters has seemed and does seem to vast numbers of people simply a mixture of uncertainty, nonsense and "miracle," the last of these in the sense of an appeal sometimes made by Christian apologists and preachers to what strikes the modern man as an absurd and unintelligible violation of the pervasive regularity which he has come to believe is a mark of the universe as he knows it to be.[2]

In speaking of the popularity of *Honest To God* by the Bishop of Woolwich[3] he says:

> It is my own belief that the explanation for the enormous sale of *Honest To God* is simply that great numbers of men and women who wish to be both modern and Christian found in that book a presentation of Christianity which on the one hand they felt was absolutely honest and which on the other hand (and for the first time) opened to them the basic meaning of what we may style "The religious question.'"[4]

Dr. Robinson relied largely on the philosophical theology of Paul Tillich. Although Pittenger expressed great respect for Dr. Tillich, he explained why he did not follow the same line of thought as that presented in *Honest To God*. He said, "It is my own conviction that there is another kind of thought which is even more suitable for use in the task of Christian reconception. This is the line taken by what in North America today is frequently described as 'process-thought'; its great exponent was the late Professor Alfred North Whitehead in his works *Process And Reality*."[5]

Pittenger is careful to point out that Whitehead does not stand alone in Process thought:

But Professor Whitehead was only one of a number of thinkers in the years 1920-35 who were taking the same general approach to an understanding of man and his world. Professor C. Lloyd-Morgan's *Emergent Evolution And Life, Mind And Spirit*, Professor Samuel Alexander's *Space-Time and Deity*, General Jan Smut's HOLISM, and other works of a similar nature were appearing during those years. While there were many differences among them, there was also a consistent use of evolutionary ideas which gave them a genuine unity. In our own decade, the works of Pierre Teilhard de Chardin, the noted Jesuit paleontologist, have been published posthumously; they too follow the same general line as the English writers I have mentioned. Furthermore, in the United States, for over a quarter of a century the writings of Professor Charles Hartshorne, including *Beyond Humanism, The Vision Of God, Reality As Social Process, The Divine Relativity, The Logic Of* Perfection, and *A Natural Theology For Our Times*, as well as many occasional articles and essay have eloquently argued the case for "process-thought."[6]

Additional contemporary writers giving consideration to process thought include Professor John B. Cobb[7] and Professor Ian G. Barbour,[8] both of whom, in addition to Pittenger, are primary sources for recent scholarly research in process thought.

Process thought is an effort to relate that which is known and experienced by modern human being to a religious faith. It is an effort to move from a dualistic philosophy of life. In dualism, religious views tend to be categorized in one area of experience while an understanding of the universe of which we are a part are kept separate in another area. Process thought, however, relies on a unified philosophical and theological approach where what is held as truth is consistent with what is believed to be known. In this latter instance, "truth" and perceived knowledge are supportive and congruent with one another, rather than in conflict or contradiction as is often the case in theology.

The "Process" approach is consistent, in principle, with that taken by our ancestors in the development of their system of beliefs about religion and their world. They developed their beliefs from what they experienced and perceived to be true. The tendency of subsequent generations, however, has been to accept as "eternal truth" that which the ancients perceived in the area of religion, even though the world has changed drastically. At one time, observation of human experience and natural phenomenon tended to support the idea of a God removed from the universe, who might if he chose, intrude into it with instantaneous and miraculous results. More recent knowledge concerning the nature of our universe tends to support the idea of a God that moves within the universe, through a slow and dependable process of evolvement which, in many ways, is open to scrutiny by the scientific mind. Process thought seeks consistency with this latter point of view.

Why, in this modern age, is this not the basis for theological thought in the church? Pittenger points out a basic reason when he says:

Another reason for the neglect of Whitehead and the other process-thinkers, especially among theologians, has been the long period (from which we now seem to be emerging) when philosophical theology itself, and especially such philosophical theology as employed scientific data as part of its material, was looked upon as a highly dangerous and even sinful intrusion of non-biblical and secular thought into the Christian faith. What some call "biblical theology" has been taken to rule out, once and for all, any such philosophical approach to faith...God has revealed himself either in the pages of Holy Scripture or in the events which the Bible records; nothing else is needed and anything else diminishes or denies the unique adequacy of biblical revelation.[9]

The Bible story is relatively simple and subject to a variety of interpretations. It is easier to keep repeating and embracing the "old" than it is to consider giving birth to the "new." When this fact is mixed with the punishment and reward system traditionally associated with Christian teaching, it is not difficult to understand why an approach like "Process thought" is either opposed or at least not given consideration.

Another reason for the church not giving general consideration to Process thought has to do with the diverse nature of the churches' compositions. While it is true that some people are searching, as is evidenced by the response to HONEST TO GOD, it is also true that many are not. Many "good" church members are genuinely distraught when anyone with, or without, clout suggests that the "old time religion" is not good enough.

It is not surprising that the church is responding slowly to Process thought. Pittenger believes that, "It would appear that evolutionary or process motifs are again being forced upon our attention; and Christian thought will neglect them to its own peril."[10] The urgency which Pittenger feels in this regard is expressed by Whitehead:

Those societies which cannot combine reverence for the symbols with freedom of revision must ultimately decay either from anarchy or from the slow atrophy of a life stifled by useless shadows.[11]

Pittenger described Process thought as based on four assumptions.[12] The first is that we are confronted with a dynamic rather than a static reality. The second is that we are in a world that is not only in dynamic movement but is an inter-related society of "occasions." The third assumption is that each series of occasions has within it a directive quality known as the "subjective aim" which is the goal or end toward which a given process moves toward actualization. The fourth assumption is that because of the nature of the world as we know it, we cannot know it with any kind of absolute clarity and therefore must always be in search of greater clarity.

The First Assumption

Few of us would argue with the first assumption. Science has demonstrated, and we thus plan and act on the knowledge, that everything is in a process of movement and change. The seasons come and go. Thoughts rapidly move from subject to subject. Moods change. Material objects which appear to be inert are composed of atoms which in turn are composed of electrons, protons, and "empty space." In sharing something of the mystery of the entities of which an atom is composed, Cobb comments:

> At first one tried to understand these new entities as particles of matter and for some purposes this imagery worked well. However, in other respects they turned out to function not as particles but more like waves...It seemed that the ultimate entities of which the world is composed are able sometimes to function as particles and sometimes as waves. To this disturbing fact was added the fact that they seemed also to be able to move from one place to another without passing through the intervening space. Further it became clear that electrons and protons are not things that carry electric charges, as a material model would require, but rather they themselves are electric charges. It seemed that something happens, now here, then there, with definite connection between one event and the next, but without continuous movement between them. Things happen in bursts or jerks rather than in even flow.[13]

We now understand with increasing clarity that not only is the tiniest "universe" within the atom that we can observe in perpetual movement and change, but that the same condition exists in the great universe in which we exist. Micro and Macro Universes are in a continual state of change.

Given the current level of knowledge, it is reasonable to conclude that everything within the universe, as well as the universe itself, is in a state of evolvement. Barbour describes our growing knowledge of this evolvement in this manner:

> Since Darwin's day there has been a vast accumulation of scientific data supporting the fact of evolution, and there have been many significant advances in understanding the factors which have contributed to evolutionary change. Moreover, there has developed a biological history of the universe, to which many fields of science have contributed. From astronomy have come theories about the origin of the universe; from bio-chemistry, clues as to the origin of life; from genetics and molecular biology, information about the role of genes and mutations in organic evolution; from paleontology, a partial reconstruction of human ancestry.[14]

Pittenger points out in support of this theory of universal dynamic change that "it is absurd to speak of 'human nature'...Man is 'on the move', he is a living, changing, developing creature. If he is to be described at all, the dynamic quality of his existence must be recognized and grasped, even if it is also the fact that through all the changes there are persistent qualities which preserve his identity as human."[15]

The Second Assumption

The second assumption is basic to Process thought. The idea of inter-related occasions provides the media through which the "process" occurs. Professor Cobb indicates that our conscious experience is concerned with groupings or societies of occasions, rather than individual occasions:

The final indivisible entities of which the world is made up are actual occasions of experience. But these occasions exist only momentarily, enjoying a fleeting moment of subjective immediacy before passing into the past. These individual occasions are only detectable either by intense introspection or by scientific instruments. None of the entities of which we are conscious in common experience are individual occasions and only rarely do these appear even in the sciences. For the most part, our conscious experience is concerned with entities that are groupings of occasions rather than individual occasions.[16]

Pittenger speaks of the importance and the function of the occasions as follows:

Not only is the world and all that is in it a dynamic movement; it is also an inter-related society of "occasions." Nor is there the possibility of isolating one occasion from another, so that each may be considered in itself alone...Into each of the given occasions there enter past events as well as the surrounding and accompanying pressures of other occasions, not to mention the "lure" of the future. To illustrate...A man does not and cannot exist in complete isolation from other men, or from his present environment, or from his own past history and the more general history of the human race of which as man he is a part, or from the natural order to which he and his whole race belong, or from the possible developments which are before him and mankind in general. Each man is a focusing, a concretizing, of all these. Thus in being "himself" he is not himself alone; he is all that has gone to make him up, all that surrounds him, all that presses upon him, all that he himself enters into and in which he shares, all that he may be. And that which is true of man is also true in its appropriate way throughout the universe. We live in and we are confronted by a richly inter-connected, inter-related, inter-penetrative series of events...This means that we are not able to make sharp distinctions of an ultimate and definitive kind. We cannot do this between "selves," for they are inter-penetrating. It also means that in the rich experience which we possess...We are given a full and compresent encounter with the world.[17]

Such an approach clearly emphasizes the individual and group responsibility that is placed upon us as human beings. We are related to the evolvement of human experience and in the same way we are related to our existential medium. This obvious responsibility thus makes our moral and religious response one of extreme importance. What the present is, and what the future becomes, is largely our own creation and that of those who lived before and who live contemporarily with us. The ecological, social, political, psychological, and spiritual overtones of this understanding of reality are readily seen.

Barbour emphasizes both the inter-relatedness and the responsibility inherent in the implications of Process thought.

Whitehead's social model of reality is developed in a detailed metaphysician system;...He uses a set of very general categories which with suitable modifications can be applied to all kinds of entity. He thinks of every entity as a series of events, each of which is to be considered as a moment of experience that takes account of other events and responds to them. Causality, in Whiteheadian thought, is a complex process in which three strands are interwoven. Every new event is in part the product of efficient causation, that is, the influence of previous occurrences upon it. There is also an element of self-causation or self-creation, since every event unifies what is given to it by the past in its own manner from its unique perspective on the world. It contributes something of its own in the way it appropriates its past, relates itself to various possibilities, and produces a novel synthesis that is not strictly deducible from its antecedents. There is a creative selection from among alternative potentialities in terms of

goals and aims, which is final causation. Every new occurrence can, in short, be looked on as a present response to past events in terms of potentialities
grasped.[18]

The Third Assumption

The third assumption, that each series of occasions has
within it a directive quality known as the subjective aim which
is the goal or end towards which a given process moves toward
actualization is less amenable to empirical verification than the
first two. Nevertheless, it serves to explain why the first two can
be experienced in an orderly manner in a way that provides
meaning instead of utter and unending chaos. Pittenger asks
and answers the question:

> But what secures such persistence or identity in occa-
> sions as we do in fact know, both from observation and
> from our own experience of ourselves? The answer to
> this question is given in the concept of the "subjective
> aim" which is proper to each series of occasions. This
> aim, which has always about it a directive quality, is to
> be understood as the goal or end towards which a
> given process moves, yet it must also be seen as in
> some sense imminently at work in that process moving
> it towards its goal or end or actualization...But this
> does not mean that each set of occasions is "conscious"
> in anything like our human sense, of the aim which is
> before it and which gives it the distinctive identity that
> it possesses. An acorn is certainly not aware of the
> "aim" which keeps it moving towards its proper devel-
> opment into an oak-tree. But none the less, what does
> thus keep it moving towards its proper development is
> the given subjective aim which is proper to the acorn.
> And so, in appropriate measure and of course with
> vast differences at each level, throughout the cos-
> mos...God himself is possessed of a subjective aim;
> and every entity in the process, understood as dynamic

inter-related, inter-penetrative of every other entity is also characterized by such an aim.[19]

When speaking of the complexity of the occasion of experience, Cobb points out that "the whole experience is governed by some purpose...some end is in view,...This purposive element Whitehead affirms as present in every occasion and is what he calls its 'subjective aim.'"[20]

Everything is therefore understood to be "going somewhere" and for some purpose. Nothing is happening without the potential for meaning. Nothing is designed to be a fruitless expression. The "subjective aim" inherent in the very nature of reality is that which protects the individual entities and the sum total of reality, from chaos and meaningless wandering.

The Fourth Assumption

The fourth assumption, i.e., that because of the nature of the world as we know it, we cannot know it with any kind of absolute clarity, and therefore must always be in search of greater clarity, is what tends to impress one of the open mindedness and honesty of the Process approach to Theology. It is an admission that regardless of how intensely we search for final knowledge concerning the "nature of things," clarity of understanding is never fully attained. It is this assumption that makes process thought different in spirit, and in its application to theology, than most approaches taken by the church. Process thought is always open to new insights. It recognizes that in the experience of new knowledge the door is opened ever wider to the possibility of limitless new knowledge. This includes, but is not limited to, knowledge about God, about human beings, and all inter-relatedness of God and human beings and human beings to one another. It is this assumption that creates a spirit in Process thought that makes it a natural co-searcher with, and provides meaning for, the scientific method so effectively used in our modern world.

Pittenger describes this assumption thus:

Finally, because of the nature of the world as we know it, we cannot grasp it with that kind of absolute clarity which a Cartesian type of thinking would demand. Indeed we must always seek clarity, as Whitehead once said; but he went on to say that at the same time we must always distrust it. For the difficulty is that simple explanations, are likely to give us falsely simple explanations. If we accept experiences as we know it, there will be some things which will appear relatively clear, but they will be set in contexts which are not so clear. Hence the picture of truth is much more that of a small area of fairly straightforward knowledge which shades out into more and more mysterious and unclear knowledge or intimation or hint or apprehension, than it is that of "clear and distinct ideas" which leave no room for doubt and presume to give a simple and direct explanation of any given moment of experience.[21]

Theological Process Thought adjusts well to the contemporary expansion of knowledge concerning ourselves and the world of which we are a part. The challenge is to take this realistic approach to theology and relate it to the values and tradition of our faith in a manner which creates a transition that is defensible. Such an approach can be rooted in the good things that have provided a basis for values that are important to us contemporarily and encourage us as we move forward into the unknown of time, space, and experience.

Appendix II

Although other, or more passages of Scripture might have been chosen, I have associated Scripture with each Chapter in Part II for those who appreciate such scriptural association with basic ideas of theology and/or a philosophy of life.

Chapter V   Micah 6:6-8; Matthew 7:12

Chapter VI   Exodus 34:18; Leviticus 1:1; Amos 5:21-24; Matthew 21:12-13; Romans 12:1

Chapter VII   Psalm 119:11-16; Matthew 5:17, 18, 21a, 22a; II Timothy 3:16; Revelation 11:18, 19

Chapter VIII   Deuteronomy 6:1-9; Matthew 7:24-28

Chapter IX   Deuteronomy 7:9, 11-14a; 19, 28; I Corinthians 3:10-14

Chapter X   Matthew 6:12, 14, 15; 18:21, 22

Chapter XI   John 3:1-8; II Corinthians 5:17

Chapter XII   Luke 4:1, 14; Galatians 5:22-25

Chapter XIII   Luke 2:52; Galatians 5:1

Chapter XIV   Luke 4:16-21

Chapter XV   Exodus 20:3; Judges 2:11-15; Acts 17:22-30

Chapter XVI   II Chronicles 20:20b; Habukkuk 2:4; Romans 1:17; Hebrews 11:1,2

Chapter XVII   Hebrews 11; Matthew 17:14-21

Chapter XVIII   Matthew 6:5-13

Chapter XIX   Ephesians 4:25-5:2

Chapter XX   John 8:31,32; Galatians 5:1

Chapter XXI   Luke 19:28-38; 22:1-6

Chapter XXII   Ecclesiastes 11:9-12:1; John 20:1; Revelation 21:1-4

Chapter XXIII   Joshua 24:15; Matthew 4:18-22

Chapter XXIV   Matthew 16:13-20

Appendix III

For Those Who Wish Additional Supportive Reading

Barbour, Ian. *Religion in the Age of Science*, San Francisco; Harper San Francisco.

_____ *Myths, Models, and Paradigms*, NewY9ork, Evanston, , Lond: Harper & Row, 1974.

Bellah, Robert N. *Beyond Belief*, New York: Harper & Row, 1970.

Cobb, John B. *A Christian Natural Theology*, Philadelphia: The Westminster Press, 1974.

_____ "Can the Church Think Again?" *The United Methodist Reporter*, Vol. 3 Number 29, 2 July 1976, p. 1.

_____ *Is It Too Late?* Beverly Hills: Bruce Inc., 1971.

Hartshorne, Charles. *Aquinas to Whitehead: Seven Centuries of Metaphysics of Religion*. Marquette WI: Marquette University Press, 1976.

Pittenger, Norman. *Process-Thought and Christian Faith*. Digswell Place, Welwyn, Herts: James Nisbet & Company Ltd., 1968.

Robinson, John A. T. *Honest to God*. London: SCM, 1963.

Sagan, Carl. *The Demon-Haunted World: Science as a Candle in the Dark*. New York: Random House, 1995.

Spong, John Shelby. *Rescuing the Bible from Fundamentalism: A Bishop Rethinks the Meaning of Scripture*. San Francisco: Harper San Francisco, 1991.

_____ *Why Christianity Must Change or Die: A Bishop Speaks to Believers in Exile*. San Francisco: Harper San Francisco, 1998.

Whitehead, Alfred North. *Process and Reality*. 1929. Reprint New York: Free Press, 1978.

Footnotes

1   Norman Pittenger, *Process-Thought and Christian Faith*, (Diswell Place, Welwyn, Herts: James Nisbet & Co. Ltd, 1968)
2   Ibid., p. 2.
3   John A. T. Robinson, *Honest to God* (Philadelphia: The Westminster Press, 1963.
4   Pittenger, pp. 2-3.
5   Ibid., p. 3.
6   Ibid., p. 4.
7   John B. Cobb Jr., *A Christian Natural Theology* (Philadelphia: The Westminster Press, 1974).
8   Ian G. Barbour, *Myths, Models and Paradigms*, (New York, Evanston, San Francisco, London: Harper & Row, 1974).
9   Pittenger, pp. 5-6.
10 Ibid., p. 8.
11 As cited in Pittenger, p. 11.
12 Ibid., pp. 11-17.
13 John B. Cobb, Jr., pp. 25-26.
14 Barbour, *Issues In Science and Religion*, (Englewood Cliffs: Prentice Hall, 1966), pp. 365-366.
15 Pittenger, p. 12
16 John B. Cobb, Jr., p. 40.
17 Pittenger, pp. 13-14.
18 Barbour, *Myths, Models and Paradigms*, P. 163.
19 Pittenger, pp. 15-16.
20 Cobb, p. 35.
21 Pittenger, pp. 16-17

About the Author

Vernon Goff was born in 1928 on a farm in northwest Nebraska that was homesteaded by his grandfather. He was a child of the depression, a teenager during World War II, and was nurtured in a fundamentalist, interdenominational, brand of Christianity until young adulthood. He was a traveling evangelist in the early years of his ministry and received his education in secular, biblical literalist, and progressive schools of higher education. He received a BA degree from Taylor University, Upland Indiana, a Master of Theology from Iliff School of Theology in Denver, Colorado, and a Doctorate of Ministry from San Francisco School of Theology in California.

He has been pastor to both small and large churches. In 1965, he was the founding pastor of St. Lukes United Methodist Church in Omaha, Nebraska, and continued as senior pastor of that church for thirty-five years. His ministry spans over fifty years.

Making God Talk Make Sense is an effort to bring together a meaningful understanding of spirituality in God with the wonderful, contradictory, and fast-changing contemporary world.